DATE DUE

Demco, Inc. 38-293

ESRI STUDIES ON AGEING

Editorial Board

Olivia S. Mitchell, *Executive Director, Pension Research Council, International Foundation of Employee Benefit Plans and Professor of Insurance and Risk Management, Wharton School, University of Pennsylvania, USA*

Ralph C. Bryant, *Senior Fellow, Brookings Institution, USA*

Paolo Onofri, *Professor of Economics and Director, Department of Economics, University of Bologna and General Secretary, Prometeia Associates, Italy*

Koichi Hamada, *Professor of Economics, Yale University, USA and former President, Economic and Social Research Institute, Japanese Cabinet Office, Japan*

Hiromi Kato, *Deputy Director General, Economic Assessment and Policy Analysis and former Executive Research Fellow, Economic and Social Research Institute, Japanese Cabinet Office, Japan*

In April 2000 the Japanese government launched a series of comprehensive, interdisciplinary and international research projects called 'the Millennium Projects' and as part of this initiative the Economic and Social Research Institute (ESRI) of the Cabinet Office of Japan initiated a two year project entitled 'A Study on Sustainable Economic and Social Structures in the 21st Century', which focuses on ageing and environmental problems in the Japanese and international context.

The *ESRI Studies Series on Ageing* provides a forum for the publication of a limited number of books, which are the result of this international collaboration, on the three main issues of macroeconomics, pension and social security reform, and the labour market. The series is invaluable to students and scholars of public economics and public finance as well as policymakers and consultants.

Titles in the series include:

The Economics of Social Security in Japan
Edited by Toshiaki Tachibanaki

The Economic Impacts of Population Ageing in Japan
Landis MacKellar, Tatiana Ermolieva, David Horlacher and Leslie Mayhew

The Economics of an Ageing Population
Edited by Paolo Onofri

The Economics of Social Security in Japan

The Economics of
Social Security in
Japan

Edited by

Toshiaki Tachibanaki

Professor of Economics, Graduate School of Economics, Kyoto University, Japan

THE ESRI STUDIES SERIES ON AGEING

Edward Elgar
Cheltenham, UK • Northampton, MA, USA

© Toshiaki Tachibanaki 2004

Published by
Edward Elgar Publishing Limited
Glensanda House
Montpellier Parade
Cheltenham
Glos GL50 1UA
UK

Edward Elgar Publishing, Inc.
136 West Street
Suite 202
Northampton
Massachusetts 01060
USA

A catalogue record for this book
is available from the British Library

Library of Congress Cataloguing in Publication Data

The economics of social security in Japan / edited by Toshiaki Tachibanaki
    p. cm. — (ESRI studies series on ageing)
  Includes index.
  1. Social security—Japan. 2. Pensions—Japan. I. Tachibanaki, Toshiaki, 1943–
  II. Series.

 HD7096.J3E26 2004
 362.952—dc22

                                                                  2004040442

ISBN 1 84376 682 5

Printed and bound in Great Britain by MPG Books Ltd, Bodmin, Cornwall

Contents

Contributors

Henry J. Aaron Senior Fellow, Brookings Institution, Washington, DC, USA.

Ales Cerny Lecturer in Finance, Tanaka Business School, Imperial College London, UK.

Robert L. Clark Professor of Economics and Business Management, North Carolina University, Raleigh, NC, USA.

Benjamin H. Harris Research Analyst, Brookings Institution, Washington, DC, USA.

Yasushi Iwamoto Professor, Department of Economics, Hitotsubashi University, Kunitachi, Japan.

Akira Kawaguchi Professor, Faculty of Policy Studies, Doshisha University, Kyoto, Japan.

David Miles Professor of Finance, Tanaka Business School, Imperial College London, UK.

Olivia S. Mitchell Professor of Insurance and Risk Management, University of Pennsylvania, Philadelphia, PA, USA.

Yasushi Ohkusa Senior Researcher, National Institute of Infectious Disease, Japan.

Fumio Ohtake Professor, Institute of Social and Economic Research, Osaka University, Osaka, Japan.

John Piggott Professor, School of Economics, University of New South Wales, Sydney, Australia.

Sachi Purcal Lecturer, School of Actuarial Studies, University of New South Wales, Sydney, Australia.

Toshiaki Tachibanaki Professor of Economics, Graduate School of Economics, Kyoto University, Kyoto, Japan.

Matthew Williams Research Assistant, School of Economics, University of New South Wales, Sydney, Australia.

Tadashi Yagi Professor, Department of Economics, Doshisha University, Kyoto, Japan.

Hisaki Yamaga Assistant Professor, Institute of Policy and Planning Sciences, University of Tsukuba, Tsukuba, Japan.

Preface

At the beginning of the twenty-first century the world must place the highest priority on constructing a sustainable socioeconomic system that can cope with the rapid ageing of populations in developed countries and with the limited environmental resources available in both developed and developing countries. At first glance, the problems of ageing and the environment may seem to be quite separate issues. However, they share a common feature: they both deal with intergenerational problems. The essence of the ageing problem is how to find effective ways for a smaller, working generation to support a larger, ageing generation. The crux of the environmental problem is to find a feasible way to leave environmental resources to future generations. Moreover, in terms of consumption, slower population growth may slow consumption and help to alleviate environmental problems. On the other hand, a rapidly ageing society may use more energy-intensive technology to compensate for the inevitable labor shortage, and thus cause a deterioration in the natural environment.

Today, these concerns are highly applicable in Japan. The pressure created by the rapid ageing of the Japanese population is becoming acute; Japan must construct a sustainable society that does not create intergenerational inequity or erode public welfare. At the same time, Japan cannot deplete its environmental resources and energy, as this would leave future generations with an unbearably heavy burden.

The Japanese government has recognized the vital importance of both problems. To explore and implement solutions for this difficult task, in April 2000 former Prime Minister Keizo Obuchi launched several comprehensive and interdisciplinary research projects known collectively as the 'Millennium Project'. As a consequence, in the same month, the Economic and Social Research Institute (ESRI), Cabinet Office, Government of Japan, initiated a two-year project entitled 'A Study on Sustainable Economic and Social Structure in the Twenty-first Century'. While the Millennium Project covers a wide range of topics and disciplines such as natural science and technological innovation, the project conducted by ESRI places major emphasis on social science. While taking into account technological innovation and feasibility, it focuses on ageing and environmental problems. It aims to design a desirable socioeconomic structure under the pressure of an ageing population and environmental constraints by identifying the necessary policy tools to attain stable and sustainable growth.

This project is being implemented with close collaboration among Japanese as well as foreign scholars and research institutes. Besides Japanese scholars and institutes, foreign participants have been involved from, among others, the United States, the United Kingdom, Norway, Austria, Italy, Australia, Korea and Thailand. In total there are ten countries and 30 working groups.

AGEING SOCIETY

The Japanese population is graying rapidly, and the elderly are expected to account for a quarter of the nation's total population in 2020. Japan needs to reform its social security system, pension management schemes, financial/capital markets and labor markets if it hopes to create a better and sustainable future society. When looking at Japan's problems head on, we see giant fiscal deficits, bad-loan problems, and long-term structural problems that must be fixed aggressively or suffered indefinitely. The clock is ticking, and the time to act is short, but our problems are not insurmountable. Pessimism is not our rallying call. Rather, we are optimistic, and encouraged by the European example. In Europe, countries have worked hard to improve fiscal conditions and social security, and they have attained positive results and succeeded in uniting their separate markets.

Studies on ageing populations can be divided roughly into three categories: (i) macroeconomic problems related to the decline in the workforce due to ageing; (ii) social security systems, with many of the studies looking at pension systems; and (iii) the labor market, for example, employment of the elderly, competition with younger workers, the female workforce, and immigrant workers. We have made a specialized study of our theme from these perspectives.

Many people are pessimistic about the effect of ageing on the macro economy due to the reduction in the labor force. However, in this study, there were others who expressed a challenging view that various impacts, including those on economic growth, can be coped with fully and overcome by technological progress and other measures. Some strongly suggested that the current economic and social system would need to be reformed to achieve the flexibility required. Accelerated return to prosperity and the realization of economic growth at a comparatively high level would reduce costs and alleviate the distress that a change in the system in the transition period would involve, helping to carry forward the reform smoothly. In other words, measures to be taken to improve the present situation of the

Japanese economy do not differ significantly from what is required to build the future sustainable economy and society.

In order to emerge from the current stagnant state of the macro economy as soon as possible, it is necessary to reconstruct the financial system in such a way as would bring about efficiency of fund allocation and recover efficiency of the labor market. Some also pointed out that it will be difficult to achieve economic growth amid an increasingly ageing population unless a sound labor market and an efficient financial and capital market are established. Finding solutions for the bad loans and forming an efficient financial and capital market will not only make it possible to diversify portfolio selection and pension asset management of individuals but will allow enterprises to raise their funds efficiently. At the same time, there were many who expressed the opinion that the soundness of the Japanese economy would be recovered and a sustainable economy and society will be realized by defining public participation in the social security system (defining the roles which the public and the private sectors should play in social security) and building a safety net against various risks. As a timeworn story, it is pointed out that the formation of an efficient market through the improvement of various regulations and systems in the labor market will not only stimulate participation of the aged and women in the market and make up for the labor shortage but will also make a variety of employment forms feasible and contribute to the formation of a society in which people will feel that their life is worth living. There are also some who see the necessity of establishing the concept of equity in the social security system and employment of the aged, since these factors bear a significant relationship to the age at which payment of pensions is started, sustainability of the system and fair sharing of the pension cost between the young and the aged.

RESOURCE AND ENVIRONMENTAL PROBLEMS

Studies on resource/environmental problems reflect a closed-loop model of the economy and society. These studies are divided into four themes: (i) studies on waste management, which cover a wide variety of empirical studies; (ii) studies on sustainability and technological innovation related to resources/energy; (iii) studies on potential policies for addressing changes in climate; and (iv) studies on the relationship between environmental policies and economic policies, including employment policies.

From the standpoint of long-term sustainability of global resources, official involvement including policy measures and the development of new technology to remove environmental restrictions will be called for. There is a high possibility that new technology creates new products, stimulating demand, developing new industries with high productivity, and bringing about a renewed sustainable economic growth. New technology in the twenty-first century should contribute to the construction of the closed-loop economy and society and enhance resources and energy efficiency, properly dispose of waste and increase efficiency of reusing resources. Furthermore, it must generate renewable energy efficiently and on a large scale. It may sound paradoxical, but past experience suggests that various restrictions imposed on economic activities, and the existence of regulation actually stimulates new technological development which helps to break through the restrictions.

Today, environmental issues encompass a very wide range of problems from territorial disposal of waste to the global environmental issues. It has been pointed out that a policy mix ingeniously combining such methods as regulatory and economic instruments, voluntary agreements and international emissions trading is essential for coping with these issues. What is important then is a policy which skillfully uses incentives, making use of market mechanisms. Japan is one of the most advanced countries in environment-related technology in the world. However, further technological breakthroughs will be called for in the future and it has been pointed out that use of market incentives and official support is essential in the fields where long-term risks are uncertain. It is suggested that concrete behavior by a community based on shared information (bottom-up approach) and a change in the behavior of individuals as consumers provide one of the keys in the closed-loop economy and society. Such a change in the behavior of individuals is caused by the diffusion and permeation of concepts such as the precautionary principle, one of the environmental principles in the European Union.

Addressing the construction of the closed-loop materials-cycle economy and society is important in the Japanese economy, which is faced with restrictions on resources and energy; it may be a way by which we can seek sustainable progress and growth of a Japanese type. Furthermore, some pointed out that, given its climatic and topographical conditions and its population density, the waste management system in larger Japanese cities could be a model for Asia and Japan will play an important role in the Asian area in coping with global environment issues.

SYNTHETIC CONSIDERATION

None of the various issues addressed in this project can be seen in isolation. They are closely related to one another and they will require simultaneous decision making by different parties when a desirable scenario is to be visualized. Ageing and the environment will both have a strong impact not only on the welfare of people today but also on that of future generations. An awareness of issues that are common to the ageing population and the environment is the context in which we should make use of market mechanisms.

There is a case for saying that we should make good use of market mechanisms by utilizing economic means in order to efficiently attain goals in health care and annuity, employment of the aged, women in the labor force, climatic change and waste disposal. However, many of these issues are examples of market mechanisms not functioning efficiently, or a 'failure' of the market. Utilizing market mechanisms in this domain involves various difficulties such as internalizing externalities and we cannot avoid classical problems such as efficiency and equity and what roles should be played by the public and private sectors.

Research into the ageing population and the environment has thrown into relief the importance of technological innovation. Looking back on human history, we find that restrictive conditions gave birth to technological innovation which presented a way out of the difficulties faced. Although the twenty-first century has severe restrictions imposed upon it such as resources, energy, labor force and population, we may also take a positive view and say that, conversely, the conditions are ripe for technological innovation. If we could achieve such innovation in this global situation, then a more enriched economy and society would develop.

In the short term, countries with ageing populations are likely to consume more energy – without any thought to the long-term impact of their consumption patterns and economic activity. This tendency must be offset by a new sense of sustainability, one that looks to the future, that thrives on improved resource/energy efficiencies, and that is based on eco-friendly waste disposal and new eco-friendly technologies. Without lowering living standards, we must solve global environmental problems, and overcome the constraints of limited energy resources. To do so will require the creation of a closed-looped economy/society. Failure to do so may spell the end to our way of life in the not-so-distant future.

In this project, we explore optimal solutions to social optimization problems. After taking into account the political and social constraints we face, and after alignment and coordination of the results of the studies, we will sketch out an ideal design and examine the possible direction of future research.

The project came to an end in March 2002. It solved many theoretical and empirical issues, but has created new areas for debate. Twice a year, all the members of the project, along with selected participants, met to discuss the results of the research. Unfortunately, it has not been possible to reproduce the fruitful discussion in this volume.

Overall, the studies presented in the project were extremely challenging, and covered a wide range of topics. We hope that we shall soon have the opportunity to discuss the research once more from a common standpoint. The results are presented here as part of the ESRI studies series, available to policy makers, academics and businesspeople with a keen interest in these subjects. The series on ageing problems covers macroeconomics, social security and the labor market. Unfortunately, because of space limitations we are able to publish only some of the total output, selected by the members of the Editorial Board. We would like to acknowledge the ceaseless efforts of ESRI members throughout the project period, especially those from the Department of Administrative Affairs. Last but not least, we would like to thank Dymphna Evans, Matthew Pitman and Karen McCarthy from Edward Elgar Publishing.

Yutaka Kosai, President, ESRI

Acknowledgments

This book is the outgrowth of work that was undertaken in the context of a two-year research project conducted by the Economic and Social Research Institute (ESRI), Cabinet Office, Government of Japan, entitled 'A Study on Sustainable Economic and Social Structure in the Twenty-first Century'. I would like to express my sincere gratitude to all staff members of the Institute for their support throughout the project and during several conferences held in Osaka and Tokyo, among others. I thank in particular Koichi Hamada, Hiromi Kato and Mitsuo Hosen of ESRI for their continuous encouragement and suggestions during the course of this research project.

The book contains ten of the large number of studies presented to the project, and concentrates on the subject of Social Security in Japan. Following the introduction, the chapters fall into two groups: the first selected from the Social Safety Net in Japan project under the direction of Toshiaki Tachibanaki, and the second from other projects. I am grateful to all the authors for their contributions.

Toshiaki Tachibanaki

1. Introduction

Toshiaki Tachibanaki

1. MOTIVATIONS OF THE BOOK AND SEVERAL FEATURES OF SOCIAL SECURITY SYSTEMS IN JAPAN

Historically, Japan has not been a welfare state, which is a country where the public sector (central government and/or local governments) provides citizens with considerable welfare provision. This can be clearly seen in Table 1.1, which gives an international comparison of the share of social security benefits over national incomes, and the rate of tax revenues and social security contributions. The table shows that Japan is in the lowest group together with the United States, where it is regarded as a typical non-welfare state country. Note that Japan is even somewhat lower than the United States.

Why has Japan been seen as a typical example of the non-welfare state?

Table 1.1 *Rate of social security benefits over national incomes (A), and rate of tax revenues and social security contributions over GDP (B) (%)*

	A		B		
			Total rates	Taxes	Social security contributions
Japan	1993	15.2	2002	38.3	22.9	15.5
	1997	17.8				
USA	1992	18.7	1997	37.0	26.2	9.8
UK	1993	27.2	1999	50.0	40.0	10.0
Germany	1993	33.3	1999	56.7	25.7	31.0
France	1993	37.2	1999	66.1	40.6	25.5
Sweden	1993	53.4	1999	75.4	55.8	19.7

Sources: (A) National Institute of Social Security and Population, *Social Security Benefits*, Tokyo 2000. (B) Ministry of Welfare and Labor, *White Paper*, Tokyo 2002.

1

There are four possible reasons. The first is that families have traditionally been responsible for providing for their members. This is due partly to an East-Asian cultural heritage which emphasizes family ties. Second, enterprises, in particular larger ones recognized the benefit of making welfare provision available to their employees – in short, there was an economic incentive. Good economic conditions due to their higher productivities cannot be ignored as an additional cause. Third, the main goal of the government during the post-war period was to promote strong industrialization and thus higher economic growth. Thus, the government did not concern itself over people's welfare, and the private sector (for example, families and large enterprises) has responded to the government attitude. Fourth, Japan did not have an ageing population in the 1960s and 1970s, when strong industrialization and rapid economic growth was achieved. Also, life expectancy was not as high at that time, although it is now one of the highest in the world. These phenomena imply that the demand for welfare services such as old-age pensions, medical care, home care for the elderly and so on was relatively less, although it is very high currently because of the ageing trend in population structures.

Tachibanaki (1996a and b, 2000, 2002, 2003) has discussed these issues fully, in particular the reasons why families and larger enterprises were committed to making welfare provision. It must be emphasized, however, that citizens' and families' attitudes towards this phenomenon is currently undergoing a serious transition process; in other words, the degree of family ties and thus mutual help among family members is weakening considerably. At the same time, industrial sectors benefited from families' commitment to welfare provision, and from the relatively lower financial burdens of employers' contributions to various social security systems in order to achieve good economic performances. However, industrial sectors are still suffering from the current serious recession which has continued for the past ten years, and are reluctant to accept a possible increase in the financial burden of employers' contribution to the social security system during the current ageing trend. In sum, various changes in both family structure and enterprise conditions demand a reconsideration of Japanese welfare provision systems.

The purpose of this book is to examine how social security systems are facing a serious transition process in Japan as described above, and to propose various policy recommendations. It does not address general issues which would be useful to an understanding of the entire welfare provision as a whole, but rather examines various components separately, such as the public pension, the enterprise or occupational pension, medical care, child care, and a barrier-free infrastructure for the disabled. A few chapters, however, such as those by Tachibanaki (Chapter 2) and Yagi (Chapter 11), touch on general issues such as the Japanese social security system as a whole, and the concept of capability according to Amartya Sen.

One important feature of this book is that contributions have been made by both Japanese and non-Japanese specialists. Japanese authors, needless to say, know the system well, and thus are able to investigate issues in depth regarding the advantages and disadvantages of the system. Non-Japanese authors may not be as familiar with the system, but they are able to evaluate it without prior prejudice, using their own countries' experience for a comparative perspective. I hope that readers can appreciate the subtle differences between Japanese and non-Japanese writers, all of whom are leading specialists in their field.

Before presenting a summary discussion of each chapter, several features of the Japanese systems of public pension, enterprise pension, medical care, child care and a barrier-free infrastructure for the disabled are examined very briefly as a reference point for readers.

1.1. Public Pension

There are two elements to this pension: the first is the basic part which pays a flat rate to each retiree, and the second is the proportional part. One-third of the basic part is financed by tax revenues, and the remaining two-thirds by social insurance contributions. The second part functions principally as a pay-as-you-go scheme with a modified version of a funded scheme. The serious ageing trend demands radical reforms in both payment structures and financing methods.

There are three different proposals. First, modifying from a pay-as-you-go to a funded scheme, which includes a reduction in benefits and an increase in contributions. Second, keeping the contribution rate at 20 percent in the final stage, and raising it gradually every year before the final stage of 20 percent. The benefit level would fluctuate according to each year's budget. This is the Swedish type of reform, and the current government seems to prefer it. Third, introducing drastic tax measures instead of social security contributions, and maintaining the current benefit level.

1.2. Enterprise Pension

Historically, enterprise pension programs evolved from a one-off retirement payment, which was the system commonly used by larger enterprises. Payment was made at the time of retirement to a life-time employee. There was a gradual shift from a one-off lump sum to an annual pension payment for a limited duration. The basic scheme, therefore, has been a defined benefit (DB) type. Since the influence of the US-type defined contribution

(DC) plan is strong, a large number of enterprises contemplate introducing a defined contribution type, or shifting from the former to the latter, or introducing a hybrid of the two.

There are several reasons and motivations for these policy reforms. First, there is a significant degree of uncertainty associated with the future course of the public pension program. It would be necessary to rely on enterprise pensions in the future, if the benefit level of public pensions were cut. Second, the ageing trend within each enterprise would result in financial difficulty in the management of an enterprise pension program. Third, the current low interest rate and low return on equities would also lead to financial difficulty for enterprise pension programs in particular when a defined benefit plan is the basic scheme. Employers would have to contribute significantly in such a case in order to improve the financial situation, and they hope, naturally, to avoid having to make such contributions.

1.3.   Medical Care (or Insurance)

The most important feature of the medical insurance system is the existence of a large number of independent insurance programs, which are differentiated by participants' age, occupation, enterprise size and so on. Since age structure, earnings capacity, financial conditions of employers and so on vary so widely among the programs, the rates of benefits and contributions, and financial conditions also differ considerably from program to program. Some internal financial transfers among various programs have been made to help financially troubled programs. This is an imperfect arrangement, and thus more reliable reforms are called for.

Another important feature is that government regulations concerning the medical sector and health insurance programs are strict. In other words, patients and medical insurance participants are unable to express their hopes and demands effectively, and insurers cannot play a significant role. Another obstacle is the strength of medical doctors' and pharmacy associations. Asymmetrical information between specialists and patients, of course, is one of the causes of the difficulty in the medical insurance system. Far-reaching policy reforms are necessary.

1.4.   Child-care System

A system of leave for child care has been uncommon because married women have traditionally been responsible for taking care of babies and children at home. Many women retire from the labor market when they get married, or give birth. They stay at home to take care of the children, and return to working activities after their children have grown up. Of course, there have always been a certain number of women who continue to work and combine it with marriage and child-bearing.

There is now a strong demand for introducing and strengthening a child-care leave system for the following reasons. First, many married women want to continue working without any interruptions for marriage and child care. Second, the current birth rate is very low at 1.34 births per woman. This low rate is regarded as a serious problem by the majority of concerned people. It is believed that one of the causes is insufficient provision for child-care leave, although there are many other concerns. There is a consensus that society should take care of children. The issue is, 'Who takes the initiative, who bears the financial burden, and how are children cared for?'.

1.5. Barrier-free Infrastructure for the Disabled

Barrier-free infrastructure systems have been underdeveloped for various reasons. First, the economy and society regarded strong industrialization as the top priority during the entire post-war period. Consequently, no serious attention has been paid to the disabled, and thus public expenditure on easy accessibility and quality of life has for them been quite limited. Second, many people felt that families and relatives should be responsible for providing them with various services. This idea came from the general understanding that families were responsible for providing the needy with various welfare services, and this also included the elderly disabled. It is now time to reconsider such a limited infrastructure, and society has started to recognize it.

2. SUMMARY OF THE CONTENT

In Chapter 2, Tachibanaki is concerned with the problem of pension programs. He presents two major reforms in social security in Japan. The first one is to switch the public pension system from the current pay-as-you-go insurance principle to the tax financing method at least for the basic part of the pension benefit. More concretely, it is recommended that progressive consumption tax or progressive expenditure tax is introduced. The second reform is to allow and even encourage firms to withdraw from welfare provision programs. Tachibanaki examines the present status of social security systems in Japan, and concludes that Japan is not a welfare state. The major providers are families and firms, particularly large firms. The chapter also discusses various issues of public pension and enterprise pension reform in the advanced countries, including privatization, efficiency–equity trade-off, tax incidence, and so on. It presents a scheme for reform in the public pension system, and a recommendation of withdrawal from firms' contribution to welfare provisions. It is proposed that such reforms and recommendations are useful to maintain the standard of living for the aged in an uncertain world, and improve the economic prosperity of firms which are currently in serious recession and facing acute competition internationally.

In Chapter 3, Aaron and Harris are concerned with uncertainty in public pension programs because the balance between pension contributions and benefits varies considerably because of uncertainty. Demographic uncertainty is, in particular, crucial under pay-as-you-go or partial-reverse financing because changes in fertility and mortality rates and other related variables affect both revenues and benefits in view of the long-run contracts of the system. One way to deal with these demographic uncertainties is to introduce indexed pensions and wages, and indeed many countries have introduced them. Aaron and Harris evaluate various indexing methods such as 'retrospective' indexing based on past changes in wages and prices, and 'prospective' indexing based on anticipated deviations of key variables from expected values. Also, other possible forms of indexing on labor force participation, productivity growth and so on in addition to traditional demographic variables are evaluated for both DB and DC plans. One attractive feature of their study is to evaluate the situation in both the United States and Japan. They conclude that indexing with respect to projections is technically problematic, which is understood as political rather than economical. This means that economists cannot make well-informed decisions on the timing and magnitude of indexing. Bearing this in mind, it is questionable whether a 'correct' political decision is possible.

Miles and Cerny (Chapter 4), present a comprehensive study on public pension programs, which includes a rigorous simulation study based on their economic model for Japan, and concrete policy recommendations. Their model is complex, and of a stochastic general equilibrium type. Emphasis is placed on uncertainty associated with labor income, returns on financial assets, efficiency in annuity markets, probabilities of surviving and so on. The model is a significant extension of the Auerbach–Kotlikoff model. The simulation results suggest several useful implications for Japan. For example, a long-run implication of a switch from a pay-as-you-go scheme to much greater reliance on a funded scheme is prudent because an increase in consumption and welfare for future generations would be considerable. This is provided through a higher personal saving rate, and thus a higher capital–labor ratio. The extent of financial risk or return on various financial assets is crucial in their exercise. One important finding is that there would be no intergenerational income transfers if the timing of contributions and of receiving benefits were adhered to rigorously. Also, there was no indication that reform would have any adverse distributional consequences. In sum, Miles and Cerny proposed that Japan should switch from a pay-as-you-go to a funded scheme in the management of public pensions.

In Chapter 5, Ohtake and Yamaga examine the effect of a public pension on labor supply. More specifically, they analyze the impact of the old-age pension system for active employees on the employment behavior of the elderly using the difference-in-differences method and the estimation of dynamic labor supply models. Data were obtained from 'Surveys on the Employment of Older Persons'. Both the difference-in-differences method and the estimated dynamic labor supply models show that the old-age pension system for active employees influenced the supply of workers in their early sixties (60 to 65 years of age). Effects of the reform of the system in 1995 are analyzed. The difference-in-differences method revealed that the reform affected the decision of whether to work, especially for elderly persons on a small pension, but did not affect working hours. The estimated dynamic labor supply models revealed no significant marginal tax rate effects of the pension system around 1995. The wage elasticities, which were estimated by pooling data for 1988, 1992, and 1996, were relatively high, ranging from 0.2 to 0.6. Since the ageing trend implies that labor supply will be limited in future, it causes a slower economic growth rate. It is expected that the aged labor force will continue to work if they remain in good health. This would also alleviate a serious shortfall in the public pension budget. These findings should be borne in mind when policy reforms of the public pension program are being considered.

In Chapter 6, Clark and Mitchell compare both the public pension system and the enterprise (or company) pension program in the United States and Japan. Emphasis is placed on the enterprise pension program, and one of the objectives of such a comparison is to highlight several advantages in the US program and to suggest that some of these can be useful for policy reforms in Japan. The authors compared various institutional settings of enterprise pension programs, historical developments, their economic motivations, both employers' and employees' views and preferences on pension programs and so on. Emphasis is placed on a comparison between a DB plan and a DC plan for both the United States and Japan. Clark and Mitchell recommended that Japan should adopt the US-type DC plan in view of three success stories: first, the US regulatory and tax policies (the famous 401(k)) were successful; second, changes in the composition of the US labor force and industrial relations favored a DC plan; and third, the US economy has recently been buoyant. Finally, they evaluated the 2001 legislation in Japan which approved a DC plan; they found that it was a 'big-bang' reform that would convert Japanese workers from savers to investors.

In Chapter 7, Piggott, Purcal and Williams are concerned with Japanese asset allocations, and evaluate whether different financial investment strategies and activities produce considerably different outcomes in pension benefits. This kind of simulation is quite important because in the past households and even financial institutions adopted a fairly risk-averse attitude to investment; quite simply, they preferred the concept of safety to that of risk. After examining and reviewing various theoretical financial investment theories, Piggott, Purcal and Williams choose the following four investment strategies as the fund management formula for a DC plan in an enterprise (occupational) pension program: (i) an all-equities strategy at the Nikkei, (ii) a division strategy between stocks and bonds, (iii) a long-term phased strategy in which the proportion of the portfolio invested in stocks is gradually reduced over the life cycle, and (iv) a safe strategy in which all contributions and earnings are held in short-term bills. Their comprehensive simulation, which covers the past 30 years, suggests that, based on a simple stochastic model of investment return innovations, increasing the sophistication of the investment strategy generates outcomes, or distributions of outcomes, which dominate those implied by simple constant-proportions positions. They recommend that Japanese investors should be more sophisticated in order to enjoy higher pension benefits under a DC plan.

Iwamoto (Chapter 8), discusses past national medical-care expenditure and its possible future path. It is an important subject because the ageing trend will increase medical costs in the future. About 30 percent of past growth was due to population ageing and the remaining 70 percent to technological change. Technical progress in the medical sector is rapid, and this has contributed to prolonging life expectancy considerably. Medical expenditure will increase by 40 percent in 30 years due to population ageing. The second half of the chapter focuses on a reform of health insurance for the elderly, and presents some policy recommendations. One of the most serious problems in the health-care market is that virtually nobody evaluated or attempted to improve the quality of medical services. It is not clear whether the rising medical costs are a result of waste or of necessity. It has been suggested that the government and the medical doctors' association colluded to maximize their regulation rents. A desirable direction of reform is that rather than relying on the government (that is, the regulator) and the doctors' association, the insurers will play a more active role in the health-care market as informed agents for patients. Since the public sector has dominated the health insurance business, large-scale outsourcing of the health insurance business to the private sector should be promoted.

In Chapter 9, Ohkusa examines one of the most important current policy issues in Japan: its very low birth rate. One of the useful tools is to introduce and strengthen the child-care system. Ohkusa uses a new technique, 'conjoint analysis', which enables economists to estimate changes in the birth behavior under several alternative and hypothetical conditions. Several conditions were controlled, and additional economic and social variables were taken into account. The empirical results show that increasing child-care leave by one year increases the mean number of children by 0.12–0.14. Income support during child-care leave also has a positive effect on fertility but a 10 percent improvement in the replacement rate of only 0.04 children. The condition of admission to the day-care service has a significant effect: the 'waiting list' cases decrease by 0.34–0.39 and the 'very difficult' cases decrease by 0.52–0.58 in comparison with the 'easy' cases. Financial rewards for bearing children have a positive effect, and increasing them by ¥34–40 thousand boosts the average number of children in a family by 0.1.

In Chapter 10, Kawaguchi examines the child-care leave system, which might encourage married women to return to work. According to Kawaguchi, problems with the current system are as follows: the atmosphere in the workplace is not sympathetic to those who wish to take child-care leave; the amount of benefit for such leave is small; there is no guarantee for those who take leave that they can return to the same job; casual workers are not eligible for leave; and wages may decline after taking leave. He shows that the interruption of women's careers after childbirth was the biggest cause of the large gender wage gap. However, an econometric analysis shows that the immediate wage reduction after taking child-care leave is not significant, but the opportunity of off-the-job training declines significantly later. The last result should result in a large wage reduction. Kawaguchi examines various institutional child-care leave systems, and evaluates them carefully. He concludes that we need a more comprehensive child-care benefit system which supports the harmonization of work and family. The proposed child-care benefit system shares the risk of raising children, and changes the traditional gender division of labor by encouraging male as well as female workers to take child-care leave. He suggests that firms should take strong action to support female employees taking leave, and that the government should endorse such actions.

Finally, in Chapter 11, Yagi investigates the rate of social infrastructure in an ageing society where there are a large number of disabled people. Before presenting his theoretical and empirical discussions, he raises the importance of the concept of 'capability', after Amartya Sen, and suggests that the capabilities of the disabled differ greatly depending upon how well accessibility to services is implemented. Yagi presents a theoretical model which analyzes the effect of introducing barrier-free infrastructure into a society where there are two types of people, non-disabled and disabled. The social optimization procedure for public expenditure and tax revenue is examined, and the conclusion is that the government should invest more than the amount indicated by residents, including the able-bodied. Yagi conducted his own survey on this issue, and presents several useful findings based on the contingent valuation method. Among them, it is proposed that able-bodied people have a strong feeling of responsibility for improving accessibility for the disabled. Also, some attempts are made to estimate the willingness to pay for barrier-free investments by both the non-disabled and the disabled, which could provide policy authorities with useful information on how much investment should be made, and who should bear the financial and tax burdens.

3.   OVERALL SUMMARY

The above is a brief summary of the chapters in this book, each presenting different views on the evaluation of the social security system in Japan, and various useful policy reforms. I shall not outline general conclusions, but hope that readers will draw their own after reading the content of the book.

Nevertheless, several important remarks can be added, based on my reading of the entire manuscript, which may be a somewhat personally biased view. First, Japan faces a crucial decision: whether to continue with its traditional feature of welfare provision, that is, relying on families and enterprises, or shift to a welfare state in which the public sector plays a major role in welfare provision, or to the American-type self-support and privatization of welfare provision. Which direction the country takes must be decided soon. This requires a careful evaluation of each possible route by specialists, and then the Japanese people can reach a democratic decision based on these evaluations and comprehensive discussions by all fellow citizens. Once the direction is determined, concrete reform policies for each social security program can be proposed fairly easily and precisely because everybody will understand the general principles involved.

Second, there are two conflicting views even in this book about the role of the market mechanism. One view stresses the importance of deregulation policies, and the merit of the market mechanism, in other words, a diminishing role of public sector welfare provision. Thus, a DC type and a funded scheme are preferred in pension programs, for example. It is interesting to note that the great majority of non-Japanese and some Japanese authors prefer these reforms. The other view, which stresses the importance of the public sector, does not advocate the merit of the market mechanism so strongly. Recommendations of public policies for welfare provision are presented by several Japanese authors. The distinction arises from individual value judgments, and decisions about welfare provision should be reached according to the majority principle.

The studies included in this volume help us to understand the advantages and disadvantages of the Japanese social security system, and to evaluate various policy reforms. I believe that readers have much to learn from this book, and will obtain useful information on the determination of future policy reforms in social security systems.

REFERENCES

Tachibanaki, T. (1996a), *Wage Determination and Distribution in Japan*, Oxford: Oxford University Press.

Tachibanaki, T. (1996b), *Public Policies and the Japanese Economy*, London: Macmillan.

Tachibanaki, T. (2000), *The Economics of a Safety Net*, Tokyo: Nihon-keizai-shinbunsya (in Japanese).

Tachibanaki, T. (2002), *The Economics of Mind in Safety*, Tokyo: Iwanami-shoten (in Japanese).

Tachibanaki, T. (2003), 'The role of firms in welfare provisions', in S. Ogura, T. Tachibanaki and D. Wise (eds), *Labor Markets and Firm Benefit Policies in Japan and the United States*, Chicago: University of Chicago Press, pp. 315–38.

2. Social security reform in Japan in the twenty-first century

Toshiaki Tachibanaki

1. INTRODUCTION

One of the most serious social and economic problems facing Japan in the twenty-first century is the ageing trend in the age–population structure. In particular, it has a serious effect on the social security systems for pensions, medical insurance, old-age caring, growth rate of the economy and so on. The purpose of this chapter is to examine the pension program that supports a comfortable standard of living for the aged.

The ageing trend is likely to reduce the pension benefit level if the current pay-as-you-go system is retained without any modification. This author believes that it is important not to reduce the benefit level because the public pension benefit is the major source of income for the aged. By maintaining the present benefit level, the elderly will not have to face uncertainty and anxiety concerning their standard of living. The chapter presents two major policy reforms to support this assertion. The first is to switch the public pension system from the current pay-as-you-go method to the tax financing method at least for the basic part of the benefit, and the second is to allow firms to withdraw from welfare provision programs.

2. CHARACTERISTICS OF WELFARE PROVISION IN JAPAN IN COMPARATIVE PERSPECTIVE

2.1. Japan Is Not a Welfare State

Japan has never been a welfare state, according to various criteria of welfare provision. The United States and Japan, contrary to other industrialized countries, mainly in Europe, are the only two nations that are non-welfare states. A welfare state is defined as a country where the public sector

Table 2.1   Social expenditures (% of GDP)

	1980	1985	1990	1993	1994
Austria	22.3	24.0	23.6	25.6	–
Belgium	25.4	28.2	26.4	27.2	–
Denmark	27.6	26.5	28.2	31.0	–
Finland	18.9	23.5	25.3	34.8	34.1
France	23.5	27.0	26.0	28.7	–
Germany	25.8	26.5	24.8	29.8	–
Greece	10.8	16.2	17.1	16.9	–
Ireland	19.7	23.3	19.3	21.3	20.7
Italy	18.4	21.7	23.1	25.0	–
Luxembourg	24.8	24.6	23.9	25.3	–
Netherlands	28.5	28.9	29.2	30.5	–
Portugal	11.6	11.9	14.4	17.5	–
Spain	16.5	18.7	19.8	22.5	–
Sweden	28.9	30.4	31.6	37.5	–
UK	18.7	21.5	20.2	24.0	–
USA	12.7	12.9	13.8	15.3	–
Japan	10.2	11.3	11.2	12.5	13.0

Source: Organization for Economic Cooperation and Development, *Public Management Reform and Economic and Social Development*, Paris: OECD, 1998.

plays a significant role in welfare provision, both in designing the system and providing actual services.

Let us confirm the above by looking at the quantitative evidence. Tables 2.1 and 2.2 show the size of social expenditures, and the size of both tax and social security contributions, respectively, for the Organization for Economic Cooperation and Development (OECD) countries. These tables clearly indicate that in Japan and the United States, the public sector plays only a small role in social expenditure and welfare provision because the two governments collect only a small amount of funds from the private sector and provide fellow citizens with very minor social services.

Tachibanaki (2000a) concluded that families and enterprises were the two main suppliers of welfare provision, which compensated for the lower degree of social service supplied by the public sector in Japan. It would be feasible to assert that fellow citizens and enterprises are both responsible for old-age pensions and medical care in the US. There is an American tradition that self-support is a dominant principle.

The so-called 'libertarianism' appears to be the most preferred philosophical doctrine in both Japan and the United States, while 'liberalism'

Table 2.2 *Weights of a tax revenues and social security contributions (% of GDP)*

	Gross revenue			Personal income tax			Social security contribution						Other tax		
							Employee			Employer					
	1991	1993	1995	1991	1993	1995	1991	1993	1995	1991	1993	1995	1991	1993	1995
Austria	41	43	42	9	9	9	6	6	7	7	7	7	20	21	20
Belgium	45	45	46	14	14	15	5	5	5	10	10	9	16	17	17
Denmark	49	50	51	26	26	28	1	1	1	–	–	–	21	22	22
Finland	45	47	46	17	16	16	0	1	2	11	10	10	19	18	18
France	44	44	45	6	6	6	6	6	6	12	12	12	20	20	21
Germany	38	39	39	10	11	11	6	7	7	8	8	8	14	14	14
Greece	38	40	41	5	4	5	5	6	7	5	6	6	23	24	24
Ireland	35	35	34	11	11	10	2	2	2	3	3	3	19	19	19
Italy	40	44	41	10	12	11	3	3	3	9	9	9	17	20	19
Luxembourg	43	44	44	9	9	9	5	5	5	6	6	5	23	24	24
Netherlands	47	47	44	12	12	8	11	11	12	3	3	3	20	21	21
Portugal	32	31	34	6	6	6	3	3	3	5	5	5	18	17	19
Spain	35	35	34	8	8	8	2	2	2	9	9	8	16	15	15
Sweden	54	50	50	18	18	18	–	1	2	15	13	12	21	18	18
UK	36	33	35	10	9	10	2	2	3	4	3	3	19	18	20
USA	27	27	28	10	10	10	3	3	3	4	4	4	10	11	11
Japan	31	29	29	8	7	6	4	4	4	5	5	5	14	13	13

Source: Organization for Economic Cooperation and Development, *The Tax/Benefit Position of Employees 1995–1996*, Paris: OECD, 1997.

seems to be the most popular doctrine in Europe. This distinction regarding a social principle and a philosophical thought between Japan/United States and Europe reflects one of the causes for the differences in the size of the public sectors in welfare provision, although I accept that it is too simplistic to attribute the difference between the two regions only to the distinction in the preferred philosophical doctrine.

It is, nevertheless, interesting to note that both Japan and the United States have been the champions of capitalism or the free market economy, while many countries in Europe have been suffering from slower growth rates and higher unemployment rates. It is possible to conjecture that the feature of the welfare states, which normally demand a higher financial burden from both individuals and firms, is responsible for this weak economy in Europe. In fact, the welfare state has been attacked not only by politicians but also by economists in Europe, for example, by Margaret Thatcher in the UK, and Lindbeck (Lindbeck et al. 1994) in Sweden.

We should add a reservation about the comment that both Japan and the United States have been the champions of capitalism or the free market economy. In the 1990s, the United States enjoyed a very strong competitive edge, and the economy prospered due possibly to the new economic policies, while for ten years Japan suffered its worst recession since the second world war. Indeed, the United States could be regarded as the only winner in the world economy in the 1990s. The other countries, including both developed and developing ones, are possibly all losers. There are, of course, several problems even in the United States, for example, a widening income distribution and a large difference in the life expectancy between the rich and the poor, if we are concerned with social issues. These problems, however, may be regarded as minor because the average citizen can enjoy the current economic prosperity.

The success of the US economy, moreover, may lead to the suggestion that the welfare state is harmful to the overall economic performance. In other words, a trust in non-welfare states or a dislike of welfare states would exert a strong power. In fact, such a feeling or a movement is now gaining ground in America, as shown by several phenomena. The first is the failure to create a nationwide public health insurance program, and the second is the recent proposal to privatize the old-age pension program. Other countries, both developed and developing, are influenced by the US privatization plans. In particular, the latter countries have received a strong recommendation to privatize from the International Monetary Fund (IMF) and the World Bank, where US influence prevails (see, for example, World Bank 1994). Japan is no exception. Several economists have proposed privatization of the public pension program influenced largely by the US economic success.

I concluded above that both families and enterprises, and not the public sector were responsible for welfare provision in Japan. Nevertheless, it is important to recognize that only large firms were suppliers of social welfare; both employees in smaller firms and the self-employed were outside the area of generous welfare provision. I called this phenomenon the 'dual structure of social services' (see Tachibanaki 2000b).

It is quite easy to recognize this dual structure. First, large firms normally have their own housing facilities for married employees and dormitories for non-married employees. The rents are generally very cheap. Second, large firms operate and manage their own health insurance systems, although officially they belong to the public health insurance system. Very large firms have their own hospitals, and cultural and athletic facilities for their employees. Third, the level of pension payments and health services to employees and retired employees in larger firms is considerably higher than those in smaller firms or for self-employed people.

These observations can be confirmed statistically. Table 2.3 shows the amount of non-wage payments by firm size, and its components. It is possible that non-wage labor payments are largely related to welfare provision. The most striking result in the table is the large difference (almost double) in monthly per-employee payments between very large firms (more than 5000 employees) and very small firms (30–99 employees) – ¥116 949 and ¥57 710, respectively. In addition, although the table does not show the difference in the actual payment, it is well known that there is a large difference in severance payments. Table 2.3 supports this indirectly because the rate is 5.6 percent for very large firms, and only 2.8 percent for very small ones.

Table 2.4 presents the figures of non-statutory fringe benefits by each component. Non-statutory fringe benefits imply voluntary payments to employees. A more striking difference can be seen in Table 2.4, where the monthly amount in the largest firms is ¥23 601, while it is only ¥6907 for the smallest ones. The difference is nearly 3.0 times higher. The largest difference appears in the amount of housing costs, as indicated previously. Employees in larger firms enjoy higher housing subsidies than those in smaller firms, including a generous housing mortgage system with a very low interest rate.

Why do enterprises pay non-wage labor costs? Why are there large differences according to the size of the firm? Tachibanaki (2003) discusses this issue extensively, so here we shall merely list the reasons without any explanation: (i) agency model (that is, deferred payment); (ii) tax advantage theory; (iii) worker preference; (iv) cost saving other than to gain a tax advantage; and (v) better industrial relations.

In addition there is a sixth factor, that is, 'ability to pay'. Larger firms can enjoy higher productivity for various reasons, which enables them to pay a

Table 2.3 Components of non-wage labor costs (¥) and total labor costs (%)

Items Size	Total (per month) Amount	(%)	Real goods	Severance payment	Statutory	Non-statutory	Education & training	Hiring cost	Other
Total	82360	17.1	0.5	4.3	8.9	2.8	0.3	0.2	0.2
Over 5000	116949	19.0	0.6	5.6	8.4	3.8	0.3	0.1	0.2
1000–4999	92531	17.5	0.4	4.5	8.4	3.3	0.3	0.2	0.3
300–999	76743	16.5	0.5	3.9	9.0	2.4	0.3	0.2	0.4
100–299	64627	15.6	0.3	3.5	9.3	2.0	0.2	0.2	0.1
30–99	57710	15.2	0.3	2.8	9.8	1.8	0.2	0.1	0.1

Source: Ministry of Labor, 1996 General Survey on Wages and Working Hours, Tokyo.

Table 2.4   Components of non-statutory fringe benefits (%)

	Total	Over 5000	1000–4999	300–999	100–299	30–99
Total	100.0	100.0	100.0	100.0	100.0	100.0
Housing	46.3	49.6	54.1	51.8	33.8	19.4
Medical insurance	5.6	7.9	4.7	3.5	4.7	3.3
Food	10.6	9.8	9.4	10.4	12.7	14.8
Culture and athletics	8.6	8.1	7.1	7.8	9.9	14.1
Private insurance	8.4	3.2	6.8	9.3	14.6	22.5
Additional casualty payment	1.7	0.4	0.6	2.1	3.9	5.8
Congratulations and condolences	3.4	2.7	3.7	3.2	4.0	4.8
Aid to saving	3.9	6.0	3.3	3.1	2.4	1.3
Other	11.6	12.3	10.3	8.7	13.9	13.9
Amount per month (¥)	13682	23601	17439	11317	8069	6907

Source: Ministry of Labor, *1996 General Survey on Wages and Working Hours*, Tokyo.

higher remuneration, in the form of both wages and non-wages, than smaller firms, as shown by Tachibanaki (1996b).

2.2.   Current Problems in Japan

The most serious problem currently facing Japan with respect to socio-economic issues is the lack of confidence in the public pension program by the Japanese people. Particularly the young and the post-baby boom generations fear that their future pension benefits will not be sustained. They anticipate that under a continuation of the pay-as-you-go system their benefit level after retirement will be lowered significantly because of the forecast pension budget deficit.

The various reasons for this deficit may be summarized as follows: (i) excessive payment to previous generations (that is, retired people); (ii) unanticipated slower growth of the economy following the oil crisis and very slow growth rates (sometimes negative) in the 1990s; (iii) very low rates of interest in the 1990s; (iv) a significantly more rapid ageing trend in population–age structure than expected; and (v) no financial contributions to the system by some participants, and a considerable number of people who refuse to participate in the system. The last item is the result of a lack of confidence in the public pension system. An irony is that it also contributes to the predicted budget deficit.

Since the first four items have been discussed and documented fairly well, and are easily understandable, I shall address only the last one. Data on no contributions and/or non-participation are scarce. The media are concerned with this issue, and publish estimated figures of no contributions and/or non-participation. I am obliged to rely on these because the government does not disclose such figures officially.

What is the current situation, and who are the non-contributors and/or non-participants? First, the most serious problem for the basic part of the public pension system is that in 1998 the total number of non-contributors and non-participants was 23.4 percent. According to several casual observations, it could be as high as a third. A survey released by the Social Insurance Agency in 1999 shows that the principal reason for making no contributions, given by 63.8 percent of respondents, is due to insufficient income during the period which makes it difficult for them to contribute. The second most important reason (41.7 percent), is that people do not trust the public pension system. Multiple answers were allowed in this survey.

Second, about 15 percent of firms that are required to participate in the public pension system by law, do not in fact do so. Moreover, the current serious recession means that some participating firms are unable to contribute financially.

Third, the great majority of housewives, who do not work, are exempted from contributing financially, but are entitled to receive the pension benefit. This principle is not applied to women who work. Certainly, the lack of contributions by a certain percentage of women is one of the causes of less revenue in the system. Although the third problem is important, and requires policy reform, I shall not develop it here because of space limitations.

The second and third problems are so serious that a free-rider problem and/or no pension benefit for some retired people might arise in the future. Also, they inevitably contribute less revenue to the public pension system, and thus aggravate the problem. I shall put forward a reform plan later to cope with this problem.

3.   REFORM IN WELFARE PROGRAMS

Nearly all countries experience a predicted budget deficit in their public pension system for the following reasons. First, the pay-as-you-go system provides a favorable benefit to the first generation who did not contribute sufficiently. Second, the ageing trend observed in many countries aggravates the budget deficit because of higher aggregate payments to a large number of retired people and lower aggregate contributions by fewer young people. Third, slower growth rates of the macro economy in the 1980s and 1990s, observed in many countries, also exacerbate the difficulty.

There are various proposals, suggestions and schools of thought with regard to policy reforms in welfare programs in advanced countries. One is the privatization movement in the public pension system. The UK made the first attempt in this field when a shift from the pay-as-you-go system to the funded system with individual freedom of financial management was implemented. The United States has made similar attempts. The issue receives serious attention in Kotlikoff (1996), Feldstein (1998), Diamond (1999), Aaron and Shoven (1999), and some others. The idea of privatization has also received some support from several specialists in Japan (see, for example, Oshio 1999).

Another proposal is to delay the starting age of public pension payments. A large number of countries facing predicted budget deficits have delayed the starting age for benefits. Needless to say, several countries have lowered the pension rate. Japan, in fact, has opted for both these policies, namely delaying the starting age and a cut in benefits.

A third school of thought is represented by several proposals which demand a reduction in the size of welfare programs in general, such as pensions, medical care, unemployment benefit and so on. This point of view can be seen mainly in Europe where the welfare state has been dominant. It proposes that a higher burden of both taxes and social security contributions is harmful to overall economic performance because it is likely to discourage households and firms. A moral hazard problem has also been raised in this connection.

A fourth area concerns the financing method for welfare programs, in particular pension programs. Japan is currently engaged in this debate. One proposal to deal with the anticipated budget deficit in the pension program is to replace social security contributions by general tax revenues. One-third of the basic part (that is, the first tier) is financed by tax revenues in Japan. It has been suggested that all of the basic part should be so financed.

There are several advanced countries such as Australia, Canada, Denmark, Finland, Iceland, New Zealand, Norway and Sweden, where tax revenues are the only source for financing the basic part of the public pension. The reason why I mentioned the names of the countries where tax revenues are used is somewhat ironic; at the hearing organized by the Ministry of Finance I spoke of my tax financing proposal. A comment by one official at the ministry was, 'The countries to which Mr Tachibanaki referred are non-G-five countries like France, Germany, Japan, the UK and the US, and thus smaller countries. Japan should pay more attention to the system in the G-five countries.' I accept that the size of the country matters to a certain extent when we discuss the pension system. However, I do not accept the idea that a larger country cannot implement a tax-financing system. The UK is notable as a country where tax revenues are used to finance the basic part of medical care, as the National Health Service demonstrates.

Why are reforms in welfare programs proposed? As mentioned above, some strong negative opinions and criticism against generous welfare programs, in particular welfare states, have been expressed in Europe. Atkinson (1999) called this 'Rolling back the welfare state'. Atkinson's (1996, 1999) defense of the welfare state included two points: first, such criticism often ignores the virtue or benefit of the welfare state, and over-emphasizes the negative side; and second, the cost of the welfare state, that is, the negative side, as suggested in various critical evaluations has not been verified either theoretically or empirically. Atkinson prefers a more balanced view of the welfare state.

In principle, I am in agreement with Atkinson, and presented my personal views on Japan in Tachibanaki (2000b). Several critics have demanded a lower level of welfare provision even in Japan. At the same time, it has been proposed that the government become less involved, that is, a reduced public role in welfare provision and deregulation policies in many fields. I do not disagree with the necessity of deregulation in industries and other areas in Japan. I do not, however, share the notion that the role of the public sector must be reduced in welfare provision. The main reason for refuting such a proposition is that the role of the public sector in welfare provision is still very minor in Japan, compared to that of other advanced countries. It might be more justifiable to accept some criticism against the European welfare states where the role of the public sector is much more significant in welfare provision than in Japan where there is no sign of a welfare state.

Several reasons have been presented in Japan to explain why a higher rate of tax and social security contributions would be detrimental to labor supply and savings incentive. The negative effect caused by a possibly higher financial burden for households is likely to be harmful to the growth economy, namely to the overall economic performance. This is the main justification for reducing the public sector's role in welfare provision.

I do not agree with this justification or proposition for the following reasons. First, there is no empirical proof to support the negative effect of taxes and social security contributions on labor supply. It is possible that several demographic groups such as married female part-time workers and older workers are concerned about the burden of making tax and social security contributions, and in fact it has been reported that several empirical studies support a minor negative effect. The effect on prime-age male workers, however, has not been demonstrated empirically. Therefore, a possible detrimental effect often suggested for them is merely a hypothetical dissatisfaction that does not have any empirical support. Note that lowering the income tax rate in the United States has made little change in the labor supply behavior of the rich, as shown by Moffitt and Wilhelm (1998).

Second, a possibly detrimental effect of a higher income tax on savings motivation is not supported empirically in Japan. The interest rate elasticity with respect to savings is normally very low, as suggested for example by Tachibanaki and Suruga (1999), and thus it is impossible to predict that a change in the income tax rate on the rate of interest would alter the amount of savings. In other words, savings are unaffected by the burden of income taxes. Consequently, the rate of capital accumulation, which determines the growth rate of the economy, is not influenced by the financial burden of tax and social security contributions, at least in Japan.

Third, somewhat related to this second point, it is necessary to evaluate a proposal to replace state pensions, that is, public pensions, by a means-tested private funded pension. This is common in the United States (for example, see Feldstein 1987, and the World Bank 1994). The idea behind the proposal stems from a fear that a generous state pension, more broadly speaking the welfare state, is likely to reduce the amount of personal savings. Thus, it may be harmful to the growth economy.

Atkinson (1999, ch. 6) showed that the savings trap would matter, if this policy reform were introduced. Under the model of two different representative groups whose wages are above and below a critical level, the former group may raise their savings rate while the latter may reduce theirs to zero. Atkinson concludes that whether aggregate savings increase depends on the number of people above and below the level, these relative wages and the other parameters. In sum, it is premature to draw a definite conclusion about the influence of state pensions on personal savings.

Fourth, as stated above, Japan is not a welfare state. Thus, neither individuals nor enterprises are paying higher taxes and social security contributions to the government. Both sides, nevertheless, complain that the government levies higher burdens, in spite of the fact that they contribute very little to the government, statistically speaking.

There are several reasons for this misunderstanding or misconception. First, people do not know the exact use made of their tax payments and social security contributions, in particular from the international perspective. They do not know exactly how the welfare state in Europe works, or that it raises a considerable amount of tax and social security contributions from the private sector. Related to this argument, people are more familiar with the US situation, that is, it is a non-welfare state. More information on the United States is released to the public because it is regarded not only as the main competitor but also as the 'ideal'. Consequently, it is natural that people should want to keep the burden of taxes and social security contributions to a minimum, as in the United States.

A second reason is that Japanese people are suspicious of government activity in relation to both public expenditure and welfare provision. They regard the government as inefficient, and at the same time they receive little satisfaction. For example, there is a belief that the private sector is more efficient in productivity than the public sector. Some people resent the internal benefits enjoyed by government employees, who sometimes receive extra incentives. There is a common understanding that those who receive benefits from public expenditure are limited to certain groups such as the construction and financial industries, and some others. In sum, people are dissatisfied with the returns on their financial contributions to the public sector.

Third, the second reason is also applicable to welfare. Various welfare programs such as unemployment compensation, public pensions and health insurance are normally financed by social security contributions from both individuals and enterprises. Therefore, the amount of these benefits is determined largely by their contributions, although each person's contribution–benefit relationship is not inflexible, as shown by the existence of both intergenerational and intragenerational transfers. Another difficult issue is the contribution of the general tax revenues to welfare provision, which makes each person's contribution–benefit relationship obscure. By evaluating the above points, it is possible to conclude that the Japanese are suspicious about their return on social security contributions because they feel that they do not receive sufficient benefits compared with their contributions. This feeling is much stronger in the young than in the retired generation. The latter group received a considerably higher level of benefits in both public pensions and medical care, while it is predicted that future retirees, that is, younger generations, would receive a considerably lower level as was described previously.

Fourth, there is a misconception that the benefit of social welfare programs comes from 'heaven'. In other words, a significant number of people feel that they should be able to enjoy the benefit of social welfare programs, but that other people should pay for it. This is because they regard social welfare provision as an extension of social assistance programs such as poverty relief, payment for the disabled and so on, which are normally financed by general tax revenues. In sum, there is a feeling that 'Others should pay for social welfare programs', and at the same time 'I would like to minimize my contribution'.

Finally, the position of enterprises is complicated for the following reasons. Enterprises do not complain formally about their financial burdens to social security systems because there has been general support for the Bismarckian tradition which demanded that both employers and employees in social insurance systems should shoulder the burden equally. A voice of dissatisfaction from the employers is beginning to be heard, as in Europe. The current serious recession, the largest and longest in the postwar period, has intensified such a voice, with many firms facing difficult financial conditions and a risk of bankruptcy. This observation is confirmed by a recent trend which showed an increasing rate of no contributions and/or non-participation of enterprises in social insurance systems, as was disclosed previously. Although this trend is not yet predominant, it suggests a necessity for reform in the future. We have to understand that the role of enterprises is vital in the economy because they guarantee both economic prosperity, and thus employment. Thus, it is desirable to prepare a social welfare program that does not damage the active role of enterprises. I shall discuss this issue below.

4.   POLICY REFORM IN PENSION PROGRAMS

This section discusses reforms in public pension systems, and presents my own policy reform measures, particularly for Japan.

4.1.   Arguments for Policy Reforms

I have discussed briefly several policy alternatives for public pension programs. One major issue was a shift from the pay-as-you-go to the funded system with personal financial management. The latter is frequently called privatization. Thus, such an issue may be characterized by the public pension with a pay-as-you-go scheme versus the privatized pension with a funded scheme.

Disney (2000) classified the treatment of public pension systems into the following: (i) 'parametric' reform of the unfunded program; (ii) 'actuarially' fair; (iii) 'clean break' privatization; and (iv) partial privatization. The first two retain a strong unfunded component, while the last two involve a strong private component. The funded scheme is superior to the unfunded scheme for ten advanced countries, if the real return to pension assets exceeds the sum of the growth rates in the working population and in labor productivity, as shown by Blake (2000). At the same time, Blake shows that the unfunded scheme is not viable for ten advanced countries if real pensions grow in line with productivity.

The above studies as well as those in the United States cited previously seem to suggest that a shift from an unfunded to a funded scheme is unavoidable. However, there is some disagreement on the issue of privatization, for example, see Diamond (1998) and Aaron and Shoven (1999) for the United States, Atkinson (1999) for the UK and Sandmo (1991, 1999) for Scandinavia.

Since the purpose of this chapter is not to compare these two different opinions extensively, I shall describe only briefly my personal judgment on the issue. A crucial issue is the disadvantages of privatization. In particular, since privatized pension funds hold a greater portion of shares in an equity market under privatization, face an increased cost of monitoring shares and have an interest in a short-term view of equity returns that maximize share values, then a long-term view may result in a lower growth rate of the corporation, and thus of the macro economy. This fear was articulated in Atkinson (1999, ch. 7), who analyzed the relationship among investment, pension funds, and the capital market. Atkinson cautions that privatized pension funds may exhibit a slower growth rate than state pension programs.

There are several other reasons why privatization would not work so well, at least in Japan, as expected by advocates of privatization. Also, I would like to propose a different policy reform that avoids the alternatives of the unfunded and the funded schemes – that is, replacing the social insurance principle by the tax principle; in other words, the financing method for pension benefits is shifted from social security contributions to general tax revenues.

The first reason why privatization is problematic is that the Japanese are not ready to invest their funds in the financial market. The investment behavior of the average Japanese is characterized by extremely large quantities of financial assets being deposited at banks and postal saving accounts as time deposits. There is a very low rate of investment on equities and bonds, which normally give a higher rate of return but have a larger fluctuation. This can be verified by, for example, Tachibanaki (1996a), who discusses why the Japanese have not taken risks in financial investment. If individual households had to make an asset commitment under privatization, it is likely that their return on financial investment would be lower. In other words, a higher financial return cannot be expected under privatized pension funds. It would take much longer if a higher financial return on asset investment by ordinary people were one of the targets of privatization.

Second, it is possible that privatization would lead to an increase in the number of people who do not participate in the pension program because it is anticipated that participation enforcement will be very weak. I suggested earlier that the number of no contributions and/or no participations in public pension programs would increase fairly rapidly, even under a strict rule of mandatory participation. Under a privatized pension program such non-participation may lead to an increase in the number of people who have little or no income after retirement. Higher public expenditure may be necessary to support these people. Such public expenditure, which should be financed from general tax revenues, may be regarded as a moral hazard by those who have not only participated in privatized programs, but have also paid general taxes. Simply, it is unfair.

Third, a considerable reduction in the role of firms in welfare provision would entail a fairly drastic policy reform in welfare systems in general. This would suggest a departure from the Bismarck and Beveridge traditions of a social security system in which both employers and employees are expected to contribute financially.

Tachibanaki (2003) has discussed at length the reasons why enterprises can evade social security systems, and these are summarized here. First, it is logical to have a social security system where beneficiaries are the sole financial contributors. In other words, financing for social security benefits should be borne by beneficiaries. Firms are not direct beneficiaries, although they enjoy some indirect benefits.

Second, the intrinsic role of firms is to enhance economic activity, and thus to boost employment. Thus, worrying about employees' welfare should not be the first priority of firms' management policy. Responsibility must be borne by society as a whole. The existence of firms' contribution to social security may be distortional for efficient allocation of labor and capital.

The third reason for proposing a very limited role for firms in welfare provision is that the degree of benefit levels differ greatly not only from occupation to occupation but also from firm size to firm size both in statutory and non-statutory welfare benefits, as was discussed previously. Self-employed workers receive no support from firms, while employees in large firms receive an excessively high level of benefits. This may be regarded as unfair.

In sum, there is no strong justification to support the notion that firms should be responsible for welfare benefits of workers. I believe that the benefit should be financed by an individual's contribution through the public sector's transfer to each beneficiary.

4.2. An Actual Reform Policy

This section outlines my proposal for reforming social security systems in Japan, in particular the public pension system, and presents several simulation results which support such a proposal.

The overall proposal may be summarized as follows. The current financing method, namely the pay-as-you-go system, could be replaced by the (general) tax revenue method, that is, full (100 percent) financing by progressive value-added tax or progressive expenditure tax levied on individuals, for the first tier (that is, the basic part of the pension benefit). The second tier might be abolished, if the payment amount of the first tier were sufficient, or might be modified to a privatized funded scheme, if the amount of the first tier were not sufficient. I estimate that the desirable monthly amount of the first tier is ¥170 000 for a couple, and ¥90 000 for a single person. Firms' contribution to social security is no longer expected. Implementation would require careful policy reform, particularly in the early stages in order to minimize excessive welfare loss in transitory generations.

I shall explain why such reform is desirable, and present supporting evidence. I shall also address some anticipated reservations about and critical comments on my arguments.

The reasons for reform can be summarized as follows. First, it is likely that people, in particular the younger generation, would be reassured in the knowledge that a basic level of income for all retirees is guaranteed, because funding would be provided by general tax revenues rather than by social security contributions where a shortfall is expected.

Second, there is serious concern about intergenerational inequality in the rates of return on public pension premiums, which has been caused by many factors. Adopting general tax revenues makes the calculation of the rates of return impossible or unreliable, and thus obscures the inequality argument. Similarly, no one calculates the rate of return on educational expenditure financed by general tax revenues. In other words, pension benefits could be regarded as a public good like public expenditures on education, if general tax revenues are used.

Third, there are, in principle, two public institutions which collect funds from the private sector, namely the tax bureau, which collects taxes, and the social insurance bureau, which collects social security contributions. My proposal suggests an integration of these two institutions, thus contributing to a reduction in the administration cost, and individual households and enterprises would also benefit because of administrative simplification.

Fourth, the amount of the basic part, that is, an estimated ¥170 000 per month for a retired couple, can be regarded as the national minimum that would justify the existence of a social security system, or social safety net for all citizens. This would eliminates poverty, and has been a tradition since Beveridge. Although I proposed a departure from the Bismarck and Beveridge traditions in the sense that employers can withdraw from contributing financially to the social security system, I would like to retain the Beveridge tradition regarding the concept of a national minimum amount for benefits.

Fifth, as described above, Japan was not a welfare state in which the public sector was responsible for welfare services; traditionally, both families and enterprises have been the main providers. The recent social and economic phenomena in Japan can be characterized by the following trends: (i) erosion of solidarity and family ties, and (ii) weakness of enterprises' financial and management conditions. These phenomena imply that both families and enterprises cannot support family members and/or employees, and thus an alternative method must be introduced to compensate for the decreasing rate of such welfare provisions. I believe that the public sector should be actively involved in collecting funds from individuals and providing them with a minimum level of welfare services.

Sixth, there is an economic justification because replacing social security contributions by general tax revenues provides an economy with a better allocation of resources regarding the public pension system. In particular, several simulation studies indicate that social welfare is greatly improved when a progressive value-added tax or a progressive expenditure tax rather than social insurance premiums is used to finance pension benefits. Efficiency is assured by virtue of the indirect nature of value-added taxes and/or of an expenditure tax rather than the direct tax, and equity is assured by virtue of the nature of progressivity (see Okamoto and Tachibanaki 2002).

Okamoto and Tachibanaki (2002) undertook a simulation study, utilizing an extended life-cycle general equilibrium model of overlapping generations with heterogeneous households. 'Heterogeneous' here implies that households differ according to their income level. They considered four cases of policy reforms in public pension programs (see Figures 2.1 and 2.2).

- Case B: partial integration and a progressive income tax. 'Integration' implies that a tax system and a social insurance system are combined. Thus, 'perfect integration' signifies that only tax revenues are used, and thus social security contributions are no longer used. 'Partial' signifies that 50 percent is tax revenues, and thus the remaining 50 percent is social security contributions. 'Progressive' implies that the tax rate for higher-income households or higher expenditure households is higher than that for lower ones.
- Case C: partial integration and a proportional expenditure tax.
- Case D: perfect integration and a proportional expenditure tax.
- Case E: perfect integration and a progressive expenditure tax.

Cases B, C, D and E in Figures 2.1 and 2.2 are classified by the following three elements: (i) tax base – income or expenditure, (ii) tax rate – proportional

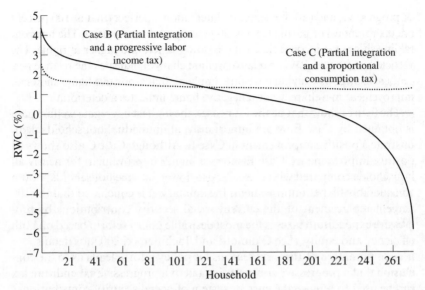

Figure 2.1 Changes in welfare of 275 households, by income (cases B and C)

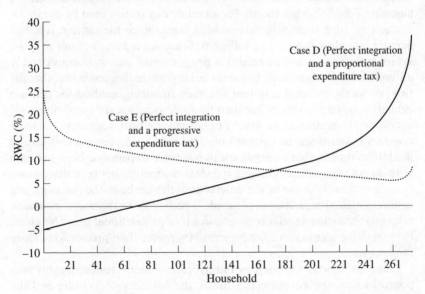

Figure 2.2 Changes in welfare of 275 households, by income (cases D and E)

or progressive, and (iii) the degree of integration – perfect (that is, 100 percent are tax revenues) or partial (that is, 50 percent are tax revenues). The horizontal line shows the income class (that is, lower at left and higher at right). The vertical line (that is, RWC = relative welfare change) indicates the relative percentage change in individual welfare, implying that a positive figure shows an improvement in welfare, while a negative figure indicates a deterioration.

The figures show that of the four cases, the highest aggregate welfare gain is obtained by Case E. More importantly, all individual households demonstrate a positive improvement in Case E. Although Case C also shows all positive improvements, Case E shows a higher improvement for nearly all households compared with Case C. Also, lower-income households show a considerably higher improvement. In summary, it is concluded that the 100 percent replacement of the current social security contributions by progressive expenditure taxes is the most desirable policy reform based on both efficiency and equity. (See Okamoto and Tachibanaki 2002 for details.)

A combination of these six reasons for policy reform leads us to the conclusion that a progressive consumption tax or a progressive expenditure tax can be used to replace the current system of social security contributions.

There is various supporting evidence that consolidates the policy reform. First, Denki-Rengo (2000) released a document which proposes that the amount of ¥170000 per month for a couple can be financed by the introduction of 10 percent rate value-added taxes. Since the current rate is 5 percent, doubling it would be sufficient. Since the report does not propose a progressive tax rate but retains a proportional rate, it is considerably different from my proposal. It should be emphasized, nevertheless, that the two proposals are similar in that the main financing method for pension benefits is through taxes rather than through social security contributions.

Second, Ushimaru et al. (1999) published a report suggesting that tax revenues rather than the current one-third rate of tax revenues should be used to finance the basic part of the public pension benefits. Their tax base is an income tax. Although there is a clear distinction between this proposition and mine because of the difference in the tax base, the two suggest a common idea, that is, the tax principle is preferable to the social insurance principle. Also, they prefer a progressive to a proportional tax. Therefore, the two share a preference for progressivity rather than proportionality in the tax rate.

There are various reservations and critical comments concerning my proposal. In fact, the government (that is, the Ministry of Welfare and the Ministry of Finance), does not accept this proposal, but continues to support the social insurance principle.

There are several reasons for the government's antipathy. First, it claims that the pension benefit financed only by tax revenues is nearly equivalent to the social assistance program to the poor. Retaining the insurance principle makes the relationship between benefits and contributions straightforward, and thus it fits well with the idea of self-support after retirement. In other words, a benefit financed only by taxes may lead to a moral hazard problem, as observed in various social assistance programs. Second, a means test may be required if all retirees are entitled to receive the same amount of basic pension. After all, should rich retired people receive a pension benefit based on tax revenues?

These two reservations come from a fairly common background, namely that the pension is not a public good which can be financed by general tax revenues. Although I shall not discuss this idea theoretically and extensively, I believe that the tax principle for pension benefits overrides various shortcomings of the current public pension program, and the advantages outweigh the disadvantages. Incidentally, I am inclined to support a means test even for the basic part of pension benefits.

Third, employees at the Social Insurance Bureau in the Ministry of Welfare are concerned about the loss of their jobs because there are no social security contributions. This problem would easily be solved by integrating the Social Insurance Bureau with the Tax Bureau, as was done in the UK recently.

Fourth, the Ministry of Finance does not like the idea that a large amount of tax revenues from value-added and/or expenditure taxes should be used for pension benefits. The ministry, implicitly, assumes that an increased amount of tax revenues induced by an increase in the value-added tax rate should be used to reduce Japan's huge budgetary deficit. The answer to this problem is simple. It is rational to think of the overall government budget as including the social security account, rather than seeing the latter as a budget administered in isolation by the Ministry of Finance. At the same time, if the overall benefit caused by a change in the financing method for pension payments is positive, the ministry has no reason to object since the government exists for the benefit of citizens.

5. THE ROLE OF FIRMS IN WELFARE PROVISIONS

5.1. Introduction

Section 2 showed that Japan was not a welfare state, and it also discussed the role of firms in welfare provisions.

There are basically four important components of firms' contributions to welfare: (i) statutory contributions to social security, accounting for about 50 percent of non-wage labor payments; (ii) non-statutory fringe benefits; (iii) retirement allowances (or severance payments); and (iv) the sum of payment as a form of real goods, expenditures on education and training for employees, hiring costs and so on.

5.2   Why Firms Contribute to Welfare Provision

This section presents economic theories and/or reasons that can explain why there is a considerably high share of non-wage payments, in particular non-statutory fringe benefits.

It is crucial to understand that a large part of fringe benefits such as payment to private retirement systems (including severance payments), life insurance systems, health benefits and other agreed-upon plans, are *deferred* compensations. Thus, the intrinsic nature of deferred compensations is the main reason for both employers' and employees' preferences, although the factors that are not associated with deferred payments also have to be examined.

In an early study, Rice (1966) put forward four factors to explain the growth of fringe benefits in the United States: (i) preferential treatment under federal personal income tax laws; (ii) savings that are made possible by group purchase of some benefits, notably insurance; (iii) efforts to reduce turnover in the face of rising costs of labor turnover; and (iv) unionization. Woodbury (1983) added three more factors: (v) preferential treatment under federal corporate income taxes since contributions by employers to pension funds and insurance benefits are largely deductible from employers' taxable income; (vi) the changing age composition of the labor force; and (vii) the effect of rising income. Hart (1984) provided a useful survey for these results in the 1960s to early 1980s, and analyzed non-wage labor costs.

These factors were recently examined in an attempt to understand the rationales of fringe benefits, and new results were added which can be summarized as follows: (i) agency theory; (ii) tax advantage theory; (iii) worker preference; (iv) cost saving other than to gain a tax advantage; and (v) better industrial relations. These factors explain the *level* of fringe benefits; however, by reinterpreting them, they may also be used to explain the *growth* of fringe benefits. Each heading is discussed below.

Agency model
This model was developed by Lazear (1979, 1981) as an extension of Becker (1964). Basically, the optimal age–earnings strategy for a firm is to pay workers less than their marginal value product in their early years within the firm and more in their later years. There are several reasons for supporting this strategy. First, an employee who has received costly training may

quit before the firm has recouped the cost of training, or may engage in a suboptimal level of shirking. Lazear emphasized the importance of deferred compensation to increase the employee's opportunity cost of quitting or shirking, with its attendant prospects of being discharged. Second, fringe payments may directly increase workers' productivity. Third, somewhat contrary to the second view, there is a finding that productivity grows far less in proportion to earnings by length of service in the firm (see Medoff and Abraham 1980). If this finding were true, a more steeply rising age–earnings profile would increase a worker's incentive to shirk.

Several reservations may be expressed for agency theory. First, the model refers implicitly to total labor compensation rather than to fringe benefits only. Second, the causal mechanism is less clear. Third, some empirical evidence on the difference in working hours between younger and older workers is contradictory with the theory. Fourth, it is not easy to identify whether human capital theory or agency theory based on empirical wage data is more appropriate.

Tax advantage theory
Three basic arguments are possible under the tax advantage model. First, it benefits from the fact that most forms of non-wage compensation are not taxed as income. By applying a standard microeconomic theory, it is possible to conjecture that employers could reduce compensation costs without reducing employee utility by offering compensation packages which contain non-wage costs, when these costs are free from income taxation. This provides employers with an incentive to raise the rate of non-wage compensation.

Second, somewhat related to the argument of the agency model, Mumy (1985) has shown that deferred payment has a clear advantage when all the factors about payroll taxes, social security benefits, and income taxes are taken into account. This is because when wage income is deferred, the present value of the payroll taxes on wage income declines, but a later wage income enters the calculation of average earnings for social security payment in an undiscounted manner. In other words, the social security and payroll tax incentive is to defer compensation early in working life, and avoid payroll taxes and allow pension benefits to accrue, while the concentration of compensation in later life raises the average earnings base for social security benefits. Again, the reservations on the agency theory may be applicable here.

Third, corporate tax laws favor employer contributions to social security and pension funds because such contributions are tax deductible.

In sum, the tax advantage model is quite promising for interpreting the rapid growth of non-wage labor costs, particularly pensions. We can see a good example of the usefulness of this tax advantage theory in the rapidly growing enterprise pension systems such as 401(k) in the United States (among others see, for example, Poterba et al. 1994).

Worker preference
A large number of empirical studies such as Freeman (1981), Lester (1967), and Woodbury (1983) propose that unionized firms have a higher proportion of total compensation in the form of fringe benefits in comparison with non-unionized firms. An exception is Reynolds (1974). Since the union gives greater weight to the preference of older workers and permanent workers, who are likely to want to substitute more deferred compensations such as health insurance and pensions for lower wages, than to younger and more mobile workers, unionized firms tend to have higher fringe benefits. This argument is an application of the median voter model advocated by Freeman and Medoff (1979). See Tachibanaki and Noda (2000) for unions in Japan that prefer such arrangements. Interestingly, large Japanese firms reacted positively to their unions' preferences.

It must be noted, however, that although the theory of union preference is reasonably persuasive, we have to offer adequate explanations as to why even non-unionized firms in some countries prefer fringe benefits, and why highly unionized countries such as Germany and Sweden have a lower rate of voluntary non-wage labor costs.

The case of Germany and Sweden is straightforward. Those countries which have a lower rate of non-statutory social programs have a higher rate of statutory social welfare programs. Thus, the necessity for non-statutory social programs is greatly reduced. However, it is open to question whether reliance on statutory social welfare programs or on non-statutory programs is the more efficient and productive method of strengthening a national economy.

The case of non-unionized firms is not so simple. The tax advantage model may be working quite adequately for non-unionized firms as well. In other words, both employers and employees agree upon raising the rate of deferred payments in order to benefit from the more favorable tax treatment. It is possible that firms also pay fringe benefits on a purely 'voluntary' basis outside the system of collective bargaining to encourage employee loyalty.

Cost saving other than to gain a tax advantage
A specialized agent, such as an insurance company, can provide insurance with lower charges. The employee's risk would be reduced if a large number of workers were to join a group insurance program with the consent of an employer. The management cost of pensions and insurances can also be

reduced if an employer and its employees administer, monitor and evaluate their programs collectively. These cost-saving features encourage an employer and its employees to increase the number of fringe programs and the employer's expenditure on these programs.

Better industrial relations
Larger firms tend to provide a considerably high share of non-statutory fringe benefits to their employees. One of the reasons for this is that such firms want to improve industrial relations. Generous treatment, such as better housing facilities, medical insurance, canteens, cultural and athletic facilities and so on, can reduce turnover by attracting more qualified workers and encouraging employees to stay in their firms. Loyalty to firms can also be expected, and thus employers can benefit from their employees' high motivation and hard work. Also, firms were reluctant to be the only ones to pay higher wages to employees, because harmony in the industry was believed to be important. These are the main reasons why larger firms provide a considerably high share of fringe benefits. Trade unions in these firms responded positively, and thus both employers and employees cooperated (see Tachibanaki and Noda 2000).

6. TAX INCIDENCE

Several criticisms have been made against the high share of social security contribution, in particular employers' contributions and non-statutory fringe benefits. First, this high rate increases labor costs in general. It is detrimental to the financial condition of a firm, and thus to employment. Second, it may encourage a firm to employ a more capital-intensive rather than a labor-intensive technique because of an increase in labor costs. Again, this is harmful to employment. Third, related to the second point, labor-intensive industries are affected more severely than capital-intensive industries. Fourth, non-manual (or skilled) workers will be preferred to manual (or non-skilled) workers due to a wage ceiling in determining the contribution rate. Fifth, since welfare provisions are enjoyed almost entirely by individuals, it is conceivable that firms could be relieved of the burden of making contributions to welfare provision. The reduction in these contributions could be used to finance an increase in the number of employees and/or in the per hour wage.

There is one extremely important subject which must be considered before proceeding to these questions: payroll tax incidence. It is crucial to understand who actually bears the burden of employer contributions. There are three possible scenarios: (i) backward shifting, which means that a firm can pass on employer contribution (payroll tax) to its employees; (ii) forward shifting, which specifies that a firm can pass on the tax to consumers in the form of price increases; and (iii) no shifting at all. The five propositions regarding the effect on employment are made under a presumption that a firm does not shift the burden at all. Therefore, when tax shifting does occur, the propositions must be modified according to the direction and the degree of tax shifting. Several theoretical results and empirical evidence about payroll tax incidence are reviewed.

In a world of competitive markets the incidence of a payroll tax depends upon two parameters, namely the labor supply elasticity and the labor demand elasticity. If capital is considered as an additional input factor, the substitution possibility between capital and labor also plays an important role. The common technique to estimate the payroll tax incidence was initiated by Brittain (1972), who formulated a labor demand equation derived from a production function. The effect of a payroll tax was estimated indirectly. There was a common understanding based on this technique that payroll taxes are mostly borne by labor in the long run because long-run labor supply elasticity is perfectly inelastic or very low, as Break (1974) found mainly for the United States. In other words, it had been believed that employer contributions were fully shifted backward to workers' real wages.

Feldstein (1974) proposed a model of the incidence of the payroll tax which assumes that the supply of labor is not necessarily inelastic. He also introduced a growth dynamic through capital accumulation. When the estimates on labor supply elasticity and labor demand elasticity are applied to the model, a slightly different result is obtained. For example, for the United Kingdom data, Beach and Balfour (1983) estimated that only 45–60 percent of prime-age males and 14–19 percent of married women were shifted back to labor. Since the value of labor supply elasticity is considerably higher for married women, say 0.8–1.1 percent compared with 0.08–0.20 percent for men, only a small portion is shifted back. Thus, the effect of the payroll tax is shared equally between wage rate loss and employment reduction for married women, while the major effect is on wage rate loss for men. Irish results show a similar story. Kirwan (1979) adopts a higher value of labor supply elasticity, 0.74, while Hughes (1985) applies a lower value, 0.21. The estimated results of shifting turned out to be considerably different between the two. Consequently, a possible reduction in the employer contribution produces a different result in the estimate of job creation. Those two studies clearly show the importance of labor supply elasticity in estimating the effect of the payroll tax on shifting and on the number of possible job creations (or job losses) due to a change in the rate of the employers' contribution.

Hamermesh (1979) estimated labor supply elasticity for the United States, and obtained the result that 36 percent of payroll taxes is borne by labor in the form of lower wage rates for white males. Although his 1979 paper recognized the difference in labor supply elasticity among demographic groups, he failed to take account of such differences. His emphasis was placed upon the adjustment process of labor demand and supply. Extending the idea of the adjustment process, Hamermesh (1980) obtained the result that the impact of a change in the payroll tax rate on a change in the wage rate is delayed for several years because the adjustment of both labor supply and labor demand is not instantaneous in reality. He applied the recent estimated values of the adjustment coefficients to estimate his result.

Another important finding derived from Hamermesh (1980) is that the response to a decrease in the payroll tax is much slower than to an increase. This asymmetric nature arises from the fact that the adjustment of actual to desired labor supply is slower than that of actual to derived labor demand because he adopted the Barro and Grossman (1976) employment model. The Barro–Grossman model specifies that actual employment must be the minimum of amounts supplied and demanded. This asymmetry has an important policy implication: when the tax rate is increased, the employment rate adjusts quickly (that is, employment is cut quickly because labor demand is the binding constraint). When the tax rate is decreased, employment increases only slowly because the labor supply is the constraint. Thus, a policy which aims at lowering the payroll tax rate in order to increase employment has only a limited value, while increasing the tax rate is quite detrimental to employment.

Two reservations are necessary. First, it may still be effective to decrease the payroll tax rate in order to increase employment for an economy where the observed rate of unemployment is very high, such as in several European nations. Second, it is necessary to bear in mind that the supply elasticities for both men and women are considerably higher in a country where the average tax burden (both income and payroll taxes) is heavy. See, for example, Blomquist (1983) in Sweden. In those cases employment adjustment (cut in employment) may be made more quickly than the adjustment suggested by the model.

What happens in an economy in which both factor and product markets are imperfectly competitive with respect to the incidence problem? Unions may resist the lowering of real wages to maintain their real purchasing power. Firms with monopoly power may raise the product price, and pass on the tax increases to consumers, that is, forward shifting. For example, see Leuthold (1975) who tackled this problem in the United States. Although she concluded that labor contracts and union actions effectively prevented real wage from falling rapidly, much work is needed to obtain a more conclusive result.

Apart from the common technique described above, another estimation method has been applied by several authors. This may be called a macro-economy, or Phillips curve, approach. Perry (1970) proposed that an increase in employers' contributions did not show any decrease in wage. Gordon (1971), on the contrary, suggested that employers' contributions were shifted back to wages entirely. Vroman (1974) showed a result somewhere between these two. All the studies were conducted for the United States, and the outcome is quite mixed. Holmlund (1983) made estimations for Sweden, using a similar but more sophisticated method. He concluded that only a fraction (roughly about 40 percent) of post-war Swedish payroll tax increases had been directly shifted back onto labor as lower wage increases. Incidentally, he also showed that around 30 percent of employers contributions in the United States were shifted back.

In sum, the studies on the analysis of the payroll tax incidence tends to suggest that only a small portion of employers' contributions is shifted back onto labor. The degree depends on many factors, and is very sensitive to the adopted elasticity parameters. However, it must be emphasized that no studies except for one (that is, Perry 1970), have shown that there is no backward shifting at all. Some backward shifting must be kept in mind.

Interest in the study of the payroll tax incidence has diminished in recent years. There are two reasons for this: first, there is a widespread belief that only a small portion of employers' contributions is shifted back onto labor, thus, there is no strong incentive to add a new result; and second, several technical issues have not yet been solved. Thus, unless a new estimation method is devised, the existing results will prevail.

Finally, the estimated result in Japan (see Tachibanaki and Yokoyama 2002) suggests that no major portion of employers' contributions to social insurance is shifted back onto labor. In other words, nearly all of the employers' contribution is borne by employers (that is, firms). Since few studies have estimated the degree of tax incidence in Japan, it is somewhat risky to rely only on the study by Tachibanaki and Yokoyama, and some reservations are necessary.

7. POLICY RECOMMENDATIONS FOR FIRMS

This section presents policy reforms regarding the role of firms in welfare provision. There are three possible options: first, abandon or reduce the burden of firms' contributions to social security if it is believed to be too heavy, and thus expect employees to accept a lower level of social security benefits. Since it is not, however, desirable to lower the level of social security benefits, somebody has to accept a higher financial burden to compensate for the reduction in social security benefits, in other words, everybody; second, only a part, namely non-statutory fringe benefits, should be transformed into wage payments; and third, consider a new financing method for social security, if employees do not accept a lower social security benefit level.

My own preference is to propose a combination of these three choices for the following reasons. First, it is desirable to reduce the burden of firms' contributions to social security financing in order that firms can concentrate on engaging in their own business activities more easily. We can add the fact that firms' contributions to social security are likely to make a distortionary impact on labor allocations, as was proposed previously.

Second, there is no strong justification to believe that firms are required to be responsible for workers' social security benefits. I believe that firms' responsibility is to ensure prosperous economic activity, thereby maintaining employment levels with possibly higher wages. It should be noted that self-employed workers and farmers have no outside support such as employer contributions on which they can rely.

Third, it is desirable to have a social security system whose financing is borne by beneficiaries. One way to have such a system is to shift the financing method from the social insurance principle to the tax principle, as proposed in this chapter.

8. CONCLUDING REMARKS

This chapter has presented two major reforms in social security in Japan. The first one is to switch the public pension system from the current pay-as-you-go method to the tax financing method at least for the basic part of the pension benefit. More concretely, it is recommended that progressive consumption tax or progressive expenditure tax should be introduced. The second is to permit and even encourage firms to withdraw from welfare provision programs.

The chapter examined the present status of social security systems in Japan, and concluded that Japan was not a welfare state. The major providers were families and firms, in particular large firms. The chapter also discussed various issues of public pension and enterprise pension reforms in the advanced countries, including privatization, efficiency–equity trade-off, tax incidence and so on.

A fairly concrete reform in the public pension system, and a recommendation of withdrawal from firms' contribution to welfare provisions was proposed. I believe that such reforms and recommendations are useful to support the standard of living of the aged in an uncertain world, and improve the economic prosperity of firms which are currently in serious recession and facing acute competition internationally.

REFERENCES

Aaron, H.J. and J.B. Shoven (1999), *Should the United States Privatize Social Security?*, Cambridge, MA: MIT Press.

Atkinson, A.B. (1996), *Incomes and the Welfare State*, Cambridge: Cambridge University Press.

Atkinson, A.B. (1999), *The Economic Consequences of Rolling Back the Welfare State*, Cambridge, MA: MIT Press.

Barro, R.J. and H.J. Grossman (1976), *Money, Employment and Inflation*, Cambridge: Cambridge University Press.

Beach, C.M. and F.S. Balfour (1983), 'Estimated payroll tax incidence and aggregate demand for labour in the U.K.', *Economica*, **50**, 35–48.

Becker, G.S. (1964), *Human Capital: A Theoretical and Empirical Analysis with Special Reference to Education*, New York: National Bureau of Economic Research.

Blake, D. (2000), 'Does it matter what kind of pension scheme you have?', *Economic Journal*, **110** (461), F46–F81.

Blomquist, N.J. (1983), 'The effect of income taxation on the labour supply of married men in Sweden', *Journal of Public Economics*, **22**, November, 169–97.

Break, G. (1974), 'The incidence and economic effects of taxation', in G. Break et al., *The Economics of Public Finance*, Washington, DC: Brookings Institution.

Brittain, J.A. (1972), *The Payroll Tax for Social Security*, Washington, DC: Brookings Institution.

Denki-Rengo (2000), 'A report on the issues of fewer children and more aged people, and policy reform for public and occupational pensions', unpublished (in Japanese).

Diamond, P. (1998), 'Economics of social security reform', in R.D. Arnold, M.J. Graetz, and A.H. Hunnell (eds), *Framing the Social Security Debate: Values, Politics, and Economics*, Washington, DC: National Academy of Social Insurance.

Diamond, P. (1999), *Issues in Privatizing Social Security*, Cambridge, MA: MIT Press.

Disney, R. (2000), 'Crises in public pension programmes in OECD: what are the reform options?', *Economic Journal*, **110** (461), F1–F23.

Feldstein, M.S. (1974), 'Tax incidence with growth and variable factor supply', *Quarterly Journal of Economics*, **87**, November, 551–73.

Feldstein, M. (1987), 'Should social security benefits be means tested?', *Journal of Political Economy*, **95**, 468–84.

Feldstein, M. (ed.) (1998), *Privatizing Social Security*, Chicago: University of Chicago Press.

Freeman, R.B. (1981), 'The effect of unionization on retirement,' *Industrial and Labour Relations Review*, **34**, July, 489–509.

Freeman, R.B. and J.L. Medoff (1979), 'The two faces of unionism', *Public Interest*, **57**, 69–93.

Gordon, R.J. (1971), 'Inflation in recession and recovery', *Brookings Papers on Economic Activity*, **1**, 105–66.

Hamermesh, D. (1979), 'New estimates of the incidence of the payroll tax', *Southern Economic Journal*, **45**, April, 1208–19.

Hamermesh, D.S. (1980), 'Factor market dynamics and the incidence of taxes and subsidies', *Quarterly Journal of Economics*, **95**, December, 751–64.

Hart, R.A. (1984), *The Economics of Non-wage Labour Costs*, London: George Allen & Unwin.

Holmlund, B. (1983), 'Payroll taxes and wage inflation: the Swedish experience', *Scandinavian Journal of Economics*, **85** (1), 1–15.

Hughes, G. (1985), *Payroll Tax Incidence, The Direct Tax Burden and the Rate of Return of State Pension Contributions in Ireland*, Dublin: Economic and Social Research Institute.

Kirwan, F.X. (1979), 'Non-wage costs, employment and hours of work in Irish manufacturing industry', *Economic and Social Review*, **10**, 231–54.

Kotlikoff, L.J. (1996), 'Privatizing social security at home and abroad', *American Economic Review*, **86** (2), 368–72.

Lazear, E.P. (1979), 'Why is there mandatory retirement?', *Journal of Political Economy*, **87**, December, 1261–8.

Lazear, E.P. (1981), 'Agency, earnings profiles, productivity, and hours restrictions', *American Economic Review*, **71**, September, 606–20.

Lester, R.A. (1967), 'Benefits as a preferred form of compensation', *Southern Economic Journal*, **33**, April, 485–95.

Leuthold, J.H. (1975), 'The incidence of the payroll tax in the United States', *Public Finance Quarterly*, No. 1, January, pp. 3–13.

Lindbeck, A. et al. (1994), *Turning Sweden Around*, Cambridge, MA: MIT Press.

Medoff, J.L. and K.G. Abraham (1980), 'Experience, performance, and earnings', *Quarterly Journal of Economics*, **95**, 703–36.

Moffitt, R.A. and Mark Wilhelm (1998), 'Taxation and the labor supply decisions of the affluent', NBER Working Paper No. 6621, National Bureau of Economic Research.

Mumy, G.E. (1985), 'The role of taxes and social security in determining the structure of wages and pensions', *Journal of Political Economy*, **93** (3), 574–85.

Okamoto, A. and T. Tachibanaki (2002), 'Integration of tax and social security systems: on the financing methods of a public pension scheme in a pay-as-you-go system', in T. Ihori and T. Tachibanaki (eds), *Social Security Reform in Advanced Countries*, London: Routledge, pp. 132–60.

Oshio, T. (1999), 'An economic welfare analysis of pension privatization', *JCER (Japan Center for Economic Research) Economic Journal*, No. 39, 1–20 (in Japanese).

Perry, G. (1970), 'Changing labour market and inflation', *Brookings Papers on Economic Activity*, No. 3, 411–41.

Poterba, J.M., S.F. Venti and D.A. Wise (1994), '401(k) plans and tax-deferred saving', in D. Wise (ed.), *Studies in the Economics of Aging*, Chicago: University of Chicago Press, pp. 105–38.

Reynolds, L.G. (1974), *Labor Economics and Labor Relations*, Englewood Cliffs, NJ: Prentice-Hall.

Rice, R. (1966), 'Skill, earnings and the growth of wage supplements', *American Economic Review*, **80**, 1120–43.

Sandmo, A. (1991), 'Economists and the welfare state', *European Economic Review*, **35**, 213–39.

42	*The economics of social security in Japan*

Sandmo, A. (1999), 'Public economics of redistribution and the welfare state', *Quarterly Journal of Social Security Research*, **35** (1), 13–23 (in Japanese).

Tachibanaki, T. (1996a), *Public Policies and the Japanese Economy*, London: Macmillan Press.

Tachibanaki, T. (1996b), *Wage Determination and Distribution in Japan*, Oxford: Oxford University Press.

Tachibanaki, T. (2000a), 'Japan was not a welfare state, but . . .', in Ch. 11, R. Griffiths and T. Tachibanaki (eds), *From Austerity to Affluence: The Transformation of the Socio-economic Structure of Western Europe and Japan*, London: Macmillan, pp. 188–208.

Tachibanaki, T. (2000b), *The Economics of a Safety Net*, Tokyo: Nihonkeizai shinbunsha (in Japanese).

Tachibanaki, T. (2003), 'The role of firms in welfare provisions', in Ch. 11, S. Ogura, T. Tachibanaki and D.A. Wise (eds), *Labor Markets and Firm Benefit Policies in Japan and the United States*, Chicago: University of Chicago Press, pp. 315–38.

Tachibanaki, T. and T. Noda (2000), *The Economic Effects of Trade Unions in Japan*, London: Macmillan.

Tachibanaki, T. and T. Suruga (1999), 'Consumption functions, interest rates and transitory consumption', mimeo.

Tachibanaki, T. and Y. Yokoyama (2002), 'The estimation of the incidence of employer contributions to social security', Kyoto Institute of Economic Research, Discussion Paper No. 528.

Ushimaru, S. et al. (1999), 'Policy reforms in basic pension systems', Economic Policy Analysis No. 13, Economic Planning Agency (in Japanese).

Vroman, W. (1974), 'Employer payroll taxes and money wage behaviour', *Applied Economics*, **8**, 189–204.

Woodbury, S.A. (1983), 'Substitution between wage and non-wage benefits', *American Economic Review*, **73**, March, 166–82.

World Bank (1994), *Averting the Old Age Crisis*, Washington, DC: World Bank.

3. Uncertainty and pension policy

Henry J. Aaron and Benjamin H. Harris*

1. INTRODUCTION

Governments in most developed countries face serious problems in financing their public pension programs. Falling fertility and mortality rates are pushing up the costs of government-managed pension programs, none of which has built up full reserves. The problem is widely perceived as one of population ageing, which is certainly one legitimate way of viewing the situation. But the problem can equally well be interpreted as a result of legislative intent. In every case, pension laws could have been drafted to avoid these problems. The most obvious way would have been to build up full actuarial reserves.[1] Such funding could have boosted national saving and productive capacity, but it would not have lowered the shift of real resources from active to inactive members of the population. Legislatures elected not to build such reserves for what, at the time, seemed to be good and sufficient reasons.

Alternatively, plans could have been drafted with automatic adjustment provisions that would have forestalled the emergence of deficits and the need to amend pension laws to maintain financial balance. Had such adjustment provisions been enacted in the past, they might have reduced the current political divisiveness associated with pension reform. But they would not have reduced the cost of providing the elderly and disabled with a given standard of living. In fact, such automatic adjustment provisions might well have forestalled desirable debate about changes in pension structure now occurring in many countries, a debate that many regard as long overdue.

Of equal and perhaps greater significance, nothing can be done to reduce the uncertainty attending projections of the future costs of pensions. These projections depend sensitively on forecasts that are subject to considerable error. In this chapter, we examine (i) the sources of inaccuracy in forecasts of pension costs with special attention to demographic uncertainty and (ii) a variety of automatic adjustment provisions that could help maintain financial balance in pension plans.

We shall review demographic projections for the United States and

43

Japan. The range of uncertainty surrounding these projections has probably increased for two opposing reasons. First, elimination or drastic reduction of the major sources of mortality and control of ageing have become realistic possibilities. If these possibilities are realized, the result could be unprecedented increases in longevity. Second, and in frightening contrast, globalization and terrorism have increased the risks of lethal pandemics. Together with continuing uncertainty regarding economic events, these demographic uncertainties raise the question of whether pension rules should contain provisions for automatic plan modifications in response to projection errors. If automatic rules are to be adopted, what forms should they take?

2. INESCAPABLE UNCERTAINTY

Demographic and economic projections are critical to pension policy and debates about pension policy. Pension commitments are among the longest that people and governments make. Workers begin making contributions or paying taxes to support pensions as adolescents or young adults. They continue making payments throughout their working lives. They begin to draw benefits, typically during their sixties. Workers, their spouses, or other close relatives may continue to collect benefits for three or even four decades. For workers who reach benefit eligibility, the entire process consumes a minimum of five decades and, as mortality rates fall, as many as nine decades.

If workers are to be assured a pension of some amount, the *ex ante* uncertainty about how high tax rates will have to be is enormous. The sources of the uncertainty depend on whether the pension benefit or the contribution is defined (see Appendix 3A1). In all cases, however, pension planners can anticipate with a high degree of reliability that their projections will be highly unreliable. No one is able to forecast accurately the economic and demographic variables upon which the actuarial balance of pensions depends. Forecasts of economic events, even a few months or years into the future, are prone to enormous error. Demographic projections have been wildly inaccurate even a few years into the future.[2] Indeed, both economists and demographers have long studied forecast inaccuracy. Nonetheless, the literature on how policy makers should incorporate such uncertainty into their planning is slender indeed.

Despite the dominant importance of forecast uncertainty, public pension plans rarely contain automatic adjustments for projection errors. Instead, pension planners seem to behave either as if they believe that their projections will be accurate or that all responsibility for correcting errors should be left to their successors. This position should be scrutinized for at least two reasons. First, individual workers make long-term saving, residential, retirement and other plans that public pensions influence. Having reliable information about likely responses to unforeseen economic or demographic events can reduce the risks with which workers, their employers, insurance companies and others must cope during a period when, by definition, anticipations are not being realized.[3]

Second, the nature of default policies influences the way in which future decision makers will respond to imbalances that emerge. Unless current policy makers are indifferent to how future decisions are made, they should be interested in shaping the framework within which those decisions will be made. For example, a rule that committed workers to pay increased taxes whenever a projected deficit emerged in a pension plan would be likely to produce a different outcome from a rule that committed pensioners to take reduced benefits whenever a deficit emerged. Legislators *could* achieve the same outcome in either case, but would be unlikely to do so.

Although forecasting techniques have improved, a claim that forecasts have become more accurate would be hard to sustain. Unforeseen events, rather than poor technique, usually explain the inaccuracy of forecasts. Given the enormous uncertainty of underlying events, it is not even clear that improved techniques will improve forecast accuracy in the near term. However, advances in forecasting techniques have improved understanding of the *pattern* of errors in past forecasts. If one is willing to assume that the processes producing volatility in underlying events has not changed, analysis of errors of past forecasts should permit one to project a penumbra of uncertainty surrounding point estimates that will encompass a measurable fraction of outcomes. Should the underlying variability of outcomes change, the fraction of outcomes that falls within this penumbra may be somewhat higher or lower than historical experience suggests. But such stochastic forecasts create an empirical basis for writing adjustment rules that would alter pensions or other public policies automatically in response to expected errors in current projections.

3.   DEMOGRAPHIC SCENARIOS

Well-regarded demographers disagree profoundly on two quite different questions: whether there is a limit to human life span (and what that limit might be); and what course human mortality rates will follow in the future. Even if one believes that maximum human life span is fixed or evolves glacially, one may hold that such a limit is so far above currently realized life expectancies that rapid – even accelerating – improvements in life expectancy will occur. Conversely, one may deny that there is any limit to human life span but hold out little hope that any major increase in life expectancy will occur soon.

The disagreement on trends in life expectancy can be cast in terms of two concepts of life expectancy in common use – 'period' life expectancy and 'cohort' life expectancy. Period life expectancy is computed on the basis of mortality rates for all age cohorts *at a given point in time*. Cohort life expectancy is computed on the basis of mortality rates for age cohorts at each successive point in time as the cohort ages. Period life expectancy excludes the reductions in mortality rates that are expected to occur over people's lives, while cohort life expectancy includes these anticipated improvements. If no reduction in mortality rates were anticipated, cohort and period life expectancies would be identical. The difference between them is a measure of the reduction in mortality rates anticipated over time.

3.1. The Natural Limit Hypothesis

Several population analysts hold that mortality rates will fall little in the future. According to this view, biological organisms, in general, and human beings, in particular, are genetically programmed to have a limited life. Beyond a certain age, internal biological processes make early death inevitable. This view goes back to the late nineteenth century, when August Weismann originated the theory that animals die because cells become incapable of mitosis after a certain, biologically determined number of divisions. This theory enjoyed considerable popularity early in the twentieth century but lost favor.[4] It has enjoyed a resurgence since 1961 when Leonard Hayflick and Paul Moorhead claimed experimental support for the proposition that normal human cells can divide only a finite number of times *in vitro* (cancer cells suffer no such limit) and inferred that similar limits applied *in vivo*. Hayflick later modified this proposition to hold that cell division slows with age but does not entirely stop.[5]

A large literature has emerged on the possible role of *telomeres* in this process. Telomeres are end-pieces of chromosomes that are essential for cell division, but that become progressively shorter with repeated cell division. Eventually telomere shortening inhibits or prevents cell division. One strand of this literature holds out the hopeful, but still speculative, possibility that the number of telomeres can be increased, thereby facilitating continued cell division and – by inference – slowing or reversing senescence.

The underlying evolutionary rationale for biological limits on lifespan is that no simple evolutionary process would tend to eliminate harmful mutations that diminish viability of the organism after the completion of reproduction. Furthermore, it is held, nothing in natural selection would reward indefinite life after the end of reproduction.[6] On the contrary, evolution might have favored mutations that hasten death after the completion of reproduction because they would reduce competition for food or other biologically necessary resources. Some theorists have speculated that natural selection could favor survival of the elderly if the elderly enhance survival of others by caring for children or by preserving information that is valuable to survival, but evidence for this view is scant.

Whatever the rationale for a biological limit, those holding this view maintain either that cessation of cell division leads to the death of the organism or that slowing down of cell division contributes to senescence and a greatly heightened vulnerability to disease.[7]

Without two additional assumptions, however, the implication of a natural limit to human life for future increases in human life expectancy remains unclear. The first assumption is that the natural limit is not materially greater than current life expectancy in populations with the highest observed life expectancy. In fact, some who believe that human life has a biological maximum place that maximum so high that it constitutes no effective barrier to large and continuing declines in human mortality rates. A lifespan limit of, say, 120 years – approximately the highest documented age of death[8] – would not materially impede rapid and prolonged reductions in human mortality rates. In contrast, James Fries suggested that the limit to human life was approximately 85 years, which is close to the current period life expectancy of Japanese women. A survey of estimates compiled in 1989 contained ten estimates of lifespan limits of 120 years or more (excluding an eighteenth-century estimate of 200 years and a biblical maximum of 120 years). Were mortality rates in Japan, the country currently with the world's highest life expectancy, to fall 2 percent a year – an extremely high and unprecedented rate of improvement for periods of several decades – it would take 75 years for female cohort life expectancy and 180 years for period mortality to reach 120 years.

The second assumption is that prospects for modifying that limit are poor. If advances in biomedical science made it possible to manipulate previously immutable biological processes – the modifications of cell senescence by manipulating telomeres is just one such possibility – then pessimism regarding the possibility of extending human life expectancy would also be unjustified.

3.2. Historical Extrapolation

At least four types of statistical evidence have led many demographers to project steady reductions in mortality rates and corresponding increases in life expectancy, continuing throughout this century and beyond.

1.   If a limit on life expectancy were near, then one might expect rates of improvement to be lowest in countries with the highest life expectancies. Such is not the case.
2.   If humans were nearing a natural lifespan limit, one would expect the decline in mortality rates among the elderly to be slowing. Instead, it seems to be accelerating.
3.   The trend of falling mortality rates in most developed nations is remarkably lengthy and shows no signs of flattening out completely.
4.   If developed countries have life expectancies near a biological limit, one might expect male and female life expectancies to converge. In fact, such convergence is not apparent. In Japan, they have diverged for roughly a century.

Because mortality rates vary from year to year, the implications of extrapolating 'past' rates of decline depend on the period from which one extrapolates. Demographers do not agree on what the appropriate period is or even on the relative probative value of recent and more remote past improvements. Consequently, one can find in past trends 'evidence' to support a wide range of projections.

Japanese mortality rates, for example, have fallen faster than those of any other nation over the past half century. Following the second world war, Japanese life expectancy soared at rates seldom seen before or since. For two decades or more, mortality rates fell at an annual rate of more than 5 percent a year and life expectancy rose by five years a decade. The pace of advance slackened somewhat, but even in the 1990s, mortality rates fell more than 2 percent a year and life expectancy rose two years.[9] Japanese (period) life expectancy at birth, which was 79.1 years in 1990, is projected officially to reach 83.0 years by 2050, a simple average of 79.4 years for men and 86.5 years for women.[10] The US demographer, John R. Wilmoth, in 1996 used four methods and projected that life expectancy at birth would reach somewhere between 80 and 90.8 years by 2050 with a 'best guess' of 84.8 years.

Life expectancy in the United States has been lower than in Japan since 1965 and has been rising more slowly. Nonetheless, official government agencies and many private demographers project improvements in life expectancy at approximately the same rate as that foreseen for Japan. The US Social Security Administration (SSA) and Bureau of the Census, respectively, project an increase in US life expectancy at birth from 76.7 years in 2000 to 81.7 years (SSA) and 84.0 years (Census) in the year 2050. The Census projection is virtually identical to that of Ronald D. Lee and Lawrence R. Carter who in 1992 extrapolated past improvements in US mortality rates to projected life expectancy at birth in 2050 of 84.3 years.[11] On the other hand, Allburg and Vaupel projected far more rapid reductions in US mortality rates – 2 percent a year; they project life expectancy at birth in 2080 of 100 years for females and 96 years for males. Were this rate of improvement to prevail in Japan, cohort life expectancy in 2050 for females/ males would reach 115.1/111.1.

3.3. Population Prometheans

Some demographers and a growing number of biological scientists project massive increases in life expectancy. It is important to distinguish between projections of very high life expectancy and estimates of high lifespan limits. Some life expectancy pessimists may be found among the ranks of those who put maximum lifespan at well above 100 years.[12] All populations, even ones that are genetically identical, exhibit considerable dispersion in lifespan. Environmental conditions or inescapable causes of mortality can powerfully influence the mean of the lifespan. But even if conditions are optimal, deaths are dispersed widely over time. In fact, neither genetic inheritance nor environmental conditions go far to reduce variance in the duration of life, although each can have sizeable effects on the mean. The pattern of age-specific mortality rates seems to bear a considerable resemblance to decay of radioactive isotopes of particular elements, a result of a random process of decay.

This fact indicates that there is bound to be a considerable difference between lifespan and life expectancy. Advances in medical technology can increase life expectancy. Environmental changes can either raise or lower it. But unless something reduces the random component of mortality, trends in maximum lifespan will provide only limited information about trends in life expectancy.

The emergent optimism on life expectancy rests on the scientific prospect that molecular biology will unravel the basic causal mechanisms of the diseases responsible for most deaths. As scientists understand the causes of diseases, it is held, they will then move on to discover ways either to prevent the onset of the diseases or to cure them. British philosopher John Harris captures this Promethean vision:[13]

> New research now allows a glimpse into a world in which aging – and even death – may no longer be inevitable. Cloned human embryonic stem cells, appropriately reprogrammed, might be used for constant regeneration of organs and tissue. Injections of growth factors might put the body into a state of constant renewal. We may be able switch off the genes in the early embryo that trigger aging, rendering it 'immortal' (but not invulnerable).

Harris effectively applies the forecasting safety principle enunciated jokingly by Scottish economist Alec Cairncross ('Give a number or a date, but never both') when he adds 'We do not know when, or even if, such techniques could be developed and made safe, but some scientists believe it is possible'. Others, somewhat less cautious or less precise, project that living to 130 or more by the middle of this century could become routine.[14]

There are powerful reasons to doubt the vision of population Prometheans. In particular, major past advances in medical science, such as the discovery and introduction of antibiotics in the middle of the twentieth century which massively reduced deaths from infectious diseases, did not produce huge leaps in human life expectancy. Future scientific advance may generate larger effects, but until there is strong evidence of discontinuous increases in life expectancy, claims of population Prometheans should be viewed with some skepticism.[15]

3.4.   What is the Underlying Process?

Whether medical advances will have major or minor effects on life expectancy is fundamentally unpredictable for two distinct reasons. First, one cannot know at what rate medical science will advance. To know the pace at which facts can be discovered, one would have to understand the relations among those facts. But that is the currently unknown object of research. Second, no model of ageing is now generally accepted . Without such a model, one cannot know whether the discovery of a cure for a particular illness will have a large or a small effect on overall mortality rates. These two problems are interrelated. To illustrate the problem, we lay out three models of mortality.

The independent causes model
Most countries collect information on causes of death. With these data, one can attribute each death to a particular illness or cause. The US SSA, for example, groups all causes of death listed in the International Classification of Diseases (ICD) into 11 groups and reports mortality rates from each of these 11 grouped causes: heart disease, cancer, vascular disease, violence, respiratory disease, infancy, digestive diseases, diabetes, liver cirrhosis, AIDS, and all other causes. Each age and sex group has a specific annual probability of dying from each of the 11 causes. SSA projects trends in overall mortality rates by projecting rates of change in age/sex specific death rates from each of the 11 groups of causes. SSA projections of the rates at which mortality from each cause of death will change over time are based on expert judgment and past trends. The change in aggregate mortality rates for each age/sex group is the weighted sum of the change in each of the 11 age/sex-specific mortality rates.

The assumption that each cause of death operates independently is valid only if the *ex ante* probability of death from, say respiratory disease, is no higher or lower for those who, *ex post*, die from, say, heart disease, than it is for any random man or woman of the same age.[16] To put matters another way, the independent effects assumption is equivalent to saying that learning that a person died from a particular disease conveys no information about the *prior* likelihood that this person was vulnerable to other diseases.[17]

The frailty model[18]

The independence assumption fails if people differ from one another systematically and continuously in their susceptibility to illness. Suppose that people differ in some characteristic, z, so that their probabilities of dying from *all* causes differs proportionately to their endowment of z. Those members of any given cohort who are particularly frail – that is, they have high values of z – will be more likely to die in any given year than those who are less frail. Over time, the surviving members of the cohort will have progressively lower values of z – that is, they will be progressively less frail than those who died previously.

A simple inference from the model leads to the conclusion that estimates of life expectancy based on age-specific mortality rates, which ignore the declining frailty of survivors, are higher than they would be if they were based on the characteristics of the entire age cohort. The frailty model also suggests that summing projected reductions in mortality rates from individual causes is unlikely to produce accurate projections of reductions in total mortality rates. Those spared death by a medical advance that reduces mortality from any single cause will tend to keep alive members of the population cohort whose frailty differs from that of population members who would have survived without the advance. The result could be an increase or a decrease in the frailty of those whom the medical advance spares, but it is unlikely to be neutral.

The limited reliability model[19]

Human death may be analogized to machine failure, a topic that has been subject to extensive analysis by reliability engineers. Clearly, the mechanics of machines and the biology of living organisms are not identical. But they bear certain similarities. Each contains systems that must all function at least up to a minimal standard if the entity is to function/remain alive. Systems may have more or less redundancy, permitting some elements of a system to fail before the system entirely ceases to work.

The time profile of human ageing has three distinctive ranges: an early period during which death rates are relatively high and fall sharply to very low levels. This stage is analogous to the 'burn in' period with some new machines, especially electronic equipment. There follows a lengthy period during which death rates are low but climb steadily and exponentially. That period is analogous to the 'useful life' of most machines. During a third and final stage death rates are high and continue to rise, but more slowly than during the second phase. Machines exhibit a similar phase after the end of their 'useful life'.

One way to approach human mortality is to identify a type of machine for which the pattern of failure matches that of mortality rates observed in humans. Machine failure rates would resemble mortality rates of humans in at least two important cases.

In the first, the machine consists of many component systems, each of which is essential to the operation of the machine. Each component system consists of many elements, any one of which is sufficient to sustain operation of the system (that is, the systems are built with redundancy). Many of the elements are faulty at the outset and the remaining elements fail at a steady rate, k. The machine may fail from any of a wide variety of causes, but complete failure occurs only when some system fails.

The pattern of machine failure rates would resemble the pattern of human mortality rates also if the machine consists of one or a small number of essential systems, the other conditions hold, and there is population diversity with respect to the number of flawed elements in the component systems. In either case, the mathematical form of the failure rates of machines mimics the mathematical form of human mortality rates.[20]

If one assumes, in addition, that when a certain critical portion of elements of components fail, the performance of that component is degraded and that it imposes additional burdens (that is, increases the likelihood of failure in other components), one ends up with a model of senescence in which mortality rates from distinct causes are clearly interdependent.

4.   DEMOGRAPHIC UNCERTAINTY

Demographic projections differ enormously, perhaps because, as one of the founding Rothschilds observed, 'compound interest is the eighth wonder of the world'. Small differences in assumptions regarding the rate of decline of mortality rates produce enormous differences in populations and age distributions when compounded over many years. If one adds in plausible variations in fertility and net immigration, the range of possible outcomes becomes enormous.

Table 3.1 shows just a few projections of population size and age composition in the United States for the years 2025 and 2050. The first two are official projections of the US Census Bureau and of the SSA, the agency

Table 3.1   Population projections, United States

Projection	2000			2025			2050		
	Total population (m)	Population 65+ (%)	Population 85+ (%)	Total population (m)	Population 65+ (%)	Population 85+ (%)	Total population (m)	Population 65+ (%)	Population 85+ (%)
US Census Bureau	281.4	12.4	1.5	337.8	18.5	2.2	403.7	20.3	4.8
Social Security Administration				342.2	17.9	1.8	376.8	20.5	3.9
2 percent annual reduction				345.8	18.7	2.4	399.5	24.4	7.1
Expert medical judgment				342.5	18.1	2.1	392.4	23.3	6.2
Expert medical judgment + doubling of legal immigration				371.4	17.4	2.0	456.4	21.9	5.5

Note: See Appendix 3A2 for methods.

53

responsible for projecting the costs of the US national pension. The next two projections retain the SSA's assumptions regarding fertility and net immigration, but assume somewhat faster rates of improvement in mortality rates. The third projection follows the assumption of two well-regarded US demographers who suggest that mortality rates could easily fall at an annual rate of 2 percent.[21] This rate of improvement exceeds recent US experience, but is in line with average improvement in Japan since 1980. The fourth projection embodies the judgment of two medical scientists on the possible trend in age- and sex-specific mortality rates from specific diseases.[22] Truly dramatic progress in prevention, diagnosis, and cure of diseases responsible for most deaths, including coronary artery disease, Alzheimer's disease, and diabetes has become a reasonable possibility through advances in molecular biology. It results in varying annual rates of decline in mortality rates, but most are less than 2 percent. The fifth projection is identical to the fourth, except that it embodies the assumption that legal immigration into the United States doubles.

Table 3.2 is organized similarly to Table 3.1. It contains an official government projection and four alternative projections. Two are based on the projections of demographer John Wilmoth that apply to Japanese data the extrapolative methods of projection developed by Ronald D. Lee and Lawrence R. Carter.[23] These methods estimate the values for the Gompertz–Makeham function based on historical data and extrapolate that function into the future. One of these projections assumes that there will be no net immigration into Japan. The other projection assumes that immigration will increase rapidly until it reaches 300 000 a year in 2010, a historically unprecedented level. The two final projections assume that mortality rates decline at an average of 2 percent a year, with no net immigration and with net immigration of 300 000 a year. As a proportion of national population, this rate of immigration would be considerably less than half the actual US rate. We include the projections with net immigration not because they seem likely, but because authorizing immigration is one way to offset low birth rates and slow population ageing.

Several patterns are apparent in Tables 3.1 and 3.2. First, as is well known and recognized, the official projections indicate a strong increase in the proportion of the population in age cohorts now regarded as elderly. Second, the trend is far more dramatic in Japan than in the United States because projected Japanese fertility and mortality rates are both lower than in the United States. Third, immigration has a large effect on population size, but little effect until after 2025 on the proportion of the population that is over age 65. Fourth, variations in mortality rates have little effect until after 2025 on the proportion of the population that is over age 65, but by 2050 the impact is considerable. Fifth, the sensitivity of the population over age

Table 3.2 *Population projections, Japan*

Projection	2000			2025			2050		
	Total population (m)	Population 65+ (%)	Population 85+ (%)	Total population (m)	Population 65+ (%)	Population 85+ (%)	Total population (m)	Population 65+ (%)	Population 85+ (%)
Official projection	126.9	17.2	1.7	120.9	27.4	4.8	100.5	32.3	6.4
Wilmoth (with increased immigration)				131.0	27.6	4.8	127.7	33.8	8.2
Wilmoth (no net immigration)				124.2	28.7	5.0	110.0	37.2	9.3
2 percent annual improvement (with increased immigration)				130.6	27.7	5.4	128.0	34.5	9.9
2 percent annual improvement (no net immigration)				123.8	28.9	5.7	110.5	37.7	11.2

Note: See Appendix 3A2 for methods.

85 – the *very* old – to faster rates of decline in mortality rates than are embodied in official projections is dramatic. A sharp increase in the proportion of the population that is very old is the natural consequence of our assumption that declines in mortality rates will be almost as high for the old as for the young. The reason is simple: a given proportional drop in mortality for the young and for the old causes a much larger proportional increase in survival among the old than among the young. In fact, drops in mortality rates among the young have little effect on life expectancy, because the mortality rates are so low to begin with. In the most extreme case, the proportion of the population over age 85 in Japan by 2050 would exceed official projections by 75 percent if mortality rates fall 2 percent annually, a rate slightly slower than actual history during the 1980s and 1990s. The proportion of the Japanese population over age 85 would be approximately the same as the proportion of the US population currently over age 65.

5.   IMPLICATIONS FOR PENSION POLICY

It is common knowledge that all developed countries face rising pension costs as their populations age. That the problems facing the United States and Japan come close to bracketing the range of those problems is also widely recognized. In the United States, rather high assumed fertility and net immigration hold down projections of the proportion of the total population that is elderly. In Japan, conversely, low assumed fertility and low net immigration lead to high projections of the proportion of the elderly population.[24] Many demographers and economists also recognize the enormous uncertainty that surrounds these summary judgments. But few analysts have incorporated this uncertainty into their policy recommendations. And elected officials in no country have taken most uncertainties into account in drafting pension legislation and rules.

5.1.   Non-demographic Sources of Uncertainty

Tables 3.1 and 3.2 understate the uncertainties. They do not allow for the possibility that fertility rates will be higher or lower than those assumed in the projections. They do not allow for economic uncertainties of any kind, such as possible variations from assumed values in the growth of productivity per worker, in interest rates, or in labor force participation. Behind projections of these variables lies uncertainty regarding ages of entry to and exit from the labor force, length of the work week and the work year, domestic and foreign saving rates, and the nature and pace of technological change.

It is possible through 'stochastic forecasting' to deal formally with such uncertainties, *provided that* one believes variations in the relevant variables will follow a probability distribution similar to their historical pattern. Given estimates of the historical relationships among variables on which the projection depends, the analyst draws repeated sample of values of the variables and projects costs from distributions of these assumptions based on the historical record. The analyst then makes hundreds or even thousands of projections based on these assumptions. The resulting distribution of forecast values contains a range of outcomes that corresponds to the actual range of underlying causes.

Using these methods, two recent studies have estimated confidence intervals for the US social security system.[25] Their results make clear the enormous uncertainty that surrounds point estimates of future pension costs. Lee and Edwards estimated that for the year 2050, the 95 percent confidence interval for cost of the US social security system ranged from roughly 15 to 25 percent of taxable payroll. For the year 2070, the range stretched from less than 15 percent to more than 35 percent of payroll. The Congressional Budget Office estimated 90 percent confidence intervals for cost measured as a percent of payroll for 2030 ranging from 13.9 to 22.9 percent and for 2075 ranging from 14.0 to 32.4 percent.

5.2. Health Costs

Uncertainties regarding the costs of pensions are much smaller than are the uncertainties regarding health outlays. The cost of health benefits is projected to grow far more rapidly than is the cost of pensions. The costs were projected to rise from less than 3 percent of gross domestic product to more than 9 percent of GDP in 2050, more than 11 percent in 2070, and nearly 20 percent in 2100. These costs are subject not only to errors in demographic projections (because health costs are largest among the elderly) but also to errors in projections of costs per person.

It is not clear that projections of health costs are plausible, as they rest on the assumption that extremely high historical rates of increase in costs will continue indefinitely. At the very minimum, the projections of protracted and very rapid growth of health-care spending is also subject to enormous uncertainty. Apart from population ageing, which affects pensions as well as health-care spending, the only additional factor driving up projected health-care spending is the assumption that the per capita cost of health care will rise indefinitely. Such increases, in turn, derive from the assumption that medical technology will continue not only to evolve but that the nature of technical advance will continue to boost spending at historical rates. In the case of trends that depend on the discovery of new knowledge, the basis for simple projections, to say nothing of stochastic projections, is highly suspect.

6.   PENSION DESIGN TO COPE WITH UNCERTAINTY

Pension plans may be designed under the fiction that parameters underlying the plan are reliably known. With the passage of time, as the value of these parameters deviates from initial assumptions, legislation becomes necessary to restore balance. Alternatively, the pension plan may be designed so that the specifications of the plan evolve automatically as values of key parameters deviate from initial assumptions. The basis for choosing between these two approaches is primarily political, not economic. Although practical problems make it impossible precisely to duplicate the effects of automatic adjustments with discretionary legislation, the two approaches could in principle yield quite similar results.

6.1.   Price and Wage Indexing

Until 1972 the US social security system was cast in fixed nominal terms. The ceiling on earnings subject to the payroll tax and the formula used to compute benefits were fixed in nominal terms. Inflation inexorably eroded the real value of earnings on which benefits were based. As a result, benefits of new claimants fell with inflation and lagged rising wage levels. After a benefit was computed, it remained fixed in nominal terms so that inflation reduced its real purchasing power. Because the benefit formula was progressive, the ratio of benefits to earnings tended to fall for the average worker as earnings grew. Because the tax schedule was proportional with respect to earnings, revenues tended to grow faster than costs as earnings increased. Surpluses tended to emerge and grow until Congress increased benefits to offset both inflation and the tendency of pensions to lag growth in wages.

In 1972 new provisions were enacted to adjust benefits automatically for inflation and real wage growth. In particular, the ceiling on earnings subject to payroll tax, each worker's earning history, and the formula used for computing initial benefits were annually and automatically adjusted for growth in average wages. Pensions being paid to retirees were automatically adjusted for increases in consumer prices. The objective was to hold constant the ratio of initial benefits to earnings for workers at a given *relative* position in the earnings distribution and to maintain the purchasing power of benefits once payment began.[26] These automatic formula changes replaced the *ad hoc* adjustments that Congress had previously made.

Most of these adjustment provisions act to maintain the size of the pension system as the economy grows. In contrast, if the wage base, earnings, and benefit formula were adjusted for increases in *prices*, rather than *wages*, the pension system would tend to shrink relative to the economy, as real incomes rose. A commission appointed by President George W. Bush recently presented two options for switching from wage to price indexing as a means of reducing the projected long-term deficit in social security. For similar reasons, the United Kingdom adopted 'price indexing' under Prime Minister Margaret Thatcher. Because of this provision, pensions for successive generations of workers in the UK will come to replace ever smaller portions of earnings. As a result, government pension costs are not projected to increase as a share of GDP in the UK, although its population ageing is similar to that of other developed nations. Of course, parliament is free to increase benefits. But there can be little doubt that the 'default' embodied in current law will profoundly affect the pensions that will actually be paid.

6.2. Other Potential Forms of Indexing

It is possible, in principle, to automatically adjust pension rules for deviations from baseline assumptions of all of the key parameters on which long-term financial balance depends. As noted in Appendix 3A1, the relevant parameters depend on the type of pension plan – defined benefit or defined contribution, funded or unfunded.

In the case of defined benefit (DB) systems, for example, the system could be indexed for deviations from baseline assumptions in mortality rates, fertility rates, net immigration, labor force participation, and productivity growth. Most systems, other than that of the United Kingdom, are already indexed for productivity growth. If reserves are sizeable, indexation could extend to deviations of interest rates from baseline assumptions.

Funded defined contribution (DC) pensions are immune to variations in labor force participation, net immigration, and fertility rates. Shifts in these parameters affect the relative size of the active and dependent populations, but they do not directly have any direct effect on the adequacy of reserves to support benefits. On the other hand, changes in wage growth and in interest rates (or, more generally, in asset values) can cause huge deviations from target reserves in DC pensions. It is possible to keep reserves on target, but only if one accepts wild swings in contribution rates.

To illustrate this sensitivity, Thompson (1998) simulated by how much actual accumulations in DC accounts would have deviated from target accumulations in four countries (Germany, Japan, the United Kingdom, and the United States) based on actual historical data under three alternative hypothetical decisions rules. The target in each case was to build up a reserve over a 43-year career sufficient to support an annuity equal to 50 percent of average lifetime earnings for a worker receiving the average wage.

Under rule 1, pension planners were assumed to know in advance the average growth of earnings and the average interest rate over the entire period. Based on this 'knowledge', the planner set contribution rates to build the target reserve. However, planners were assumed not to know the annual fluctuations in wage growth and interest rates. Because total accumulations depend on the timing of deposits, as well as the cumulative amount, and on the timing of interest rates, as well as their average value, over- or undershooting in pension fund accumulation is possible.

Under rule 2, pension planners set contribution rates to achieve precisely the desired pension fund based on actual wage growth and interest rates over the first half of the period. Since wage growth and interest rates during the final half could differ from those in the first half, accumulations could be larger or smaller than the target amount. Under the third rule, the pension planners adjust contribution rates every ten years based on wage growth and interest rates in the preceding ten years. Once again, over- or undershooting are possible because the future generally does not mimic history.

Furthermore, the order of events is arbitrary. Because events could easily have occurred in the reverse pattern, Thompson ran the simulation based both on the actual historical pattern of wage growth and interest rates and then assumed the reverse pattern.

Table 3.3 shows Thompson's calculations of the ratio of actual pension fund accumulations to the target pension fund accumulations in the four countries. As is apparent, accumulations under these rules can easily be vastly larger or smaller than target levels. Furthermore, these simulations understate possible variations for two reasons. They exclude possible capital losses from interest rates that affect asset values near retirement. And they assume that all reserves are invested in bonds whose values fluctuate less than do those of common stocks. When these deviations emerge late in a worker's career, there is nothing as a practical matter that can be done to achieve target reserves, as it would be necessary for contribution rates to fluctuate dramatically, ranging from negative values (withdrawals) to deposit rates exceeding 100 percent of late career earnings.

6.3. Indexing for Mortality

Table 3.4 shows the implications for pensions of demographic uncertainty in the United States and Japan. That pension costs will rise in both countries is well known. The range of uncertainty is not so widely recognized.

Table 3.3   Ratio of actual to target pension accumulation, four countries, 1953–1995

Simulation	Sequence	Country			
		Germany	Japan	UK	USA
Contribution set at level appropriate	Historical	137	132	140	138
for the long term (43 years)	Reverse history	88	80	73	80
Contribution set at level appropriate	Historical	261	255	233	342
for first half of period	Reverse history	41	40	43	30
Contribution adjusted every 10	Historical	163	153	165	181
years based on conditions in	Reverse history	66	68	64	58
preceding ten years					

Source: Thompson (1998, Table 3, p. 138).

The left-hand pair of columns of numbers in the table show consequences of increases in the ratio of the population over age 65 to the population aged 18 to 64 in the United States and aged 15 to 64 in Japan. Under the simplifying and unrealistic assumption that all non-aged adults are at work, that all people 65 or older are pensioners, and that the ratio of the average pension to the average wage is constant, the numbers in columns 1 and 2 show the percentage increase in the real resource cost to active workers of pensions payable to retirees in 2025 and 2050, respectively. As is clear, the cost of population ageing in Japan greatly exceeds that in the United States. In fact, the cost in Japan is close to, or slightly more than, twice that in the United States, depending on the assumed reduction in mortality rates and immigration.

Columns 3 and 4 present similar data in a different way. Based on each population projection, the numbers in columns 3 and 4 show for the years 2025 and 2050, respectively, the age until which people are all assumed to work and after which they are all assumed to retire that maintains the same aged dependency ratio as prevailed in the year 2000 in both countries at age 65. For example, the first row for Japan in column 4 reports that if everyone from age 15 to 77 worked and everyone age 78 or older was a pensioner in year 2050, the ratio of pensioners to non-aged adults would be the same as the ratio of people aged 65 or older is to people aged 15 to 64 in the year 2000. Under the previous assumptions – that all non-aged adults work, that everyone over the critical age is a pensioner and that the ratio of pension

Table 3.4   Demographic impact on pension costs, United States and Japan: ratio of population 65+ to adult population (18–64 in USA and 15–64 in Japan), 2025 and 2050

Population Projection	2025 Col. 1	2050 Col. 2	2025 Col. 3	2050 Col. 4
	Dependency ratio, percent increase over official projection in 2000		Age of pension eligibility with same dependency ratio as 2000	
United States				
Census Bureau	56	75	70	73
2 percent annual reduction	56	114	70	77
Expert medical judgment	46	105	69	75/76
Expert medical judgment + doubling of legal immigration	42	90	68/69	74
Japan				
Wilmoth (with increased immigration)	86	157	74	78
Wilmoth (no net immigration)	94	180	74	78/79
2 percent annual improvement (with increased immigration)	86	161	74	78
2 percent annual improvement (no net immigration)	94	200	74/75	79/80

Notes: Columns 1 and 2 show the percentage increase in the ratio of the population 65 or older to the population aged 18 to 64 in the United States and aged 15 to 64 in Japan between the year 2000 and the years 2025 and 2050, respectively. The population projections are those reported in Tables 3.1 and 3.2. Columns 3 and 4 show the age at which the ratio of the population above the indicated age to the population from age 18 to the indicated age in the United States and aged 15 to the indicated age in Japan will be the same as was the ratio of the population 65 or older to the population from ages 18 (USA) and 15 (Japan) to age 64 in the year 2000.

amounts to wages is constant, the proportion of earnings that would be transferred to pensioners would be unchanged. To put the point another way, if the retirement age were age 65 in 2000 and were increased to age 78 by 2050, pension costs as a percentage of earnings would remain constant. If pension laws were drafted with provisions that automatically changed benefit amounts, earmarked taxes, or the age of eligibility for pensions, demographic surprises would not require legislative changes in pension laws.

7.   HOW MUCH INDEXING IS DESIRABLE?

It is possible in principle, although it may be difficult in practice, to draft pension laws so that they respond automatically to deviations of every conceivable relevant variable from levels assumed in initial actuarial computations. But is it desirable to do so? And, if so, on what basis should legislators decide how much indexing *is* desirable?

7.1.   Uncertainty

Indexing *may* reduce *subjective* uncertainty – the range of possibilities that workers and pensioners entertain as plausible responses to future financial imbalance. The costs of subjective uncertainty could be diminished if indexing represents a pre-commitment to a policy that diffuses adjustment costs no more unequally than would occur in its absence. In that event, indexing removes one element of subjective uncertainty – the legislators' response – without increasing the range of actual adjustments. Of course, indexing does not eliminate uncertainty about the legislative response, as legislators remain free to alter the indexing rules established by their predecessors.

On the assumption that legislators, in any event, will restore financial balance, indexing does not reduce *objective* uncertainty, as pre-commitment to a given policy does not change the actual size of required adjustments.

If indexing does not reliably reduce the costs of uncertainty to workers and pensioners, it is hard to see its *economic* advantages. It may be a desirable *political* action if three conditions are satisfied. The first is that indexing increases the likelihood of adhering to a policy of dealing with 'surprises' on which there is widespread consensus. The second is that commitment will be easier – that is politically less costly – before than after the 'indexable event'. The third is that the technical problems of writing indexing legislation are not excessive, which means that the *ex ante* formula is unlikely to deviate excessively from the *ex post* desired response.

7.2. An Example: Wage Indexing

Indexing of earnings histories used in computing DB pensions illustrates each of these considerations. Failure to index earnings would (i) permit price inflation to erode the value of pensions and (ii) mean that the faster wages grow, the smaller resulting pensions would be relative to discounted lifetime earnings, for a given contribution rate.[27] Both consequences would violate widely-held norms of fairness. Adjusting earnings histories for earnings is technically easy. It requires simply that if a pension is being set in year n, then one must multiply earnings received in year w_{n-t}, by w_n / w_{n-t}.[28] Furthermore, it is technically easier to set in place a rule for wage (or price) indexing of earnings histories than it would be to legislate adjustments whenever wages or prices change. For all of these reasons, wage (or price) indexing of earnings histories has a strong presumption in its favor. A similar case can be made for updating any non-proportional DB pension formula for changes in wages, if the goal is to maintain the ratio of pensions to earnings constant at any given *relative* position on the earnings distribution (or for prices, if the goal is to hold the ratio of pensions to earnings constant at any given *real* earnings level).

7.3. Indexing for Other Economic and for Demographic Variables

Wage or price indexing are both retrospective. They involve adjusting some historical or current quantities – wages or a currently applicable benefit formula – for past or current changes in prices or wages. Adjusting future benefits or taxes for changes in forecasts of future variables such as future wages or prices, unemployment, labor-force participation, fertility, or mortality is inherently problematic. For this reason, they entail a series of complex choices for which there is no clear basis.

Consider, for example, whether or not to index a pension system for deviations of mortality rates from anticipated levels used in establishing the system. Current legislators have designed the pension system based on the best current information about the likely trend in mortality rates. But they understand that actual mortality rates may be higher or lower than current projections. As a result of the new projections, the pension system appears to face a previously unexpected imbalance. What should the legislature do with this information?

To begin with, the legislature needs to recognize that it is dealing with a projection which may itself turn out to be wrong. The actual drop in mortality rates may be larger or smaller than the current projection, in which case the surplus or deficit may be larger or smaller than the new projection indicates. If the legislature wants to act on the new projection, it must decide *what* action to take. The legislature must decide whether to adjust the system fully to eliminate all of the newly projected surplus or deficit or to implement a partial adjustment with further steps expected later. It also must decide whether to cut benefits – either by raising the age of initial pension eligibility or by lowering annual payments[29] – or to increase revenues earmarked to pay for pensions, when to phase in these changes, and how to distribute them among workers and current pensioners. They may also decide to implement automatic adjustments that change the default confronting tomorrow's decision makers but do so in a way that encourages or requires confirmatory action by the legislature before the adjustments take effect.

Demographic indexing also arises in the case of funded, DC plans when workers reach pension age. Life expectancy and interest rates determine the price of annuities and its reciprocal, the pension amount. Since the evolution of mortality rates is relatively sluggish, the impact of demographic surprises in defined contribution plans is likely to be less dramatic than in the case of DB plans.

Much the same considerations hold for indexing DB pensions for deviations in key variables other than mortality rates, such as projected growth of real wages, fertility rates, or labor-force participation rates. As noted, however, fluctuations in growth of wages and in interest rates raise extremely troublesome issues under DC plans with respect to contribution rates and age of eligibility. Workers/pensioners are vulnerable to very large changes in ratios of benefits to average earnings as a result of fluctuations in wage growth, interest rates, or asset values. Furthermore, there is no way, other than abandonment of the DC principle, to protect individual workers/pensioners from these effects, as DC plans, by definition, do not contain methods of spreading risk among workers or over time.

7.4. A Summing Up

Judicious use of indexing provisions can encourage legislatures to take cognizance of projected deficits or surpluses in a timely fashion. For example, a provision that automatically closed any projected deficit or surplus in part through benefit cuts or revenue increases triggered to take effect a few years after a projected imbalance larger than some *de minimis* amount unless the legislature dealt with it in some other way, could serve as a goad to action that otherwise might be delayed. But one should not regard such a provision as merely technical. Automatic adjustments can have profound political effects.

In contrast to the 'retrospective' indexing based on past changes in wages and prices, 'prospective' indexing based on anticipated deviations of key variables from expected values involves a host of decisions that involve guesswork and serve primarily to change the political 'default' position confronting future legislators. For all these reasons, indexing with respect to projections is technically problematic and essentially political. It is far from clear whether or when pension systems should be indexed and the decision is not one that economists are particularly well trained to make.

APPENDIX 3A1

Pension commitments involve a set of charges against workers in return for which they are promised a stream of payments after certain events, such as retirement, the onset of disability, or attaining a certain age. Pension commitments also involve implicit debt if the system is not fully funded. The debt normally occurs as a result of paying benefits to early beneficiaries that exceed the present value of payments (or contributions) made before benefit eligibility by the workers or, on behalf of them, by their employers or the general taxpayer. The funds beyond contributions to pay benefits may come from contributions of still-active workers, which by definition are *not* saved to offset the accumulation of obligations to pay them benefits later on.

The stock of debt may rise or fall over time depending on whether the payments by active workers fall short of or exceed the accumulation of pension obligations to them. Under a system in which each worker's or cohort's pensions equal contributions made on behalf of the worker or cohort, large reserves accumulate and there is no borrowing. It is not unusual for workers' payments to exceed future benefits paid to them even for early cohorts. This situation has occurred, for example, under provident funds, such as that of Singapore, where interest is credited at rates well below market rates. The same type of transfer occurs when pensions are fixed in nominal terms and inflation erodes their value.

If one focuses on the two extreme cases – an unfunded (pay-as-you-go) system and a fully funded system – the sources of risk and who bears that risk differ. We consider four cases, distinguished by whether the pension system is fully funded or entirely unfunded, and whether the system is a defined benefit or defined contribution. All four types are possible. In each case, pension actuaries or other planners typically make assumptions regarding some or all of the following variables:[30]

- mortality rates,
- wage growth,

- interest rates,
- family structure, including divorce rates, marriage rates,
- labor-force participation,
- net immigration, and
- fertility rates and the sex ratio at birth.

To the extent that the relevant variables take on values different from those the planners assumed, adjustments must be made in taxes or contributions required of workers or in payments made to pensioners. The four types of pensions differ in the 'default' adjustments that must be made to restore financial balance.

Unfunded, Defined Benefit Plan

Most social insurance plans in developed nations have been unfunded, DB systems. Balance in such systems is sensitive to all of the variables listed above, other than interest rates (if reserves are always zero). When mortality, wage growth, labor-force participation, net immigration, or fertility differs from what was assumed in setting contribution rates and benefits, the system becomes financially imbalanced, either currently or prospectively.

In a DB system there is no natural default adjustment to imbalances. Authorities may modify either contributions or pensions. If there is a current deficit and authorities lack reserves or authority to borrow from the fisc, immediate changes are inescapable. In practice, democratically elected legislators are loath to cut benefits of current retirees or of those soon to retire on the ground that these groups have little capacity to adjust to such changes. As a result, the incentive is strong in an unfunded DB system to deal with current deficits by raising contributions rather than by cutting benefits. Even modest reserves or authority to borrow from the fisc greatly relaxes this constraint in dealing with deficits, however, and enables legislatures to phase in changes in contributions or benefits. And authorities have wide discretion on whether to deal with projected deficits or surpluses by changing benefits or contributions.

Funded, Defined Benefit Plan

By definition, a funded, DB system differs from an unfunded system only in that it builds up a reserve sufficient to pay accumulated pension entitlements. Balance therefore depends sensitively on projected interest rates as well as on the variables that affect unfunded DB plans. Large reserves mean that the imperative to close projected imbalances is greatly attenuated.

Sizeable reserves enable legislators to defer action until they determine if imbalances persist. Furthermore, when action is indicated, the larger the balance the easier it is for legislators to spread required adjustments over extended periods of time.

The key aspect of a funded, as of an unfunded, DB system is that there is no clear default adjustment. Legislators may choose between changing contributions or benefits (but, again, not for current retirees or those nearing retirement) as they see fit. Because instant action is not required, the bias in an unfunded system to correct current deficits by raising taxes rather than cutting benefits is reduced.

Funded, Defined Contribution Plan

Under funded, DC pensions, the size of benefits is linked to the amounts deposited on behalf of each worker or each cohort of workers and the investment yield on these deposits. Pension actuaries deal with uncertainties about the evolution of life expectancy and of interest rates for those who are retired by maintaining sufficient reserves.

Funded DC systems are subject to large risks, as are DB systems (see Table 3.3). The difference is that DC systems have a default adjustment without legislation; benefits must change. Unanticipated declines in mortality rates or interest rates automatically generate reduced pensions. Unanticipated increases in wage growth increase pensions, but the increase is smaller than that of terminal earnings. Thus, higher-than- (lower-than-) anticipated wage growth reduces (increases) the ratio of pensions to *terminal* earnings. Each individual worker or cohort is insulated from the effects of imbalances that arise in the accounts of other workers or cohorts. Fertility rates, net immigration, and labor-force participation rates do not directly influence the balance of DC plans, in contrast to their powerful effect on balance of DB plans.

Unfunded Defined Contribution Plan

Unfunded, DC pensions are based on amounts 'contributed' to so-called 'notional' accounts. The funds collected from workers are actually used not to build reserves but for current outlays, possibly including pensions for current retirees, as under unfunded DB plans. These deposits exist only as bookkeeping entries in the ledgers of the pension plan. The resulting 'balances' accumulate at some interest rate, which may or may not be related to market interest rates. When the worker becomes eligible for benefits, the resulting balance in the notional account may be paid out as a lump sum or converted into a pension, based on an interest rate (possibly not the same as that used during the accumulation period) and estimates of remaining life expectancy. Current taxes or worker contributions, not actual reserves, pay for these benefits.

Unfunded DC and DB systems differ only superficially. In an unfunded DB system, benefits are based *directly* on the worker's earning history. For example, benefits are equal to some fraction (perhaps dependent on the duration of the working life) of earnings averaged over some number of years. In an unfunded DC system, benefits are based *indirectly* on the worker's earnings history. The linkage is through the percentage of earnings that is deemed to have been deposited and the assumed interest rate.

Actuarial balance in an unfunded DC system is subject to the same forces that buffet an unfunded DB account: mortality rates, wage growth, fertility, net immigration, and labor-force participation. Imbalances can be prevented by changes in the parameters that determine the lifetime present value of pensions, including the notional interest rate used during the accumulation period. Whether those imbalances trigger adjustments depends on the initial rules regarding the disposition of surpluses and whether the pension fund is automatically authorized to borrow to cover deficits. The 'interest rate' used in computing benefits need bear no relation to actual market rates, but serves only as a device for determining how large benefits should be, much as the benefit formula does under DB accounts.

Although unfunded DB and unfunded DC pensions are both a function of past earnings, they place the pension obligation in a different political 'frame'. The DB commitment is an obligation of the nation to deliver a specific benefit. The DC commitment is an obligation to convert the worker's own account balance into a pension, the amount of which will vary with interest rates and projected mortality rates. Although the balance between revenues and pension outlays is buffeted by similar forces in both cases, the implied responsibilities for closing any imbalances that emerge are quite different.

APPENDIX 3A2

We estimate future populations in two steps. First, we derive future age- and gender-specific mortality rates. Then we combine those rates with fertility and immigration projections to estimate future population.

Mortality Rates: United States

We start with the 1997 calendar year central mortality rates from the 2000 Old-Age, Survivors, and Disability Insurance (OASDI) Trustees Report of the Social Security Administration (SSA). The report lists, for each age/sex group, the US mortality rate per 100000 population from each of 11 causes of death: heart disease, cancer, vascular disease, violence, respiratory disease, infancy, digestive diseases, diabetes mellitus, liver cirrhosis, AIDS, and all other. For later years, we reduced each mortality rate by a given percentage depending on the forecasted parameters.

For the 2 percent annual reduction scenario, we reduced mortality rates by 2.8, 2.2 and 1.9 percent, respectively for the age categories 0–14, 15–64, and 65 and above. These rates generated a population-weighted average reduction in the mortality rate of 2 percent for the base year. For later years, the population-weighted rate of decline is slightly lower, because the average age of the population increases.

In the expert medical judgment scenario, the annual rate of reduction in mortality rates was based on estimates supplied by Dr John Potts. Where the ultimate rate of decline was faster than actual historical averages, we assumed a gradual transition from the lower to the higher rate of decline beginning in 2000. We assumed that no age/sex mortality rate from any cause increased, which is contrary to observed rates for some causes for some age/sex groups during a period from 1965 to 1995.

In order to model appropriate death rates for the population aged 95 years and above, we set mortality rates in the year 2000 rates at those forecast by the SSA in Actuarial Study 107 (Bell et al. 1992). These rates give specific death rates for each year through age 119. We assumed the maximum limit to life in 2000 to be 107 years for males and 110 years for females, and increased the maximum limit to life by one year every two calendar years until an ultimate limit of 130 years.

Mortality Rates: Japan

For the 2 percent annual reduction scenario, we assumed the base rate for Japanese mortality to be the age- and sex-specific 1999 death rates published by the Japanese Ministry of Health, Labor, and Welfare (2001). To create death rates for centenarians, which were included as a single composite rate by the Japanese ministry, we increased the age 98 mortality rate by 0.05 for each year up to 107 for males and 109 for females at which ages we set the mortality rates to 1.0 in the base year. We raised the maximum lifespan one year every two calendar years. We used the same rates of improvement as in the US 2 percent scenario.

The Wilmoth rates were derived from John Wilmoth's extrapolation of Japanese mortality trends. Using the Lee–Carter forecasting model, Wilmoth calculated mortality rates that decline linearly with time for each age/sex category. Wilmoth (1996) contains the parameters and the author provided us exact mortality rates for future years. We assumed the same maximum limits to life as the 2 percent annual reduction scenario.

Population Estimates: United States

Estimates of future population required starting population, mortality rates, immigration, sex ratio at birth, and fertility rates. Our starting population was the population in the United States on 1 January 1999. To this base population we applied the 1999 mortality and net immigration rates provided by the SSA, which provided a starting year 2000 population. We described our method of calculating mortality rates above. All other variables remained the same between the two scenarios. We set net immigration, which equals legal and illegal immigration less emigration, to the age- and sex-specific values assumed by the SSA in the 2001 OASDI Trustees Report – Intermediate Assumption. Total net immigration is assumed gradually to increase from approximately 785000 in 1999 to its ultimate level in 2008 of 900000. We assumed the same age distribution as does the SSA. Under the double immigration scenario, we maintained the age distribution of total immigration. We assumed the same sex ratio of births as did the SSA in the 2001 OASDI Trustees Report, and maintained a constant value equal to 1.05 males for every 1.00 females throughout the simulation. We also used the SSA's assumed fertility rates, as reported in the 2001 OASDI Trustees Report. Total fertility is assumed to fall gradually from 2.07 in 1999 to 1.95 in 2025 and to remain at that level.

Population Estimates: Japan

We set the Japanese starting population in 2000 at the actual population on 1 October 1999. We described above the computation of mortality rates. In the zero immigration scenario, we set net immigration at zero in all years. In the increased immigration scenario, we assumed net immigration of 50000 in 2000 through 2006, and increased the annual rate by 50000 each year until 2010, when it remained at its ultimate level of 300000. We assumed that the age distribution of immigration and the sex ratio at birth in Japan is identical to that in the United States. We set total fertility rates at those assumed by the National Institute of Population and Social Security Research in their 1997 population projections for Japan (Takahashi et al. 1999) and the age distribution of the total fertility rates at values for the United States.

NOTES

*   The authors wish to thank John Wilmoth for kindly making available data from a previous study for use in making projections, and Stephen Goss, Michael Miller, and Alice Wade from the Social Security Administration for providing valuable information and guidance.

1.   The size of required reserves depends on how the present value of accumulated obligations is computed. Under the 'closed group' approach, reserves must equal the present value of pension obligations accumulated by workers currently in the workforce and by current retirees. Under the 'open group' approach, reserves must equal the difference between the present value of pension obligations of current and future workers and current retirees and the present value of revenues that will be generated by current and future workers.

2.   Van Poppel and De Beer (1996).

3.   Of course, one can imagine rules that would increase uncertainty – such as that the pension plan would be repealed if unemployment averaged more than 5 percent for any five-year period. But pre-commitment to rules that would smooth adjustments to projected imbalances would lower uncertainty.

4.   Gavrilov and Gavrilova (1991).

5.   Ibid.

6.   Olshansky et al. (2001).

7.   Ibid.

8   Wilmoth (2000).

9.   Wilmoth (1996).

10. Throughout 'life expectancy' refers to 'cohort' rather than to 'period' life expectancy. Cohort life expectancy assumes that as members of each cohort age, mortality rates continue to fall according to some assumed pattern. Period life expectancy assumes that mortality rates for members of a cohort are the same as those that prevail for other age cohorts at the time that cohort is born. Thus, period life expectancy is always several years briefer than cohort life expectancy. The more rapid the assumed declines in mortality rates, the greater the difference.

11. Lee and Carter (1992). The procedure was to fit the logarithm of the actual mortality rates for people of age x in year t, $\ln m_{x,t}$, to a function $a_x + b_x k_t$, where k is an index of the natural logarithm of mortality rates that decreases linearly at b per year, where the bs sum to 1 and the ks sum to zero. As a result, a_x are simply the average mortality rates at time t.

12. James F. Fries cites the *Guinness Book of World Records* for the longest documented lifespan of 114, but puts maximum achievable life expectancy at not much more than 90 years (Gavrilov and Gavrilova 1991; Fries 1989).

13. Harris (2000, p. 59).

14. Schwartz (1998, p. 150) writes: 'Although Census Bureau calculations project an increase in average lifespan of only eight years by the year 2050, some experts believe that the human lifespan should not begin to encounter any theoretical natural limits before 120 years. With continuing advances in molecular medicine and a growing understanding of the aging process, that limit could rise to 130 years or more.'

15. Wilmoth (2000).

16. In symbols, $m(t,c,s) = \Sigma_c \, m(t,s)$ ($\forall \, t, s$), $c = (1 \ldots 11)$, where $m(t,c,s)$ is the mortality at time t of sex group, s, from each cause, c. Furthermore, $m_j(t,i,s) = 0$, $\forall \, i \neq j$, where $m_j(t,i,s)$ is the response of the mortality rate from cause, i, to a change in mortality from cause j.

17. For a defense of using cause-specific methods, see Caselli and Lopez (1996b).

18. Vaupel (1988); Manton et al. (1981).

19. Gavrilov and Gavrilova (1991).

20. The mathematical form is the Gompertz–Makeham function, $A + R \, e^{\alpha x}$, where A, R, and α are parameters and x is age.

21. This projection assumes continuation of the historical US pattern of mortality improvement in which mortality rates fell fastest for the young and slowest for the elderly. In particular, we assume that annual reductions in mortality rates among those aged 0 to 14 is 2.8 percent, among those aged 15 to 64 is 2.2 percent, and among those aged 65 or above is 1.9 percent.
22. John Potts and William B. Schwartz, paper in progress for a conference at the Brookings Institution under a grant from the Robert Wood Johnson Foundation.
23. Wilmoth (1996); Lee and Carter (1992).
24. The aged fraction is projected to reach even higher levels in some countries than it is in Japan. The reason is that fertility rates in those countries are assumed to remain even lower than those projected for Japan.
25. Lee and Edwards (2001); also see Congressional Budget Office (2001).
26. Earnings in year t years before the worker reached age 60 were to be adjusted by the ratio $e_{60}/e_{60-t} = IE$. The average of the highest 35 values of IE equaled average career earnings (ACE), and benefits were based on ACE. The benefit formula adopted in 1972 improperly implemented the principle of maintaining replacement rates for workers at given relative positions in the earnings distribution and tended to boost replacement rates at the relatively high rates of inflation experienced in the early 1970s. Congress rectified this error in 1977.
27. This statement assumes that the discount rate exceeds wage growth.
28. For price indexing, one would multiply by p_n/p_{n-t}.
29. Deferring the age of initial eligibility will not lower the discounted present value of benefits if benefits are adjusted actuarially for the age of initial claim. Benefits under the US pension system will be approximately actuarial at all ages after the year 2006.
30. Other variables are also relevant, depending on the terms of the pension plan. For example, if extra benefits are paid to workers with spouses not eligible in their own right or to children, marriage, divorce, and average family size would also influence pension costs.

REFERENCES

Bell, Felicitie C., Alice H. Wade and Stephen C. Goss (1992), 'Life tables for the United States social security area: 1900–2080', Social Security Administration Actuarial Study No. 107, August.
Caselli, Graziella and Alan D. Lopez (eds) (1996a), *Health and Mortality Among Elderly Populations*, Oxford: Clarendon.
Caselli, Graziella and Alan D. Lopez (1996b), 'Health and mortality among the elderly, issues for assessment', in Caselli and Lopez (eds), pp. 3–20.
Congressional Budget Office (2001), *Uncertainty in Social Security's Long-term Finances: A Stochastic Analysis*, Washington, DC, December.
Fries, James F. (1989), 'The compression of morbidity: near or far?', *Milbank Quarterly*, **67** (2), 208–31.
Gavrilov, L.A. and N.S. Gavrilova (1991), *The Biology of Life Span: A Quantitative Approach*, edited by V.P. Skulachev, Chur, Switzerland: Harwood Academic.
Harris, John (2000), 'Intimations of immortality', *Science*, **288**, 7 April, 59.
Japanese Ministry of Health, Labor, and Welfare (2001), 'Abridged life tables for Japan, 1999', http://www.mhlw.go.jp/english/database/db-hw/lifetb99_8/index.html, 1 December.
Lee, Ronald D. and Lawrence R. Carter (1992), 'Modeling and forecasting U.S. mortality', *Journal of the American Statistical Association*, **87** (419), 659–71.

Lee, Ronald and Ryan Edwards (2001), 'The fiscal impact of population aging in the US: assessing the uncertainties', paper presented at the National Bureau of Economic Research Tax Policy and the Economy meeting, organized by James Poterba, 30 October, Washington, DC, http://www.ceda.berkeley.edu/papers/rlee.

Manton, Kenneth G., Eric Stallard and James W. Vaupel (1981), 'Methods for comparing the mortality experience of heterogeneous populations', *Demography*, **18** (2), August, 389–410.

Olshansky, S. Jay, Bruce Carnes and Aline Désesquelles (2001), 'Prospects for human longevity', *Science*, 23 February, 1491.

Schwartz, William B. (1998), *Life without Disease: The Pursuit of Medical Utopia*, Berkeley, CA: University of California Press.

Takahashi, Shigesato, Ryuichi Kaneko, Akira Ishikawa, Masako Ikenoue and Fusami Mita (1999), 'Population projections for Japan: methods, assumptions, and results'. *Review of Population and Social Policy*, no. 8, 75–115.

Thompson, Lawrence (1998), *Older and Wiser: The Economics of Public Pensions*, Washington, DC: Urban Institute Press.

Van Poppel, Frans and Joop De Beer (1996), 'Evaluation of standard mortality projections for the elderly', in Caselli and Lopez (eds), pp. 288–312.

Vaupel, James W. (1988), 'Inherited frailty and longevity', *Demography*, **25** (2), May, 277–87.

Wilmoth, John R. (1996), 'Mortality projections for Japan: a comparison of four methods', in Caselli and Lopez (eds), pp. 266–87.

Wilmoth, John R. (2000), 'Demography of longevity: past, present, and future trends', *Experimental Gerontology*, **35**, 1111–29.

4. Alternative pension reform strategies for Japan

David Miles and Ales Cerny

1. INTRODUCTION

This chapter summarizes the research we have undertaken into the implications of various pension reform strategies in Japan. Reform is essential because ageing will generate extreme pressures on the public, unfunded pension system. We consider the macroeconomic, or aggregate, and the distributional implications of reforms that, to varying degrees, would increase reliance upon funded pensions. We also estimate the welfare implications of reforms by calculating the expected gains and losses to households of various generations. We take as a point of reference a scenario where unfunded pensions provide an income to the retired worth a high proportion of salaries at the end of their working life; we take that proportion to be 50 percent of gross (or around 70 percent of net) salaries.

In earlier research we have described results from a range of models. In some models uncertainty was absent but asset prices and wages were endogenous and responded to movements in savings and in labor supply generated by demographic shifts and changing pension arrangements. In other versions of the model there were multiple sources of uncertainty, none of which could be fully insured against, but rates of return and real wages evolved exogenously. In some versions of the model we were able to allow for uncertainty and to endogenize asset prices, but only by focusing on steady states. That precludes analyzing transitional periods where demographics and pension systems are evolving. Computational difficulties made it hard to simultaneously allow for multiple risks, changing demographics, and shifting pension arrangements and to also search for a general equilibrium where factor prices move as the capital stock used in production is influenced by domestic saving. Here we are able to show results for a more general calibrated model of the Japanese economy where there are all these features – there is uncertainty, endogenous factor prices and shifting demographics and pension arrangements. We use a calibrated model but vary key parameters (in particular, discount rates and rates of risk aversion) to assess how different reform strategies are influenced by preferences and by technology.

In Section 2 we give an overview of the research. In Section 3 we describe the calibrated model of the Japanese economy and discuss solution techniques. In Section 4 we focus on the macroeconomic implications of various reform strategies. In Section 5 we consider distributional effects. Section 6 looks at robustness of the main findings to variations in parameters. Section 7 summarizes and draws out the policy implications of the research.

2.   OVERVIEW

Ageing within the Japanese economy is likely to be dramatic over the next 50 years. This has obvious implications for the sustainability of pension arrangements. By far the larger part of the resources going to the retired now in Japan are unfunded, pay-as-you-go, public pensions. With a dramatic increase in the ratio of the retired to the working population, unfunded pensions can only continue to be paid at their current level of generosity (in terms of replacement rates) if contribution rates rise sharply. That is likely to have significant and undesirable impacts on competitiveness and labor supply. Reform of the system is necessary. But what sort of reform? In this chapter we consider various alternatives and estimate their impact on aggregate performance and on the distribution of gains and losses both across and within generations.

One reform strategy is to initiate a transition toward an almost completely funded system where unfunded pensions might only be set at a very low level to act as a safety net. The desirability of that policy depends on what the long-run implications of relying much more heavily on funded pensions are *and* on how a transition to greater funding is managed. The first question is about the macroeconomic and welfare implications of having made a transition to a funded system. The second is about what the transition process implies for the welfare of those generations who live through it. We consider both issues by analyzing the evolution of macroeconomic aggregates and the distribution of welfare within and between cohorts along the transition path towards alternative steady states. We also consider less wholesale reform of the system. So-called 'parametric reforms' involve some scaling back in the generosity of unfunded pensions, either by reducing replacement rates or increasing retirement ages. We consider a strategy of holding the Japanese payroll contribution rate at around its current level, thereby necessitating a reduction of unfunded state pensions, but on a scale that could not be described as 'phasing out'. We also consider the implications of trying to preserve the current generosity of unfunded state pensions with no change in the retirement age or in typical replacement rates. That will require substantial increases in contribution rates.

The welfare and macroeconomic implications of these alternative strategies for Japan are markedly different and they affect different generations in distinct ways.

A key feature of alternative pension arrangements – different degrees of reliance upon funded pensions – is that they distribute risks in different ways. For that reason any assessment of alternative pension arrangements needs to handle risk. Modeling how uncertainty about incomes and rates of return influences optimal pension arrangements is difficult. A key policy issue is what is the desirable split between funded and unfunded systems when there are sources of uninsurable risk that affect risk-averse agents and where those risks are allocated in different ways by different types of pension system. Here we try to say something about this.

3. A STYLIZED STOCHASTIC GENERAL EQUILIBRIUM MODEL OF THE JAPANESE ECONOMY

Building on the seminal early work of Auerbach and Kotlikoff (1987), many papers have used overlapping generations (OLG) models to analyze the economic impact of ageing. In this section we describe an OLG model calibrated to reflect features of the Japanese economy in which there are multiple sources of uncertainty. We then go on to describe simulations to assess the impacts of various pension policies in an environment of a rapidly ageing population.

Any model that wants to say something useful about risk and uncertainty must take account of several factors:

1. that individuals face substantial, largely idiosyncratic, uncertainty about their labor income;
2. that returns on most financial assets are volatile and uncertain; and
3. that to the extent that individuals depend upon their own accumulated funds for retirement resources the way in which annuities markets work is important (state-run, unfunded systems will be unaffected by the efficiency of annuities markets because the government is effectively providing insurance itself).

We have developed a model, calibrated to Japanese data, in which individuals face random, but persistent, shocks to labor income throughout their working life. We assume that they face uncertainty about the returns they will earn on at least some sorts of financial assets. We assume that there is a safe asset but there are also risky assets which, on average, earn higher returns. We also assume individuals are risk averse and that they understand the risks of investing in different sorts of assets and are also aware of the uncertainty over how long they will live. We use numerical techniques to calculate optimal profiles of consumption, saving and port-folio allocation for individuals over their lives. We aggregate these decisions to construct the macroeconomic aggregates. Solving this sort of model is difficult and we use numerical techniques to work out optimal paths. We set the critical parameters in the model (parameters of the utility functions such as degrees of risk aversion and rates of time preference, and charac-teristics of the labor income profile over life) by reference to recent data from the Japanese economy. The relative numbers of people at different ages at each point is set equal to estimated past, and projected future, numbers for Japan.

We then simulate the model using different settings for the key policy variables. We also consider how differences in the investment environment, particularly the efficiency of annuities contracts and the risk return trade-off on risky assets, affect the economy. We are able to show how different degrees of generosity of unfunded pensions affects the overall saving rate, the level of GDP, and the allocation of savings across different assets. We are also able to make welfare comparisons.

In this model there are stochastic processes for labor income and for rates of return. Given these, and conditional on pension arrangements and mor-tality rates, agents choose consumption (and therefore saving) and port-folio allocation in each period to maximize expected lifetime utility. We assume an additively separable form of the agent's lifetime utility function. We also assume a constant coefficient of risk aversion, the inverse of the intertemporal substitution elasticity. Agents are assumed to know the prob-abilities of surviving to given ages. Agent k who is aged j at time t maximizes:

$$U_k = E_t \left\{ \sum_{i=0}^{i=T-j} s_{ij} \left[(c_{kt+i})^{1-\zeta} / (1-\zeta) \right] / (1+\rho)^i \right\}, \qquad (4.1)$$

where T is the maximum length of life possible (which we take as 120 years of age) and the probability of surviving i more periods conditional on reaching age j is s_{ij}. ($s_{0j} = 1$.) ρ is the rate of pure time preference; c_{kt+i} is con-sumption of the agent in period $t+i$. ζ is the coefficient of relative risk aversion.

Agents face two constraints. First there is a budget constraint governing the evolution of financial assets taken from one period to the next.

$$W_{kt+1} = [W_{kt} + \exp(y_{kt}.)(1-\tau) - c_{kt} + b_{kt}].$$
$$[\lambda \exp(r_{st}) + (1-\lambda)\exp(r_{ft})], \tag{4.2}$$

where:

W_{kt} = stock of wealth of agent k in period t,

y_{kt} = log of gross labor income,

τ = tax rate on labor income; tax paid is simply a proportion of gross income,

b_{kt} = level of the unfunded, state pension received by an agent, this pension is zero until age 65,

λ = proportion of financial assets invested in risky assets,

r_{st} = one period (log) rate of return on risky financial assets between period t and period $t+1$, and

r_{ft} = one period (log) rate of return on safe financial assets between period t and period $t+1$.

For ease of notation we have not given agent-specific subscripts to asset returns but we will allow for returns to depend on characteristics of the investor; because probabilities of death are specific to agents of a given age, rates of return on assets that might have annuities features will be agent specific. We shall describe how rates of return on financial investments are determined shortly.

Agents also face a borrowing constraint; wealth cannot be negative: $W_{kt} \geq 0$ for all k and t. This constraint may bind in various periods. Whether it does so depends in a complex way upon the profile of the deterministic component of labor income, the realizations of income and rate of return shocks, portfolio choices, the degree of risk aversion and the volatility of shocks. It also depends significantly on the tax rate and the generosity of state pensions.

We also assume that agents cannot take short positions in either safe or risky assets: $0 \leq \lambda \leq 1$.

Agents work from age 20 to the end of their 64th year (if they survive that long) and are retired thereafter. We assume that the profile of gross of tax labor income reflects three factors. First, there is a time-related rise in general labor productivity. We set this at 2 percent a year. Second, there is an age-related element to the growth of labor income over an agent's life. This is modeled as a quadratic in age. The age-specific part of the log of labor income is:

$$\alpha + \gamma \text{age} - \vartheta \text{age}^2. \tag{4.3}$$

We set γ and ϑ so that the age–income profiles match patterns that have been typical. This generates a hump-shaped pattern of labor income with earnings typically peaking in the late forties. We use profiles for the deterministic part of labor income which mean that on average wages of someone at the high point in the life cycle (in their early fifties) are around double those of a new entrant to the labor market.

There is also an idiosyncratic (agent-specific) stochastic element of labor income. The log of labor income for an agent is the sum of the age-related element, the time-related element and the additive income shock. Denoting the log of gross labor income of agent k who is aged j in period t as y_{kt} we have:

$$y_{kt} = \alpha + gt + \gamma.j - \vartheta j^2 + u_{kt} \qquad (4.4)$$

$$u_{kt} = \phi u_{kt-1} + e_{kt},$$

where $e \sim N(0, \sigma_e)$, α is a constant, and g is the rate of growth of labor productivity over time (set at 2 percent). ϕ reflects the degree of persistence in idiosyncratic shocks to labor income; empirical evidence from a range of countries suggests ϕ is high and that idiosyncratic shocks to income typically have a high degree of persistence. (We will set ϕ at 0.95; we discuss calibration in detail in the next section.)

We assume that rates of return on risky financial wealth vary across periods due to random shocks that hit stock and bond markets. There may also be a slow-moving evolution of the mean rates of return on safe and risky assets due to changes in the stock of capital relative to the stock of labor. In the simulations where desired holdings of wealth by residents match the stock of capital used in production we will allow both the safe rate of return and the mean of the risky rate of return to depend upon the stock of aggregate wealth (relative to labor) held in the economy. There is an underlying production function (of the Cobb–Douglas sort) and an assumption that the capital stock used in production moves in line with the desired holding of wealth by the private sector. Movements in the aggregate capital to labor ratio are assumed to drive the mean returns on assets; they do not affect the stochastic part of the return on risky assets.

We assume that rates of return on savings at a particular time – both on safe and risky assets – differ between individuals because financial institutions take into account the probabilities of death of agents and offer age-related investment products. More specifically, financial institutions offer the following contracts. For every dollar invested in period t, with a given risky/safe split, the investor receives the market return adjusted for a probability of survival to the next period. If markets are perfect the probability used in making this adjustment is the true survival probability. But we allow for imperfections (stemming from adverse selection or some other types of cost) which mean that the two are not equal. If the agent dies the institution keeps the funds. With no bequest motives agents will always chose these contracts over ones which just pay the market rate of return. *If* the insurance element of this contract is offered on actuarially fair terms the *ex post* rate of return on a dollar invested in the risky asset during period *t* by an agent *k* who is aged *j* and who survives to the next period is given by:

$$\exp(r_{st})/s_{1j}, \qquad (4.5)$$

where s_{1j} is the probability of surviving one more year conditional on reaching age *j*.

We assume r_s is the sum of the mean log return and an unpredictable shock: $r_{st} = r_t + v_t$. r_t is the mean rate of return on risky assets at time *t* and v_t is the random element of the rate of return on assets. Furthermore, we assume *v* is iid and normal: $v \sim N(0, \sigma_r)$. We set σ_r equal to 0.175 – a value which returns on assets over the past few decades suggest is reasonable (see next section for more details).

For a dollar invested in the safe asset at time *t* the return to an agent aged *j* is:

$$\exp(r_{ft})/s_{1j}. \qquad (4.6)$$

We can write the log returns on actuarially fair investments in risky and safe assets, respectively, to an agent aged *j* at time *t* as:

$$r_t + v_t - \ln(s_{1j}) \qquad (4.7)$$

$$r_{ft} - \ln(s_{1j}). \qquad (4.8)$$

If markets are perfect this financial contract can be offered at no risk by financial institutions because they pass on all the rate of return risk to investors and are assumed to be able to take advantage of the law of large numbers and face no uncertainty about the proportion of agents who will survive. It seems natural to assume that financial firms will offer insurance against risks that are idiosyncratic (individual length of life risk) but not offer insurance against systematic risk (rate of return risk). The contracts offered by financial institutions can be thought of as highly flexible individual retirement accounts (or personal pension schemes). Effectively, agents have their own pot of assets into which they pay contributions and make deductions. Contribution rates and drawdowns from the fund are subject only to the constraint that the pot of assets can never fall below zero. The average rates of return on the fund increase with age since survival probabilities decline with age. Just as standard flat annuities available for a given sum rise with age, so the average rate of return offered by financial institutions increases with age.

In effect we are assuming that financial institutions offer one period annuities. These are the vehicles through which agents save for retirement. Agents are able to draw down such accounts in a flexible way in retirement. Individuals may decide to mimic the payments from standard flat annuities by having the 'pot' size (that is, W) decline with age at a rate that is offset by rising average rates of return.

We introduce a measure of the efficiency of annuities markets. When this measure, β, is 1 the annuities market works perfectly. When $\beta = 0$ annuities are, effectively, not offered. The survival probability implicit in the contract offered by a financial institution is a weighted average of the true survival probability, s_{1j}, and the rate when no annuity is offered, an effective survival probability of unity. β is the weight placed on the actuarially fair survival probability.

The rate of return paid on one period savings invested with λ in the risky asset and $(1 - \lambda)$ in the safe asset for an agent aged j at time t becomes:

$$[\lambda \exp(r_t + v_t) + (1 - \lambda)\exp(r_{ft})] / [\beta s_{1j} + (1 - \beta)]. \qquad (4.9)$$

This way of modeling the efficiency of annuity contracts allows the departure from actuarially fair contracts to vary with age. The greater is age, the lower the probability of surviving and for all $\beta < 1$ the greater is the departure from actuarially fair contracts.

The set of first-order conditions from individual k's optimization problem are as follows.

If:

$$c_{kt} < [W_{kt} + \exp(y_{kt}.)(1 - \tau) + b_{kt}] \qquad (4.10)$$

then:

$$U'(c_{kt}) = E_t (s_{1j} \{U'[c_{kt+i}].[\lambda \exp(r_t + v_t) + (1 - \lambda)\exp(r_{ft})]/ \\ [\beta s_{1j} + (1 - \beta)]\} / (1 + \rho)),$$

else:

$$c_{kt} = [W_{kt} + \exp(y_{kt})(1 - \tau) + b_{kt}] \qquad (4.11)$$

and

$$U'(c_{kt}) \geq E_t\,(s_{1j}\,\{U'(c_{kt+i}).\,[\lambda\exp(r_t+v_t)+(1-\lambda)\exp(r_{ft})]\,/$$
$$[\beta s_{1j}+(1-\beta)]\}\,/\,(1+\rho)),$$

where $U'(c_{kt})$ is $\partial U_k/\partial c_{kt}.$

We also require a condition for optimal portfolio allocation. Either:

$$0 = E_t\{U'(c_{kt+i}).[\exp(r_t+v_t)-\exp(r_{ft})]\}\text{ and }0\leq\lambda\leq 1$$

or:

$$0 < E_t\{U'(c_{kt+i}).[\exp(r_t+v_t)-\exp(r_{ft})]\}\text{ and }\lambda=1 \qquad (4.12)$$

else:

$$0 > E_t\{U'(c_{kt+i}).[\exp(r_t+v_t)-\exp(r_{ft})]\}\text{ and }\lambda=0.$$

Condition (4.10) holds when the borrowing constraint is not binding. When the constraint binds, complementary slackness implies that (4.11) holds. Condition (4.12) is a standard condition for optimal portfolio allocation. Corner solutions may arise where agents wish to invest only in the safe asset or in the risky asset; for an internal solution the first equality at (4.12) must hold.

Although characterizing optimal plans is easy enough, solving explicitly for optimal consumption and for the optimal accumulation path for funds is not possible. Instead we have to turn to numerical methods. We solve the problem backwards in a now standard way (see Zeldes 1989; Deaton 1991; and Hubbard et al. 1995). This involves constructing large grids in the state space and solving for optimal saving and portfolio allocation at those grid points using numerical integration and interpolation. We first solve the saving/consumption/portfolio allocation problem for a given path of interest rates and wages. We then generate life histories for cohorts each of size 7000 households born at different times. To do that we create a set of paths for the idiosyncratic shocks to income for each member of every cohort. We then work out the optimal consumption–saving–portfolio allocation profile for every agent. Then we aggregate the decisions made by all cohorts alive at each date, taking account of the relative numbers of agents of each age at each point (based on official central demographic projections for Japan). We then aggregate the saving and labor supply of all agents alive at each time and construct a time series for the aggregate stock of effective units of labor relative to capital. We calibrate the model so that during the 1990s the mean rate of return on risky assets is 6.5 percent and the safe rate is 2 percent. In the initial set of simulations we assume that investment in capital used within the Japanese economy moves in line with Japanese saving. Put another way, the capital stock used in production is equal to the stock of wealth that individuals wish to hold. This assumption is clearly at odds with the fact that Japan does not have, and has not had, a zero capital account on the balance of payments. So we consider alternative assumptions later in the chapter, where in some stochastic simulations we take the rate of return as exogenous to domestic saving. We are able to assess what difference the various assumptions about the degree of exogeneity of factor prices make. This turns out to be important and suggests that how success-ful various pension reform strategies are depends upon the portfolio allo-cation decisions of the private sector in an environment of increasing reliance upon private saving for retirement resources.

In the case where factor prices are endogenous, the future path of the mean rates of return on assets, and the evolution of mean real wages, depends upon how the aggregate capital to labor ratio evolves relative to its value in 1990. Denoting the 1990 value for the aggregate capital to (effec-tive) labor units ratio as k_0 we have that for some future date t the mean rate of return on risky assets is:

$$r_t = 0.065 \times (k_t/k_0)^{\alpha-1} \qquad (4.13)$$

where we set the coefficient on capital in the implicit underlying Cobb–Douglas production function equal to α (which is the share of profits in GDP which we set at 0.3). The safe rate evolves according to:

$$r_{ft} = 0.02 \times (k_t/k_0)^{\alpha-1}. \qquad (4.14)$$

The real wage per effective unit of labor (before we allow for the influ-ence of exogenous, time-related productivity growth) is different from the level for 1990 by the factor:

$$(k_t/k_0)^{\alpha}. \qquad (4.15)$$

Equations (4.13) and (4.14) ensure that in the simulations with endogenous factor prices the average return on assets declines (rises) if the capital to labor ratio increases (falls). We also allow for real wages to be higher the greater is the capital to labor ratio (by (4.15)).

Once we have solved the optimizing problem at a given set of average rates of return and for a given path of wages, and calculated aggregate saving and labor supply, we update the path of rates and return and wages using equations (4.13)–(4.15). We then revise the optimizing problem for each cohort, simulate the life paths for every cohort, aggregate once more and re-calculate the new paths for factor prices. This process is continued until convergence – that is until the evolution of average factor prices is consistent with the aggregate decisions made by agents who base their decisions upon that path of average prices.

In this solution procedure we do, effectively, distinguish between the market value of the aggregate financial wealth of individuals and the value of the physical capital used for production. To capture the fact that variation in the value of physical capital is likely to be lower than variation in financial wealth (there is volatility in Tobin's q), we model the value of physical capital as a moving average of the value of financial wealth. It is as if the value of physical capital is equal to financial wealth generated by zero shocks to the rate of return.

Where factor prices are exogenous the simulations are much easier since we do not iterate towards a fixed point for mean returns and wages.

Initially we will stick to the assumption that national saving is closely linked to the evolution of capital used in production – that is, that factor prices are endogenous. We consider this our base case and note that while the assumption that domestic saving and investment in domestic capital are equal is obviously unrealistic, an alternative assumption of a completely global capital market is also at odds with many facts. At the national level there remains a significantly higher correlation between savings and investment than one might expect with a global capital market – the Feldstein and Horioka puzzle remains puzzling. Portfolios of assets held by the private sector in Japan, and in other developed economies, remain substantially invested at home. Even to the extent that Japan invests overseas, it largely does so within other economies that also face an ageing problem. Arguably it is more reliable to assume that Japan is effectively a closed economy (in terms of net capital flows) rather than assume that there is some exogenous world rate of return on assets that Japanese citizens will be able to earn even as the population structure and pension arrangements change substantially.

We shall show three types of simulation. In the first, state pension generosity is preserved at roughly its current level. We assume that the unfunded pension is worth 50 percent of gross current average earnings to all those over retirement age. (This generates a ratio of pensions to net of contributions average wages of about 65 percent over the simulation period; this ratio actually rises somewhat as the contribution rate rises.) In the second set of simulations we assume that the contribution rate (the tax rate) is preserved at roughly its 2001 level. This will require that the replacement rate of the state pension declines gradually as the population ages. In the third set of simulations we assume that the government takes a radical course and announces now that from 2010 they will gradually reduce the replacement rate of unfunded state pensions in a way that leads to a fall in the replacement rate to only 10 percent by 2050.

In all simulations we use official (central) Japanese population projections to assess support ratios and calculate contribution rates needed to balance state pension systems.[1]

3.1.   Calibration

The key parameters in the model reflect degree of risk aversion and the substitutability of consumption over time (that is the intertemporal substitution of consumption), the rates of pure time preference, the degree of efficiency of financial markets and also the share parameter of the production function. There is considerable uncertainty about the magnitude of many of these parameters. Least controversial is probably the parameter from a simple Cobb–Douglas production function that reflects a share of capital income in GDP. We set this parameter equal to 0.3. In the base case we assume a relatively low intertemporal substitutability of consumption (equal to one-third, which implies a coefficient relative risk aversion of 3), we also assume a slightly negative rate of pure time preference, which may seem strange but is consistent with the limited empirical evidence available. In the absence of bequests, we find that a negative discount rate is needed to generate the level of savings observed in Japan. A negative discount rate is not inconsistent with positive equilibrium real rates of return, see Benninga (1990), and Kocherlakota (1990). Other researchers have used a negative rate of pure time preference to model Japanese household decisions. Kato (1998) calibrates an OLG model with a −7.5 percent discount rate and Kato (2000) uses the rate of −3.5 percent. Imrohoroglu et al. (1999) use a negative discount rate of just under −1 percent in their numerical simulations. The empirical work of Hurd (1989), based on US data, is also consistent with negative rates of pure time preference. We also show results with a much higher rate of pure preference where agents discount the future at +1.5 percent a year. This is a very different assumption. With a rate of pure preference of −1.5 percent an agent at age 30 attaches four and a half times as much weight to outcomes at age 80 as when the rate of pure preference is +1.5 percent.

The coefficient of risk aversion and the intertemporal elasticity of substitution (which in our specification are the inverse of each other) is also controversial; Cooley and Prescott (1995) use unity for their simulations whereas Auerbach and Kotlikoff (1987) use a coefficient of relative risk aversion of 4, implying that the elasticity of substitution is only 0.25. Empirical work by Hansen and Singleton (1983) and Mankiw et al. (1985) suggest values a little over unity for intertemporal substitutability suggesting, in our framework, a coefficient of relative risk aversion a little under unity. Hall (1980), Grossman and Shiller (1981) and Mankiw (1985) found, using US data, values between 0 and 0.4 for the intertemporal elasticity suggesting coefficients of risk aversion well in excess of 2. Hubbard et al. (1995) use a relative risk aversion of 3 in their simulations. Zeldes (1989) estimated the risk aversion coefficient as 2.3. Kato (1998) and Kato (2000) use relative risk aversion of 5 and 2.22, respectively. We consider a value of 3 for the risk aversion coefficient is a central estimate but clearly the evidence makes it hard to be confident about what a plausible figure is. We shall also show results where the coefficient of risk aversion is set equal to 6.

We also assume in this simulation that aggregate labor productivity increases at an exogenous rate of 2 percent a year. This set of parameters yields an equilibrium path in the stochastic OLG model where the savings rate over the 1990s averages about 18 percent and the capital output ratio is around 3.5.[2] These are not implausible magnitudes.

3.2. Income Profile

Cross-section profiles of Japanese incomes suggest that it is typical for earnings to peak at around age 50 when average earnings are around double the earnings of new workers (20-year-olds).[3] We set the parameters of the earnings process so that on average the income of Japanese workers peaks at the age of 50 when it is roughly double earnings at age 20. With productivity growth at 2 percent this leads to the following average income profile:

$$y_t = \ln 2 - (\ln 2)/900*(\text{age-}50)^2 + 0.02t.$$

Labor income for a particular cohort is the product of the number of units of effective labor supplied and the post-tax real wage per unit. The latter is endogenous and depends on the tax rate needed to balance the state pension scheme and on the aggregate capital to labor ratio that, via a Cobb–Douglas production function, determines the marginal productivity of labor.

One of the key assumptions in the model is that individuals typically face a hump-shaped profile of earnings. They start work in their early twenties and retire in their early sixties. Over their working life their productivity rises and then declines. This generates a hump-shaped pattern of income that, with the assumption of forward-looking behavior and consumption smoothing, generates a classic life-cycle pattern of saving. Saving is low in the early period in life, tends to be high in middle age and then is slightly negative in retirement. We assume no bequest motive so that individuals typically run down assets once they move into old age. The bequest issue is very important; it matters a lot to the economics of pension reform whether voluntary, or planned, bequests are important. In a recent paper, Horioka (2001) argues that the evidence suggests there is not a strong bequest motive in Japan. If there is not a significant bequest motive there will typically be an inverted 'V' shaped pattern of asset holdings: people start with no assets, build them up to a peak at retirement, and then run them down gradually toward death. This pattern will look different in a model with no uncertainty compared to one with stochastic factors, uncertainty about the time of death and imperfect annuity markets.

3.3. Income Volatility

Setting the volatility of the shock to labor income is particularly important for the simulations. As noted above, a significant part of the shocks to individual incomes appear to be persistent. Our strategy is to set the variance of the iid shocks so as to generate an overall degree of income uncertainty which is typical, while keeping the persistence of shocks comparable to that of other studies. Hubbard et al. (1995) use a model of income dynamics to simulate the impact of social security which is based on characteristics of US household income data. Their model is similar to that used here except that they allow for both transitory and persistent shocks, while we allow only for persistent shocks. Their model for the log income of household k at time t is:

$$y_{kt} = f(\text{age}_{kt}) + u_{kt} + w_{kt} \quad \text{and} \quad u_{kt} = \rho u_{kt-1} + v_{kt},$$

where v and w are iid shocks that are not correlated and $f(\text{age}_{kt})$ is a deterministic function.

A measure of the unconditional volatility of log income is $\sigma^2_w + \sigma^2_v / (1 - \rho^2)$. Typical values for ρ, σ_w and σ_v used by Hubbard et al. are 0.955, 0.158 and 0.158, respectively. These imply that some income shocks are highly persistent. With these values their measure of the unconditional standard deviation of the shock to log income is 0.56.[4]

The dispersion of Japanese wages is lower than in the United States. We find that setting the unconditional standard deviation of shocks to log income at between 0.4 and 0.5 for the Japanese workforce matches the empirical distribution quite well. Figure 4.1, for example, illustrates that with an unconditional standard deviation of 0.45 the implied distribution of the levels of income is very close to the actual 1996 distribution of Japanese household income. (For this comparison we adjust the intercept in our process for log income to match the mean of Japanese household

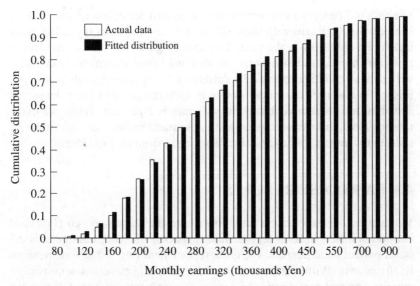

Figure 4.1   Actual income distribution of Japanese workers (1996) and its lognormal approximation with standard deviation 0.45

income in 1996.) Part of the inequality in the empirical distribution reflects the life-cycle pattern of earning rather than the impact of persistent shocks to earnings or persistent differences in earnings power. To allow for this we assume an unconditional standard deviation of log income equal to 0.40. We set the persistence parameter at 0.95 implying a standard deviation of the random (iid) income shocks of around 0.125. (In terms of parameters in Hubbard et al. we set $\rho = 0.95$, $\sigma_w = 0$ and $\sigma_v = 0.125$.)

3.4. Returns

The historical real returns on the Nikkei 225 index over the past few decades have a mean of around 7–8 percent with standard deviation of 22–25 percent depending on the precise period one considers (we have looked at 1960–2000, 1970–2000, 1980–2000). These figures are for gross returns; net of charges annual returns to individuals are likely to be lower by at least 50 basis points, and perhaps by much less.

Returns on bond portfolios are less volatile than on equity portfolios. Miles and Timmermann (1999) suggest that a mixed bond and stock portfolio in developed countries would have generated a lower average real return than an equity portfolio and have a significantly lower annual volatility. In Japan such a mixed portfolio might generate an average real return of about 6–7 percent a year with annual standard deviations of around 17.5 percent. Stock returns with these characteristics have been typical in many developed countries in the past. The above figures are before any deductions for charges, and for this reason we think of net returns on risky assets with a mean of 6.5 percent and volatility of 17.5 percent as relatively optimistic. We calibrate the model so that in 1990 the mean of the risky return distribution is 6.5 percent and the safe rate is 2 percent. When we make factor prices endogenous we adjust subsequent mean rates of return to reflect movements in the capital to labor ratio from its 1990 level.

4.   BASE CASE RESULTS

We take as our base case a situation where the pay-as-you-go (PAYGO) pension system is in balance, the annuity market efficiency parameter is 0.5 (semi-perfect annuities) and the gross replacement rate of the state pension is 50 percent. With anticipated Japanese life expectancy, a semi-perfect annuities market corresponds to a money's worth ratio of about 88 percent – a rate not unreasonable for countries with deep markets like the United States and the United Kingdom (see Mitchell et al. 1997 and Brown et al. 1999). Evidence on the money's worth ratio of Japanese annuities is hard to find. We consider below the implications of a significantly lower money's worth ratio). Perfect annuities corresponds to a money's worth ratio of 1. Unfunded, state pensions are related to final salary so as to generate the 50 percent (gross) replacement rate. (But we shall also show results for a flat rate pension scheme where each agent gets a given percentage of *average* earnings rather than a proportion of their own final salary.) We set the coefficient of risk aversion equal to 3 and the rate of pure time preference equal to −1.5 percent. We calibrate the model so that in this base situation the average rate of return on risky assets is 6.5 percent up to 1990. Thereafter the return evolves depending on movements in the aggregate capital to labor ratio.

There are three different reform scenarios. Figure 4.2 shows the replacement rate of the unfunded, state pension in each. Figure 4.3 shows the path of the contribution rate that balances the PAYGO system in each case. If the pension remains worth about 50 percent of gross income (about 65 percent of net income) the contribution rate needed to balance the system needs to roughly double by 2040 – from about 17.5 to about 35 percent. As a result, a decision to keep the contribution rate at its current level requires that ultimately the replacement rate would need to be cut in half. A decision to phase down dramatically the replacement to 10 percent would allow the contribution rate needed to balance the system to fall to about 7.5 percent – less than half its current level.

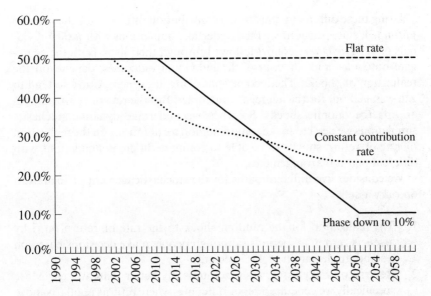

Figure 4.2   Replacement rates for state pensions

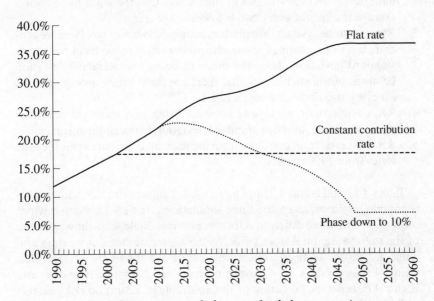

Figure 4.3   Contribution rates to balance unfunded state pensions

Using these different paths for the contribution rates and for the value of unfunded, state pensions we then undertake simulations with 7000 individuals of *each and every* cohort followed through their lives. Both the aggregate outcomes and, of course, the individual outcomes, depend on the realization of shocks. The income shocks are idiosyncratic and so tend to get averaged out for the aggregate outcomes. But the rate of return shocks are macroeconomic shocks. So when we undertake dynamic stochastic simulations we need to make some common assumptions on the realization of rate of return shocks to be able to compare different simulations with different pension arrangements.

We consider five different paths for the stochastic element of the return on risky assets:

1. The realization for the random shock to the rate of return on risky assets is zero in all periods (although people make decisions based on a standard deviation of 17.5 percent).
2. Returns on risky assets are predominantly better than average. More specifically we generate a set of outcomes where returns regularly move from being one standard deviation above the mean to being one standard deviation below it, but in such a way that there are three above-average returns for every two below-average returns.
3. Returns on risky assets are predominantly below average. Here we generate a set of outcomes where returns regularly move from being one standard deviation above the mean to being one standard deviation below it, but in such a way that there are three below-average returns for every two above-average returns.
4. Returns alternate each year between being one standard deviation above the mean, and one standard deviation between the mean.
5. Returns come from one draw from the relevant distribution for the time series from 1900 to 2150.

Tables 4.1a and b and 4.2, and figures 4.4–8 summarize the main macroeconomic implications of the three simulations. Table 4.1a shows savings rates under the three different reform scenarios; Table 4.1b shows the size of the aggregate capital stock (which is the aggregate stock of wealth); and Table 4.2 shows aggregate outcomes. Figure 4.4 shows the saving rates; Figure 4.5 shows the size of the capital stock relative to the base case; and Figure 4.6 shows the evolution of the mean rate of return on risky assets.

Table 4.1a shows that the savings rate is projected to move sharply as a result of ageing. In this table we show two simulations for each pension scenario. In one (column a) the return to risky assets is at its mean level (which is time varying) in all periods. In other words we set outturns for the

Table 4.1a   Savings rates (%) stochastic simulations

	Keep replacement rate of state pension at 50%		Keep contribution rate constant at 17.5%		Phase down replacement rate to 10% by 2040	
	a	b	a	b	a	b
2000	17.0	16.9	18.3	18.3	18.4	18.3
2005	15.6	15.5	17.8	17.7	17.4	17.2
2010	13.7	13.6	17.6	17.4	15.9	15.8
2015	11.8	11.7	17.3	17.2	15.3	15.2
2020	11.1	10.9	17.7	17.4	16.2	16.1
2025	11.0	10.8	18.1	17.7	18.0	17.9
2030	10.6	10.4	18.0	17.5	19.7	19.6
2035	9.5	9.3	17.1	16.4	20.6	20.3
2040	8.1	7.9	15.9	14.9	20.9	20.5
2045	7.4	7.2	15.0	13.9	21.8	21.1
2050	7.4	7.2	14.7	13.4	23.0	22.0
2055	7.7	7.5	14.3	12.9	22.7	21.5
2060	8.0	7.8	14.0	12.5	21.8	20.4

Notes: Column (a) shows results where the realization of the shock to the rate of return is 0 in all periods. Column (b) shows the path when shocks alternate between one standard deviation above the mean and one standard deviation below the mean. In these simulations annuity market efficiency is set to 0.5. The coefficient of risk aversion is set at 3.0 and the rate of pure time preference is −1.5% pa. State, unfunded pensions are related to final salary.

random shock to rates of return to zero. In the second column for each simulation (headed b) the return shock alternates between +1 and −1 standard deviation. On the whole the difference between the two simulations for each pension regime are fairly small, with savings rates tending to be somewhat lower when returns alternate between being above and below average. But the difference *between* pension regimes is dramatic. If unfunded pensions remain worth 50 percent of gross wages the savings rate is predicted to fall very sharply – from around 17 percent in 2000 to half that rate by 2040. If the contribution rate to balance an unfunded system is kept at 17.5 percent, the decline in the saving rate is much more gentle. The saving rate in 2040 is still around 15 percent. If the state pension is scaled back dramatically so it becomes a very small fraction of wealth at retirement (worth only 10 percent of salary at retirement) the aggregate saving rate actually rises gently over the next 50 years.

Figure 4.4 shows how influenced by the realization of shocks to rates of return on risky assets the aggregate savings rates can be. The five panels in

Table 4.1b *Aggregate stock of wealth for stochastic simulations (¥m per capita; real figures, base year 1999)*

	Keep replacement rate of state pension at 50%		Keep contribution rate constant at 17.5%		Phase down replacement rate to 10% by 2040	
	a	b	a	b	a	b
2000	11.7	11.9	10.9	11.1	11.4	11.6
2005	13.0	13.2	11.9	12.1	12.5	12.7
2010	14.4	14.6	13.3	13.5	13.4	13.7
2015	15.6	15.9	15.1	15.4	14.2	14.4
2020	16.7	17.1	17.1	17.6	15.1	15.3
2025	17.9	18.3	19.7	20.3	16.4	16.7
2030	19.3	19.7	22.7	23.6	18.7	19.1
2035	20.9	21.4	26.2	27.4	22.2	22.8
2040	22.5	23.0	30.0	31.7	26.8	27.8
2045	23.7	24.3	34.0	36.0	32.6	34.1
2050	24.8	25.4	38.0	40.5	39.9	42.0
2055	26.3	26.9	43.2	46.2	49.9	52.6
2060	28.0	28.6	48.8	52.2	60.8	64.3

Note: See note in Table 4.1a.

the figure show the evolution of savings under five different assumptions about the rate of return. If there are predominantly above-average rates of return (the second panel) savings rates will be much lower in the future; if returns are predominantly below average, savings rates are very much higher. Unusually high returns increase financial wealth substantially and encourage lower saving; bad returns erode financial wealth and households save faster to rebuild assets for retirement.

Not surprisingly when there is either a partial or almost complete switch to funding both savings and the stock of wealth (Table 4.1b) are higher. The impact on the stock of assets is particularly marked. Figure 4.5 shows the effect of different pension reform strategies on the stock of assets relative to the stock under a scenario of no reform (and a very large rise in contribution rates). With a constant contribution rate to the state pension system (a halving of the value of the state pension relative to final salaries) the stock of assets by 2060 is almost double what it would be with a constant replacement rate. (This corresponds to a value just under 1 on the vertical axis; the measure shown in the graph is k'_t/k^0_{t-1} where k'_t/k^0_t is aggregate assets relative to the base case aggregate assets in year t.) The stock of assets

Table 4.2   Stochastic simulations: aggregate outcomes

	Keep replacement rate of state pension at 50%	Keep contribution rate constant at 17.5%	Phase down replacement rate to 10% by 2040
Aggregate savings rate (%)			
2010	13.6	17.4	15.8
2030	10.4	17.5	19.6
2050	7.2	13.4	22.0
Capital/output ratio			
2010	3.6	3.2	3.4
2030	3.6	3.9	3.3
2050	3.4	4.7	4.6
Share of risky assets (%)			
2010	98	98	99
2030	98	88	97
2050	98	74	64
Mean risky return (%)			
2010	5.8	5.7	6.2
2030	5.8	4.7	5.4
2050	6.2	4.1	3.7

Notes: Figures show the simulation results when shocks alternate between one standard deviation above the mean and one standard deviation below the mean. In these simulations annuity market efficiency is set to 0.5. The coefficient of risk aversion is set at 3.0 and the rate of pure time preference is -1.5% pa. State, unfunded pensions are related to final salary.

would be well over twice as large if the replacement rate is reduced to 10 percent.

All this has implications for rates of return. Figure 4.6 shows how the mean return on risky assets evolves as a result of changes in the capital/ labor ratio. How great the fall in the rate of return over the next few decades will be, and whether that fall is reversed, depends very much on the nature of pension reform. With no reform (by which we mean a constant replacement rate) the decline is limited; mean rates of return on risky assets fall from 6.5 percent in 1990 to about 5.8 percent by 2010. But in 2050 the rate is back up at 6.2 percent. With a fixed contribution rate the decline in the rate of return is larger and more sustained. The mean rate of return falls to 4.1 percent by 2040 and stays at around that level. With an even more

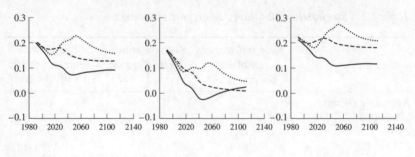

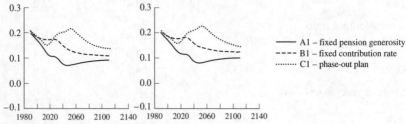

A1 – fixed pension generosity
B1 – fixed contribution rate
C1 – phase-out plan

Ex post values of aggregate savings rate for five return histories

Notes: The five panels correspond to five different return scenarios. Left to right, top to bottom they are (i) zero return shocks, (ii) 60% positive shocks, 40% negative shocks, size one standard deviation from the mean; (iii) 40% positive shocks, 60% negative shocks; (iv) 50% positive shocks, 50% negative shocks; (v) randomly generated IID shocks.

Figure 4.4   Aggregate savings rate

substantial phasing back of the role of PAYGO pensions the rate of return ultimately falls to about 3.5 percent – about half its 2001 level.

It might appear strange that the rate of return on capital (which in this model is the rate of return that people earn on savings) declines even in the scenarios when the savings rate falls significantly. One might suppose that with a lower savings rate capital would be scarce and this would drive the mean rates of return up. But with a Cobb–Douglas production function what really matters is the capital/labor ratio, or the capital/output ratio. What will happen in Japan is that the supply of labor is likely to be significantly lower as a result of population ageing than it would be if population structures were unchanging. So while the savings rate might be much lower, and this reduces the amount of capital relative to what it would have been with a constant savings rate, the impact of ageing upon aggregate labor supply is larger and the capital/labor ratio is likely to be *higher* than it otherwise would be. This means that capital becomes *relatively* abundant

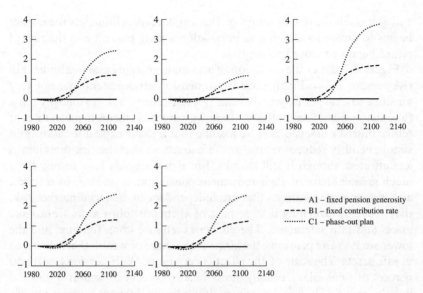

Ex post values of aggregate assets for five return histories

Note: See note in Figure 4.4.

Figure 4.5 Aggregate assets relative to base case A1

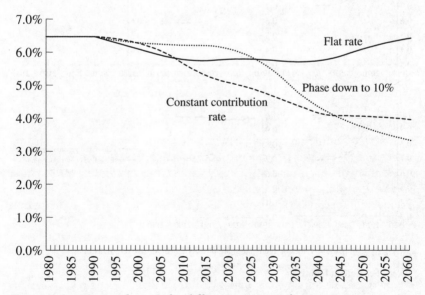

Figure 4.6 Mean risky rate for different pension reforms

and as a result the rate of return on that capital falls. Ultimately the impact begins to unwind somewhat as population ageing tails off and the rate of return begins to move back up.

Figure 4.7 shows the evolution of the share of aggregate wealth held in risky assets. This is highly sensitive to pension arrangements but not very sensitive to changes in overall mean rates of return. The reason why portfolio shares do not react strongly to downward movements in mean rates of return on risky assets is that we assume that a rising capital to labor ratio simultaneously reduces returns on safe assets so that the risk premium is less affected, though it still shrinks. But if households have to rely for a much greater share of their retirement consumption on their own funds, and less on state pensions that are independent of financial market risk, they react by switching a large part of their portfolios away from risky assets and into safe assets. The greater is reliance upon funding, and the lower are PAYGO pensions, the larger is the share of wealth that is invested in safe assets. The scale of the effect is very large. With pensions worth 50 percent of final salary, usually more than 95 percent of wealth is invested in risky assets. (Though notice how dramatically different this is if returns

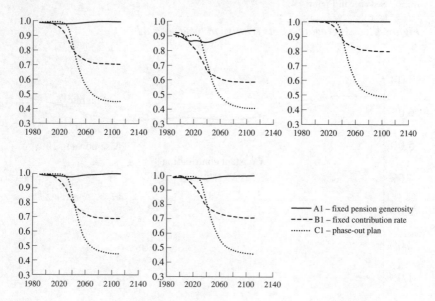

Ex post values of aggregate share of risky assets for five return histories

Note: See note in Figure 4.4.

Figure 4.7   Aggregate share of risky assets

turn out to be predominantly well above average – see the second panel of Figure 4.7.) As the replacement rate falls to 10 percent that share eventually falls to below 50 percent. Once again the results would be very different if there was a prolonged bull market or a prolonged bear market.

The evolution of aggregate consumption is illustrated in Figure 4.8. Transition towards greater reliance upon funding requires a period when aggregate consumption falls below its path under a policy of preserving the generosity of unfunded pensions. But ultimately aggregate consumption rises significantly above that level when funding becomes more important. How great the decline in consumption is, how long it takes before consumption then overtakes the path under a policy of no reform, and by how much consumption in the long term can be higher depend both upon how great the move to funding is and what happens to rates of return. Under a policy of holding the contribution rate constant, and in the absence of either unusually good or bad return outcomes, aggregate consumption is relatively low until about 2020. In the long run it is just under 20 percent higher. Under a policy of reducing the replacement rate for the state pension to 10 percent (starting from 2010) aggregate consumption is slightly lower until about 2030 but ultimately almost 30 percent higher.

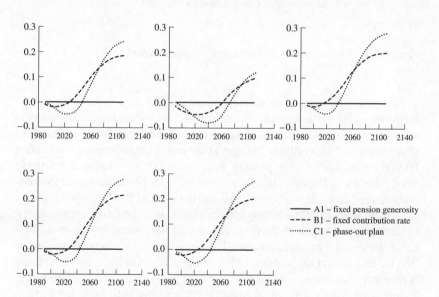

Ex post values of aggregate consumption for five return histories

Note: See note in Figure 4.4.

Figure 4.8   Aggregate consumption relative to base case A1

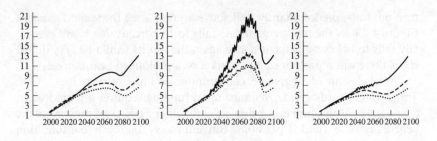

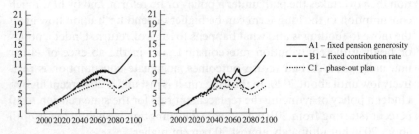

Ex post values of consumption for five return histories

Note: See note in Figure 4.4.

Figure 4.9   Consumption, cohort aged 20 in year 2000

The paths for aggregate consumption suggest that some generations might be worse off as a result of a move to funding. In particular, cohorts who are relatively early in the working lives at the initiation of reform find that they need to continue paying substantial contributions to finance PAYGO pensions to their parents' generation but will receive a relatively small pension by the time they retire 30 or 40 years hence. Consider the generation aged 20 in 2000 who have just started work at the date when reforms are undertaken. Figure 4.9 shows the evolution of average consumption for this cohort under each of the three pension scenarios and for the five different outcomes for random returns. The cross-section average of consumption for this cohort throughout its life remains lower in the case where there is pension reform and a movement towards greater reliance upon funding. Figure 4.10 reveals why: on average this cohort needs to build up a much greater stock of financial assets knowing that receipts of state, unfunded pensions will be much lower by the time it retires.

But generations born later tend to gain. One summary measure of the welfare impact of various reforms is to construct a measure of the *ex ante*

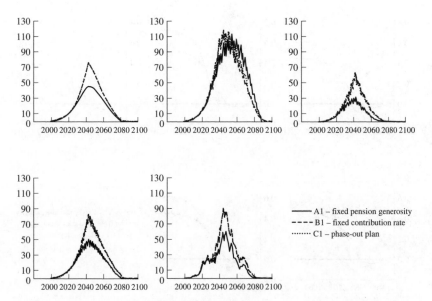

Ex post values of assets for five return histories

Note: See note in Figure 4.4.

Figure 4.10   Assets, cohort aged 20 in year 2000

expected utility of someone born at different times. Figure 4.11 shows the relative level of expected utility, at birth, for someone born at various dates under each of the two pension reform strategies that involve a move towards greater reliance upon funding. We measure the difference in expected utility from the base case of no pension reform. Our metric is the percentage difference in productivity over life that is required to make utility in the base case equal to expected utility on the reform path. The figure shows that cohorts born before 1990 are generally losers from reform. They lose out by the equivalent of up to a 10 percent decline in their lifetime labor earnings. Cohorts born after 1990 are, in an expected utility (at birth) sense, generally better off. Gains come through later when the transition to funding is announced now, but does not start to be implemented until 2010. Ultimately the gains to cohorts born after the transitions are complete (in 2050) are very substantial: of the order of a 60 percent gain in lifetime labor earnings when there is an almost complete move towards funding and around a 40 percent gain when there is a halving in the replacement rate of unfunded pensions to keep contribution rates constant.

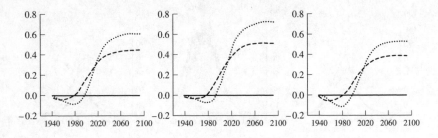

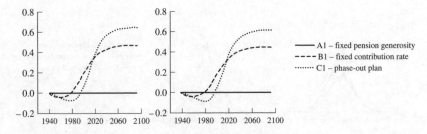

Ex post values of welfare for five return histories

Note: See note in Figure 4.4.

Figure 4.11   Expected utility by cohort: base case parameters

It is what happens to the *welfare* of agents of different generations that really matters. Table 4.3 shows in some detail how agents of different ages are affected by various reform strategies. We take as the base case a situation that we have called 'no reform' – PAYGO pensions continue to be paid at a generous level (assumed to be 50 percent of average gross wages). The table gives an indication of the effect upon the lifetime utility of people of different ages as a result of either pegging the contribution rate at its current level or scaling back pensions from 2010 towards a 10 percent replacement rate by 2050. We measure the welfare implications of phasing out pensions by calculating a measure of the lifetime utility of the representative agent of various cohorts (from those who are aged 60 today to those who will not be born for another 40 years). We compare how each cohort does in the base case where the state pension stays constant (relative to average earnings) with how they do when the ratio of the state pension to average earnings starts to fall as a move is made towards funding. In all cases we look at a scenario where the random component of the return on risky assets alternates between +1 and −1 standard deviation.

Table 4.3   Gainers and losers from pension reform (equivalent productivity gains (+) or losses (−))

Cohort age in 2002 (and year when born)	Keep contribution rate constant at 17.5%		Phase down replacement rate to 10% by 2040	
60 (1942)	L	−2%	L	−1%
50 (1952)	L	−5%	L	−3%
40 (1962)	L	−4%	L	−6%
30 (1972)	L	−3%	L	−8%
20 (1982)	G	2%	L	−9%
10 (1992)	G	11%	L	−3%
0 (2002)	G	20%	G	10%
−10 (2012)	G	28%	G	27%
−20 (2022)	G	36%	G	42%
−30 (2032)	G	40%	G	52%
−40 (2042)	G	42%	G	56%
−50 (2052)	G	44%	G	59%

Notes:
See notes in Table 4.2.
G = gain; L = lose.

The first column for each reform strategy shows whether those in the relevant age cohort gain (G) or lose (L). The second column is an estimate of the scale of the gain or loss as in Figure 4.11; it is the percentage by which lifetime resources in the base case simulation would need to have been higher or lower to generate the same level of welfare as is given by the transition path. So for people aged 40 in 2002 the average decline in utility generated by pegging the contribution rate is the equivalent of a 4 percent cut in lifetime resources. Their average loss if pensions are reduced gradually from 2010 is the equivalent of a cut in lifetime resources of about 6 percent.

Under both reform scenarios those aged just over 30 or more in 2002 lose out, to varying extents, from reform. Those just born now (2002) are better off. The gains are very substantial and increasing with time: the equivalent of 10–20 percent increases in lifetime resources for those born in 2002.

The result that the majority of those alive now would be worse off if the unfunded state scheme is phased out – even though *every* future generation is better off – illustrates the nature of the transition problem rather clearly. Democratically elected governments facing voters who focus on the direct implications to them (and not to all future generations) of changes to state pension systems would find it hard to get support for this kind of transition plan. Table 4.3 suggests that once a transition from an unfunded to a funded scheme is complete, welfare for *all* subsequent generations will be higher, but without relying on deficit financing the transition will cause certain generations to be worse off, and those generations could form a majority of voters thus permanently blocking any change.

The losses of the transition generations are relatively small and the gains of the future generations, and of the current young, are very large. So optimal policy might well be to scale back significantly the generosity of PAYGO pensions. But the table suggests that there is unlikely to be a painless (that is, Pareto improving) way of achieving this. But as we shall see, these welfare calculations are sensitive to assumptions about discount rates and rates of risk aversion.

It is important to stress that these welfare calculations are all about *expected utility at birth.* The fact that expected welfare for an agent born in, say, 2012 is higher when there has been a substantial movement towards funding and a cut in the generosity of unfunded pensions does *not* tell us that all individuals born then will turn out to be better off under a reform strategy that scales back PAYGO pensions. What it does tell us is that someone born then who understands the risks they faced *and did not know the realizations of income and rate of return shocks* would judge, at the start of their life, that they are better off in a world with more funding and less reliance upon PAYGO pensions. There will be individuals who turn out subsequently to be worse off with funded pensions. One way in which we can assess what the distribution of gainers and losers (*ex post*) looks like is to compare the distribution of retirement consumption and of *ex post* utility for different cohorts under different pension regimes. This is what we consider in the next section.

5.   DISTRIBUTION OF RETIREMENT CONSUMPTION AND OF LIFETIME UTILITY UNDER DIFFERENT PENSION ARRANGEMENTS

Different pension systems generate different distributions of retirement consumption and of *ex post* lifetime utility. Here we focus on the spread of retirement consumption and of lifetime utility for different cohorts under different pension scenarios. We consider four cohorts: those aged 60 in 2002; those aged 35 in 2002; those born in 2002 (who will not start work until 2022); and those born in 2030 who will not start work until 2050. We consider the distribution of consumption at age 65 and of lifetime utility for members of each of these cohorts under the three different pension regimes. For each pension regime there are five different sets of shocks to random returns. But for each cohort of 7000 agents we hold the history of idiosyncratic income shocks constant. Tables 4.4a and b look at the cohort not born until 2030 and who enter work when any transition towards greater reliance upon funding has been completed. There are three pension regimes, as before: a regime in which unfunded, PAYGO pensions are worth 50 percent of final salary; a regime with a contribution rate of 17.5 percent (generating a replacement rate for unfunded pensions of about 25 percent by 2050); and a regime in which PAYGO pensions by 2050 are worth only 10 percent of final salary.

The tables show that for those born in 2030 (and whose age 65 consumption is made in 2095) virtually everyone has a higher level of consumption *at retirement* if there has been a move towards greater reliance upon funding. The consumption of the household in this cohort at the lowest percentile is consistently higher the greater is reliance upon funded pensions. This is so even when we consider scenarios in which the history of rates of return is one with disproportionately below average returns (rate of return scenario 3).

In a world in which PAYGO pensions have been scaled right down (to generate only a 10 percent replacement rate) the least-well-off percentile at retirement have a level of consumption around 20 percent higher than the corresponding household in a world where PAYGO pensions continue to generate pensions worth 50 percent of final salary. The median household is better off, on average, by around 6 percent. The reason the median household gains less from a switch to funding than does the less-well-off household is that the PAYGO pension we consider here is salary related and the least well off find their state pension perpetuates the low income from work to a greater extent than does a pension which depends on contributions to a fund whose value depends on the random shocks to rates of return that are common to all agents across the income distribution.

The main point about Table 4.4a is that for the cohorts who do not live through a transition towards a more funded system (and therefore do not face the double payment burden) almost everyone is better off at retirement. Table 4.4b reinforces this message – in terms of lifetime utility all members of the 2030 cohort are better off regardless of their income, although those with lower incomes benefit more. The gains are very substantial.

But as we consider cohorts born earlier (see Tables 4.5a and b: born in 2002; Tables 4.6a and b: born in 1967 and Tables 4.7a and b: born in 1942), and who to different extents do live through the transition, the position is different. Consider Table 4.6a, which shows the cohort born in 1967, who enter work in 1987 and who are aged 35 in 2002. Right across the distribution of retirement resources we find that this cohort are worse off the greater is the scale of the move towards funding. They enter retirement in

Table 4.4a Consumption distribution for agents born in 2030 at their retirement (in 2095)

Percentile of distribution	Keep replacement rate of state pension at 50%	Keep contribution rate constant at 17.5%	% gain	Phase down replacement rate to 10% by 2040	% gain
Rate of Return Scenario 1					
1	0.407	0.472	15.954	0.490	20.588
5	0.561	0.625	11.434	0.633	12.806
20	0.795	0.868	9.163	0.873	9.755
50	1.149	1.221	6.215	1.199	4.361
75	1.538	1.603	4.229	1.565	1.803
95	2.289	2.316	1.181	2.234	−2.404
Rate of Return Scenario 2					
1	0.476	0.598	25.601	0.624	31.082
5	0.683	0.803	17.647	0.818	19.796
20	1.030	1.146	11.304	1.133	9.987
50	1.540	1.622	5.329	1.568	1.814
75	2.163	2.151	2.044	2.044	−5.489
95	3.319	3.118	−6.064	2.911	−12.286
Rate of Return Scenario 3					
1	0.360	0.393	9.072	0.414	15.150
5	0.484	0.525	8.404	0.543	12.166
20	0.678	0.724	6.720	0.742	9.485
50	0.962	1.017	5.774	1.027	6.774
75	1.270	1.329	4.649	1.343	5.736
95	1.882	1.929	2.463	1.918	1.896

Rate of Return Scenario 4

1	0.419	0.492	17.651	0.519	23.930
5	0.576	0.661	14.870	0.674	17.169
20	0.817	0.921	12.823	0.931	14.001
50	1.186	1.295	9.184	1.281	7.981
75	1.588	1.708	7.554	1.675	5.427
95	2.377	2.483	4.444	2.389	0.506

Rate of Return Scenario 5

1	0.434	0.515	18.712	0.515	18.735
5	0.599	0.685	14.291	0.675	12.755
20	0.861	0.953	10.676	0.938	8.870
50	1.249	1.339	7.147	1.305	4.482
75	1.683	1.763	4.786	1.713	1.825
95	2.518	2.560	1.686	2.474	−1.750

Notes:

Figures show level of consumption for member of cohort at given percentiles of consumption distribution.

Scenario 1: rates of return on risky assets equal the expected value in all periods

Scenario 2: rates of return are one standard deviation above average 60% of the time and 1 standard deviation below average 40% of the time.

Scenario 3: rates of return are one standard deviation above average 40% of the time and 1 standard deviation below average 60% of the time.

Scenario 4: rates of return alternate between being one standard deviation above and one standard deviation below the average.

Scenario 5: one random draw for the random component of rates of return from the normal distribution.

% gain is the percentage difference relative to a base of constant replacement rate for unfunded pension.

Table 4.4b Ex post utility of agents born in 2030

Percentile of distribution	Keep replacement rate of state pension at 50%	Keep contribution rate constant at 17.5%	% gain	Phase down replacement rate to 10% by 2040	% gain
Rate of Return Scenario 1					
1	0.028	0.041	42	0.043	52
5	0.035	0.049	41	0.053	53
20	0.044	0.063	41	0.068	52
50	0.057	0.080	39	0.086	50
75	0.070	0.097	38	0.105	49
95	0.091	0.124	36	0.134	47
Rate of Return Scenario 2					
1	0.029	0.043	51	0.048	69
5	0.035	0.053	49	0.059	66
20	0.046	0.068	48	0.075	64
50	0.061	0.087	44	0.096	59
75	0.075	0.106	42	0.117	55
95	0.099	0.138	39	0.150	51
Rate of Return Scenario 3					
1	0.028	0.038	34	0.040	42
5	0.034	0.046	35	0.049	45
20	0.043	0.058	34	0.063	44
50	0.055	0.074	34	0.080	44
75	0.067	0.090	34	0.097	46
95	0.085	0.114	34	0.125	46

Rate of Return Scenario 4

1	0.028	0.041	44	0.045	57
5	0.035	0.050	44	0.055	57
20	0.044	0.063	43	0.069	56
50	0.058	0.081	41	0.088	54
75	0.070	0.098	40	0.107	53
95	0.091	0.126	38	0.137	51

Rate of Return Scenario 5

1	0.028	0.041	42	0.043	52
5	0.035	0.049	41	0.053	53
20	0.044	0.062	41	0.068	53
50	0.058	0.080	39	0.087	51
75	0.071	0.097	38	0.107	52
95	0.092	0.126	37	0.139	51

Table 4.5a Consumption distribution for agents born in 2002 at their retirement (in 2067)

Percentile of distribution	Keep replacement rate of state pension at 50%	Keep contribution rate constant at 17.5%	% gain	Phase down replacement rate to 10% by 2040	% gain
Rate of Return Scenario 1					
1	0.428	0.465	8.587	0.441	2.962
5	0.584	0.617	5.659	0.575	−1.641
20	0.835	0.858	2.665	0.786	−5.943
50	1.207	1.205	−0.125	1.089	−9.739
75	1.617	1.581	−2.251	1.422	−12.089
95	2.411	2.280	−5.424	2.028	−15.878
Rate of Return Scenario 2					
1	0.502	0.590	17.403	0.563	12.185
5	0.722	0.791	9.549	0.729	0.913
20	1.105	1.128	2.054	1.016	−7.999
50	1.665	1.592	−4.378	1.404	−15.634
75	2.349	2.113	−10.058	1.844	−21.499
95	3.590	3.065	−14.630	2.638	−26.519
Rate of Return Scenario 3					
1	0.372	0.389	4.691	0.375	0.873
5	0.502	0.518	3.138	0.489	−2.549
20	0.702	0.714	1.818	0.670	−4.492
50	0.995	1.003	0.828	0.927	−6.829
75	1.314	1.312	−0.128	1.213	−7.643
95	1.947	1.906	−2.110	1.745	−10.399

Rate of Return Scenario 4

1	0.436	0.487	11.722	0.466	6.743
5	0.598	0.652	9.073	0.609	1.890
20	0.861	0.906	5.332	0.834	-3.105
50	1.246	1.277	2.510	1.156	-7.215
75	1.677	1.682	0.297	1.512	-9.797
95	2.507	2.443	-2.545	2.165	-13.634

Rate of Return Scenario 5

1	0.455	0.510	12.047	0.467	2.633
5	0.626	0.676	7.948	0.612	-2.317
20	0.908	0.941	3.629	0.838	-7.662
50	1.318	1.319	0.067	1.166	-11.550
75	1.779	1.734	-2.528	1.527	-14.185
95	2.672	2.519	-5.739	2.192	-17.946

Note: See notes in Table 4.4a.

Table 4.5b Ex post *utility of agents born in 2002*

Percentile of distribution	Keep replacement rate of state pension at 50%	Keep contribution rate constant at 17.5%	% gain	Phase down replacement rate to 10% by 2040	% gain
Rate of Return Scenario 1					
1	0.032	0.039	22	0.036	13
5	0.039	0.047	21	0.044	12
20	0.050	0.060	20	0.055	11
50	0.064	0.076	19	0.071	10
75	0.079	0.093	18	0.086	9
95	0.102	0.119	17	0.110	8
Rate of Return Scenario 2					
1	0.032	0.041	27	0.038	18
5	0.040	0.050	25	0.046	16
20	0.052	0.064	24	0.059	14
50	0.069	0.083	21	0.077	11
75	0.085	0.101	19	0.093	10
95	0.113	0.132	17	0.121	7
Rate of Return Scenario 3					
1	0.031	0.036	16	0.034	8
5	0.038	0.044	16	0.041	7
20	0.048	0.056	16	0.052	8
50	0.061	0.071	16	0.066	8
75	0.074	0.086	17	0.080	9
95	0.094	0.110	17	0.103	9

Rate of Return Scenario 4

1	0.032	0.039	24	0.037	15
5	0.039	0.048	23	0.044	14
20	0.050	0.061	22	0.056	12
50	0.064	0.078	21	0.072	12
75	0.079	0.094	20	0.087	11
95	0.102	0.121	18	0.112	10

Rate of Return Scenario 5

1	0.032	0.039	23	0.036	13
5	0.039	0.047	21	0.043	12
20	0.050	0.060	20	0.055	10
50	0.065	0.077	18	0.070	9
75	0.079	0.093	18	0.086	9
95	0.103	0.121	17	0.111	8

Table 4.6a Consumption distribution for agents born in 1967 at their retirement (in 2032)

Percentile of distribution	Keep replacement rate of state pension at 50%	Keep contribution rate constant at 17.5%	% gain	Phase down replacement rate to 10% by 2040	% gain
Rate of Return Scenario 1					
1	0.489	0.450	−7.872	0.421	−13.730
5	0.665	0.605	−9.079	0.567	−14.846
20	0.944	0.840	−11.012	0.784	−16.936
50	1.359	1.187	−12.643	1.108	−18.472
75	1.811	1.559	−13.919	1.455	−19.661
95	2.683	2.273	−15.288	2.121	−20.958
Rate of Return Scenario 2					
1	0.590	0.566	−4.064	0.531	−9.984
5	0.830	0.764	−7.992	0.720	−13.230
20	1.259	1.096	−12.981	1.032	−18.050
50	1.868	1.572	−15.869	1.477	−20.921
75	2.583	2.092	−18.994	1.973	−23.622
95	3.939	3.077	−21.889	2.915	−26.002
Rate of Return Scenario 3					
1	0.420	0.378	−9.842	0.352	−16.087
5	0.566	0.505	−10.804	0.471	−16.817
20	0.788	0.695	−11.769	0.649	−17.659
50	1.115	0.979	−12.207	0.913	−18.130
75	1.469	1.281	−12.777	1.192	−18.879
95	2.171	1.871	−13.801	1.750	−19.381

Rate of Return Scenario 4

1	0.500	0.468	−6.344	0.436	−12.677
5	0.681	0.632	−7.238	0.588	−13.726
20	0.975	0.880	−9.810	0.816	−16.275
50	1.406	1.246	−11.392	1.155	−17.854
75	1.884	1.641	−12.914	1.518	−19.443
95	2.804	2.399	−14.447	2.219	−20.882

Rate of Return Scenario 5

1	0.522	0.501	−4.001	0.466	−10.614
5	0.715	0.673	−5.867	0.629	−11.983
20	1.028	0.933	−9.251	0.875	−14.882
50	1.484	1.321	−10.980	1.241	−16.382
75	1.992	1.737	−12.807	1.631	−18.105
95	2.962	2.521	−14.890	2.371	−19.938

Note: See notes in Table 4.4a.

Table 4.6b Ex post *utility of agents born in 1967*

Percentile of distribution	Keep replacement rate of state pension at 50%	Keep contribution rate constant at 17.5%	% gain	Phase down replacement rate to 10% by 2040	% gain
Rate of Return Scenario 1					
1	0.037	0.037	−2	0.036	−4
5	0.046	0.044	−2	0.043	−5
20	0.058	0.057	−3	0.055	−6
50	0.075	0.072	−4	0.069	−8
75	0.091	0.087	−5	0.084	−9
95	0.118	0.111	−6	0.106	−10
Rate of Return Scenario 2					
1	0.038	0.038	0	0.037	−3
5	0.047	0.047	−1	0.046	−3
20	0.061	0.060	−2	0.058	−5
50	0.081	0.078	−4	0.075	−7
75	0.099	0.094	−5	0.091	−8
95	0.130	0.122	−6	0.118	−9
Rate of Return Scenario 3					
1	0.037	0.035	−4	0.034	−7
5	0.044	0.042	−5	0.041	−7
20	0.056	0.053	−5	0.052	−8
50	0.071	0.067	−5	0.065	−8
75	0.085	0.081	−5	0.078	−9
95	0.109	0.103	−6	0.098	−10

Rate of Return Scenario 4

1	0.037	0.037	−2	0.036	−4
5	0.046	0.045	−2	0.043	−5
20	0.058	0.057	−3	0.055	−6
50	0.075	0.073	−3	0.070	−7
75	0.092	0.088	−4	0.084	−8
95	0.119	0.112	−6	0.107	−10

Rate of Return Scenario 5

1	0.037	0.037	−2	0.036	−2
5	0.045	0.045	−2	0.043	−2
20	0.058	0.057	−3	0.055	−3
50	0.075	0.072	−4	0.070	−4
75	0.092	0.087	−5	0.084	−5
95	0.120	0.112	−7	0.107	−7

Table 4.7a   Consumption distribution for agents born in 1942 at their retirement (in 2007)

Percentile of distribution	Keep replacement rate of state pension at 50%	Keep contribution rate constant at 17.5%	% gain	Phase down replacement rate to 10% by 2040	% gain
Rate of Return Scenario 1					
1	0.525	0.499	−4.809	0.518	−1.270
5	0.715	0.676	−5.478	0.706	−1.277
20	1.006	0.942	−6.408	0.990	−1.616
50	1.438	1.338	−6.950	1.410	−1.944
75	1.909	1.763	−7.686	1.864	−2.398
95	2.812	2.589	−7.935	2.743	−2.447
Rate of Return Scenario 2					
1	0.643	0.613	−4.649	0.640	−0.550
5	0.901	0.850	−5.684	0.894	−0.801
20	1.341	1.233	−8.057	1.316	−1.877
50	1.966	1.788	−9.065	1.916	−2.519
75	2.689	2.420	−10.006	2.603	−3.198
95	4.067	3.613	−11.150	3.916	−3.720
Rate of Return Scenario 3					
1	0.445	0.424	−4.831	0.440	−1.299
5	0.599	0.567	−5.371	0.589	−1.718
20	0.832	0.786	−5.575	0.817	−1.837
50	1.175	1.109	−5.625	1.152	−1.934
75	1.544	1.448	−6.189	1.514	−1.949
95	2.272	2.139	−5.830	2.225	−2.035

Rate of Return Scenario 4

1	0.540	0.514	−4.700	0.534	−1.078
5	0.738	0.698	−5.466	0.729	−1.242
20	1.039	0.976	−6.107	1.024	−1.496
50	1.493	1.387	−7.136	1.465	−1.853
75	1.987	1.830	−7.867	1.941	−2.307
95	2.936	2.694	−8.253	2.861	−2.542

Rate of Return Scenario 5

1	0.568	0.541	−4.701	0.561	−1.302
5	0.778	0.736	−5.353	0.771	−0.923
20	1.107	1.036	−6.381	1.090	−1.522
50	1.586	1.475	−6.997	1.556	−1.935
75	2.111	1.947	−7.739	2.066	−2.119
95	3.118	2.863	−8.185	3.038	−2.585

Note: See notes in Table 4.4a.

119

Table 4.7b Ex post *utility of agents born in 1942*

Percentile of distribution	Keep replacement rate of state pension at 50%	Keep contribution rate constant at 17.5%	% gain	Phase down replacement rate to 10% by 2040	% gain
Rate of Return Scenario 1					
1	0.040	0.039	−1	0.040	−0.3
5	0.049	0.048	−1	0.048	−0.4
20	0.062	0.061	−2	0.062	−0.4
50	0.080	0.078	−2	0.079	−0.7
75	0.097	0.094	−3	0.096	−1.2
95	0.125	0.120	−4	0.123	−1.9
Rate of Return Scenario 2					
1	0.041	0.041	−1	0.041	−0.2
5	0.050	0.050	−1	0.050	−0.3
20	0.065	0.064	−1	0.065	−0.5
50	0.085	0.083	−2	0.084	−1.1
75	0.105	0.102	−3	0.103	−1.6
95	0.137	0.132	−3	0.134	−2.3
Rate of Return Scenario 3					
1	0.039	0.038	−1	0.039	−0.3
5	0.047	0.046	−2	0.047	−0.3
20	0.059	0.058	−2	0.059	−0.5
50	0.075	0.074	−2	0.075	−0.6
75	0.090	0.088	−2	0.090	−0.8
95	0.115	0.112	−3	0.114	−1.4

Rate of Return Scenario 4

1	0.040	0.039	−1	0.040	−0.4
5	0.049	0.048	−1	0.048	−0.3
20	0.062	0.061	−2	0.062	−0.4
50	0.080	0.078	−2	0.079	−0.8
75	0.097	0.094	−3	0.096	−1.4
95	0.125	0.121	−4	0.123	−2.2

Rate of Return Scenario 5

1	0.040	0.039	−1	0.040	−0.4
5	0.048	0.048	−1	0.048	−0.1
20	0.062	0.061	−2	0.062	−0.4
50	0.080	0.078	−2	0.079	−0.9
75	0.097	0.094	−3	0.096	−1.4
95	0.126	0.121	−4	0.123	−2.1

year 2032. At that point consumption is lower right across the distribution than it would be if PAYGO pension generosity had been left unchanged. The scale of the loss in consumption at retirement is substantial: generally between 10 and 20 percent with greater losses for those with more resources. Table 4.6b confirms that all members of 1967 cohort are made worse off by the reform; and the wealthy are affected more than the poor.

Table 4.7a shows that those aged 60 in 2002 (born in 1942) are also consistent losers from moves towards funding. This is true right across the income distribution. The scale of losses of retirement consumption is, however, fairly small – generally between 1 and 2 percent. Table 4.7b confirms that the welfare effect is very small for those about to retire today.

The important point to emerge from this distributional analysis is that in the longer run pretty much everyone gains from a switch to funding – even those with very low lifetime resources. But for those who face the double payment burden (at least for the fairly simple transitional arrangement simulated here) the losses are also very hard to avoid – right across the income distribution there is lower consumption at retirement. This is especially marked for those in their mid-thirties today.

6. ALTERNATIVE PARAMETERIZATIONS

In this section we consider how the simulation results are affected by changes in key parameters. We consider four alternatives. First we take a much higher rate of risk aversion, increasing the coefficient of relative aversion from 3 to 6. Second we take a much higher rate of time preference, raising the discount rate from -1.5 percent to $+1.5$ percent. Third we consider the implications of a lower degree of efficiency of annuity contracts; we reduce the efficiency parameter β from 0.5 to 0.25, which corresponds to a reduction in the money's worth ratio at retirement from an average of approximately 88 percent to around 81 percent. Finally we consider simulations where the unfunded, state pension is flat rate, rather than being linked to final salary.

Tables 4.8–11 summarize the results. In constructing these figures we once again have calculated optimal decisions for individuals based on draws for income and rate of return shocks. For each cohort we then aggregate over 7000 agents and show the average results for each regime, at each point and for a given evolution of the random rate of return. In these tables we show results where the random component of the rate of return alternates between $+1$ and -1 standard deviation.

Table 4.8 summarizes the aggregate results when the coefficient of risk aversion is much higher. Comparing those results with those in Table 4.2 reveals that with higher risk aversion a very substantially smaller share of

Table 4.8 Stochastic simulations: coefficient of risk version =6

	Keep replacement rate of state pension at 50%	Keep contribution rate constant at 17.5%	Phase down replacement rate to 10% by 2040
Aggregate savings rate (%)			
2010	9.2	13.7	11.4
2030	6.4	14.7	16.7
2050	3.2	11.3	21.7
Capital/output ratio			
2010	3.3	2.8	3.0
2030	3.3	3.6	2.8
2050	3.1	4.6	4.3
Share of risky assets (%)			
2010	76	74	81
2030	76	54	71
2050	81	42	35
Mean risky return (%)			
2010	5.8	5.5	6.6
2030	5.8	4.3	5.4
2050	6.4	3.6	3.2

Notes: Figures show the simulation results when shocks alternate between one standard deviation above the mean and one standard deviation below the mean. In these simulations annuity market efficiency is set to 0.5. The coefficient of risk aversion is set at 6.0 and the rate of pure time preference is −1.5% pa. State, unfunded pensions are related to final salary.

wealth is invested in risky assets. When state pensions are reduced sharply the share of risky assets in portfolios by 2050 falls to only around 35 percent with high risk aversion as against a figure of 64 percent with a coefficient of risk aversion of 3. The savings rate is also consistently lower with high risk aversion – the incentive to accumulate wealth is pulled in two directions by greater risk aversion. On the one hand there is a tendency for savings to rise because of greater precautionary demands. But with risky assets so much less attractive, the overall desirability of saving is actually lower. The capital output ratio is therefore slightly lower when there is more risk aversion. But the scale of the effect is fairly small.

The key welfare conclusion from the analysis is little changed with higher risk aversion. Figure 4.12 shows the time profile of expected utility for people born at different times under the three pension strategies and with

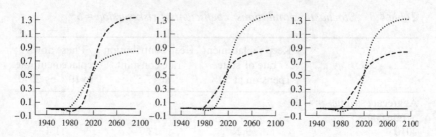

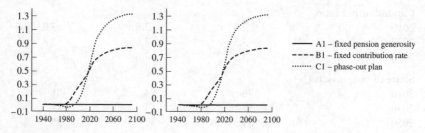

A1 – fixed pension generosity
B1 – fixed contribution rate
C1 – phase-out plan

Ex post values of welfare for five return histories

Note: See note in Figure 4.4.

*Figure 4.12   Expected utility by cohort: coefficient of relative risk
                aversion =6*

higher risk aversion. Once again we see the result that agents of working age now tend to lose out from a decision to move towards funding. Those born in the future stand to gain a great deal, and their gain is far greater than the loss of the working generations that live through the transition.

Table 4.9 shows aggregate outcomes when the rate of time preference is +1.5 percent. Now the saving rate is consistently very much lower than in Table 4.2 where the rate of time preference was *minus* 1.5 percent. (The reason for using a negative rate of preference was largely to try to match the relatively high Japanese saving rate.) As a result the capital/output ratio is much lower with positive time preference. But savings rates and capital output ratios are ultimately boosted very significantly by a move towards funding of pensions and a decline in the generosity of unfunded pensions.

The welfare implications of reform are illustrated in Figure 4.13, which again shows expected utility for someone born at different times under the three pension arrangements. The similarity of the overall shape of this pattern with that shown in Figure 4.11 (which showed results using a −1.5

Table 4.9   Stochastic simulations: rate of pre-time preference +1.5%

	Keep replacement rate of state pension at 50%	Keep contribution rate constant at 17.5%	Phase down replacement rate to 10% by 2040
Aggregate savings rate (%)			
2010	7.5	10.4	9.0
2030	5.5	11.9	12.5
2050	3.4	8.9	16.9
Capital/output ratio			
2010	2.2	1.9	2.0
2030	2.1	2.3	1.8
2050	2.0	2.9	2.9
Share of risky assets (%)			
2010	100	99	100
2030	100	95	99
2050	100	80	62
Mean risky return (%)			
2010	5.8	5.9	6.2
2030	6.0	4.7	5.4
2050	6.5	3.9	3.1

Notes: Figures show the simulation results when shocks alternate between one standard deviation above the mean and one standard deviation below the mean. In these simulations annuity market efficiency is set to 0.5. The coefficient of risk aversion is set at 3.0 and the rate of pure time preference is +1.5% pa. State, unfunded pensions are related to final salary.

percent discount rate) is clear, suggesting that the overall pattern of the welfare implications of reforms are little affected by assumptions about the discount rate. But the long-run gains are much greater with a much higher rate of time preference. The reason is straightforward. A major effect of phasing out unfunded, state pensions is that individuals do not need to make significant compulsory contributions from labor income. This is very valuable early in life to agents facing credit restrictions. The scale of those credit restrictions is greater the more impatient consumers are. It is important to note that a significant part of the gain from a switch towards giving people discretion about the scale and timing of contributions towards their own personal pension pot is the value of the flexibility this gives – something which is absent in most unfunded social security systems where contributions are typically a given proportion of earnings.

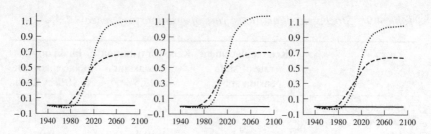

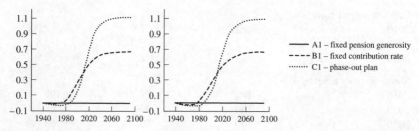

Ex post values of welfare for five return histories

Note: See note in Figure 4.4.

Figure 4.13   Expected utility by cohort: rate of time preference = +1.5%

Table 4.10 and Figure 4.14 show the impact of less efficient annuities markets. Here we cut the efficiency parameter to 0.25. This has the result of increasing savings rates slightly (as people save more to guard against unusually long lives in an environment where annuities contracts are less effective). Portfolio decisions are little changed and once again the broad shape of the welfare implications of alternative reform strategies is little affected.

Finally, Table 4.11 shows results where unfunded pensions are flat rate. In this case the main difference from the results in Table 4.2 is that savings rates and capital output ratios tend to be slightly lower. The welfare gains from pension reform if state pensions were to be wholly flat rate are somewhat greater – particularly for those that have higher earnings. Once again working generations alive at the initiation of major reform tend to lose out – the long-run gainers are the children of today and those yet to be born, and their gains are very substantial.

Table 4.10 Stochastic simulations: efficiency of annuity contracts parameter (β) = 0.25

	Keep replacement rate of state pension at 50%	Keep contribution rate constant at 17.5%	Phase down replacement rate to 10% by 2040
Aggregate savings rate (%)			
2010	14.0	17.9	16.1
2030	11.0	18.3	20.4
2050	7.9	14.7	23.6
Capital/output ratio			
2010	3.6	3.2	3.3
2030	3.6	3.8	3.2
2050	3.4	4.7	4.6
Share of risky assets (%)			
2010	98	98	99
2030	98	90	97
2050	99	76	65
Mean risky return (%)			
2010	5.8	5.7	6.3
2030	5.9	4.7	5.4
2050	6.3	4.1	3.7

Notes: Figures show the simulation results when shocks alternate between one standard deviation above the mean and one standard deviation below the mean. In these simulations annuity market efficiency is set to 0.25. The coefficient of risk aversion is set at 3.0 and the rate of pure time preference is −1.5% pa. State, unfunded pensions are related to final salary.

6.1. Small Open Economy Results

Table 4.12 summarizes the results when the rate of return on assets is independent of the domestic stock of wealth; here sharp movements in the savings rate are assumed not to influence the capital/labor ratio as flows of funds across the capital account react to swings in the domestic savings/investment balance. When we allow for movements in domestic savings and in the labor force to influence rates of return, the mean return on risky assets and the return on safe assets falls – the scale of this decline is large. When there is a wholesale move towards the funding the mean return on risky

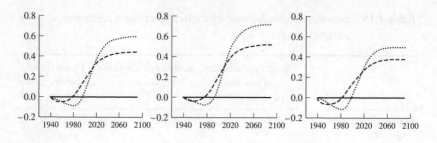

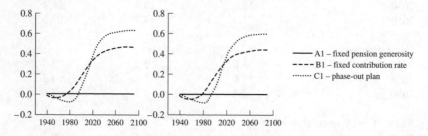

A1 – fixed pension generosity
B1 – fixed contribution rate
C1 – phase-out plan

Ex post values of welfare for five return histories

Note: See note in Figure 4.4.

Figure 4.14   *Expected utility by cohort: annuity efficiency
                parameter =0.25*

assets falls from 6.5 percent to around half that level. When the mean rate
of return is held constant, savings rates are projected to be higher. The scale
of this impact upon aggregate savings rates is significant. For example, with
the contribution rate to unfunded pensions held at 17.5 percent, the savings
rate in 2010 is projected to be around 17 percent with endogenous rates of
return but 22 percent with exogenous rates of return. The impact upon the
aggregate wealth to labor ratio is more significant. Wealth to labor ratios are
consistently higher when rates of return are assumed to be exogenous.

   There are also significant effects upon aggregate portfolio allocation.
With exogenous rates of return there is no shrinkage in the equity risk
premium as funded pensions become more important and as the labor force
shrinks. As a result the share of wealth invested in risky assets is consistently higher when rates of return are exogenous. With endogenous rates of
return the share of wealth in risky assets is 64 percent when state pensions
are run down to a low level by 2050 (see Table 4.2). With exogenous rates
of return that share is 74 percent.

Table 4.11   Stochastic simulations: flat-rate unfunded pensions

	Replacement rate on average = 50%	Contribution rate at 17.5%	Phase out pension
Aggregate savings rate (%)			
2010	10.7	18.1	14.1
2030	9.3	17.4	23.3
2050	6.1	11.8	22.0
Capital/output ratio			
2010	3.29	2.96	2.85
2030	3.21	3.72	3.00
2050	2.98	4.54	5.05
Share of risky assets (%)			
2010	95.6	92.0	98.1
2030	95.7	80.9	88.0
2050	97.4	71.5	54.0
Mean risky rate of return (%)			
2010	5.8	5.7	6.3
2030	5.9	4.7	5.4
2050	6.2	4.1	3.5

Notes: Figures show the simulation results when shocks alternate between one standard deviation above the mean and one standard deviation below the mean. In these simulations annuity market efficiency is set to 0.5. The coefficient of risk aversion is set at 3.0 and the rate of pure time preference is −1.5% pa. State, unfunded pensions are flat rate and not related to final salary.

But once again the same broad set of welfare implications of different pension reform strategies emerges. A majority of those of working age at the initiation of pension reform are worse off as a result of a switch to funding, though the average loss is relatively small and much smaller than the welfare gain to future generations. The scale of the gains is lower when we do not allow for factor prices to react to changes in savings and in the labor force. The key factor here is that labor incomes are significantly higher for future generations when the higher capital/labor ratio is assumed to boost real wages. This more than offsets the disadvantage of lower mean rates of return when factor prices are endogenous.

6.2.   Results Summary

One thing stands out immediately from the tables: the steady-state savings rate, the equilibrium stock of wealth, and the wealth to national income

Table 4.12   Stochastic simulations: small open economy assumption –
rates of return exogenous

	Replacement rate on average = 50%	Contribution rate at 17.5%	Phase out pension
Aggregate savings rate (%)			
2010	13.3	21.6	16.2
2030	10.5	20.5	24.3
2050	6.9	16.3	22.5
Wealth/output ratio			
2010	3.91	4.45	4.13
2030	3.60	5.25	4.96
2050	2.97	5.74	6.49
Share of risky assets (%)			
2010	96.5	92.2	95.9
2030	97.5	87.9	88.8
2050	98.1	83.4	73.9

Welfare gains (%) for cohorts by birth year relative to a base case of 50% pension replacement rate for unfunded pension – equivalent productivity gain (+) or loss (−)

1942	−2.6	−0.3
1967	+1.3	−2.1
1987	+10.7	+4.1
2002	+19.5	+24.0
2030	+22.8	+32.1

Notes: Figures show the simulation results when shocks alternate between one standard deviation above the mean and one standard deviation below the mean. In these simulations annuity market efficiency is set to 0.5. The coefficient of risk aversion is set at 3.0 and the rate of pure time preference is −1.5% pa. State, unfunded pensions are related to final salary. The mean of the risky rate of return is set equal to 6.5% and the safe rate is set at 2%.

ratio, are all highly sensitive to the generosity of unfunded, state pensions. When state pensions are worth around 25 percent of (end-of-working-life) gross incomes the aggregate stock of wealth is almost double its level if pensions are set to generate a replacement rate of 50 percent. With semi-perfect annuities the savings rate falls to around 7 percent by 2050 when PAYGO pensions are worth 50 percent of final salary but is 13.4 percent with 25 percent unfunded pensions and 22 percent when unfunded pensions are worth only 10 percent of final salaries. The wealth to national income ratios are somewhat less variable since with wealth so much higher when PAYGO pensions are lower, national income is also greater and the wealth to income ratio rises slightly less than the aggregate stock of wealth. With semi-perfect annuities GDP in 2020 is 7 percent higher when the contribution rate to unfunded pensions is held constant, relative to a situation with a 50 percent replacement rate. In 2050 GDP is about 16 percent higher and by 2090 around 23 percent higher. With an almost complete phasing out of state pensions, GDP in the longer term is higher again. Relative to a situation with a constant replacement rate for state, unfunded pensions GDP is 23 percent higher by 2050 and some 33 percent higher by 2090.

A second general feature of the results is that with less generous state pensions a significantly higher proportion of wealth is invested in safe, rather than risky, assets. The scale of the difference depends to a significant extent on whether rates of return are influenced by trends in savings and in the labor force. With 'semi-perfect' annuities ($\beta = 0.5$) and endogenous rates of return the share of wealth in risky assets falls from about 97 percent with a replacement rate of 50 percent on PAYGO state pensions to only 64 percent if there are only small unfunded pensions. In part the switch reflects the fact with fewer unfunded pensions the stock of wealth is very much larger and the rates of return lower. The risk premium is squeezed and this affects the portfolio allocation decision. But the major effect is a reflection of the fact that when people have to rely almost completely on accumulated savings for retirement consumption they avoid investment risk to a much greater extent than when they have substantial state pensions that are independent of rate of return risk. The results suggest that there is a powerful link between the generosity of state, unfunded pensions that are independent of asset market risk and the structure of portfolios of wealth held by households.

The welfare calculations for the simulations reveal that the long-run gain to future generations of a switch towards greater reliance upon funding is very substantial. If state pensions were set at a low rate, such that people only receive a state pension at age 65 of 10 percent of their last labor income, the expected lifetime utility of someone joining the labor force in 2030 would be significantly higher than with unfunded pensions worth 50 percent of final salary. The gain is the equivalent of productivity being higher by as much as 27 percent. With perfectly efficient annuities contracts the gains from having low state pensions and low contribution rates to a PAYGO system and relying instead on accumulated savings would be even larger.

The pattern of average savings rates over the life cycle with different generosities of flat-rate state pensions, and various degrees of efficiency of annuity contracts, is interesting. The profile of saving at the start of working life displays a pattern typical when precautionary motives are important and where income uncertainty is significant. In the first few periods in work many agents save a substantial fraction of wealth to establish a small stock of assets as a buffer to protect consumption against future labor income shocks. On average, agents then dis-save mildly for several years before starting to build up a stock of assets for retirement. But credit restrictions do affect a substantial proportion of agents in their early twenties. The proportion affected is lower with low state pensions when people can choose to delay the contributions they make towards their own retirement resources.

When savings starts to become significant, and how great the stock of wealth at retirement is, are sensitive to both the generosity of state pensions and to the efficiency of annuity markets. With no state pensions and perfect annuity markets, saving typically becomes significant from the mid-twenties. With a state pension worth 40 percent of average labor income at retirement and completely imperfect annuity markets, savings is typically not significant (after the initial establishment of a precautionary buffer at the start of work) until the thirties.

7.   CONCLUSIONS

Certain results appear to be fairly robust.

- The overall savings rate and particularly the aggregate stock of assets is likely to be *highly* sensitive to the generosity of unfunded state pensions.
- In the absence of prolonged bear markets it is likely that a long-run implication of a switch to much greater reliance upon funded pensions is that consumption and welfare for future generations will be *very* significantly higher.
- If most of the extra savings that would be generated by a switch to funding are invested within Japan the capital/labor ratio is likely to rise significantly and drive down mean rates of return. In itself this is not helpful for the whole pension reform process. But there is an upside. With a much higher capital/labor ratio wages are also higher. Indeed our simulation results suggest that the gain to future generations from higher wages more than offsets the loss from lower returns. We find that if factor prices are independent of pension reform – as they would be if Japan were a small open economy and if extra savings were largely channeled overseas – the gains to future generations of a switch to funding are actually lower.

- Yet it is likely to be hard to engineer a transition to much greater reliance upon funding without leaving a substantial proportion of today's adults at least slightly worse off.

- Annuity market efficiency is important – in a model with no bequests the degree of efficiency of annuity markets has a significant impact on the scale of the potential gains from relying more on private saving to finance retirement consumption. The more significant are bequests the less important is this factor likely to be.

- There is a powerful link between overall portfolio allocation and the pension system. The more generous are state, unfunded pensions – the value of which is only indirectly (and perhaps weakly) linked to rates of return on financial assets – the greater is the proportion of wealth invested in risky assets. If people come to rely heavily upon funded pensions which expose their retirement resources to financial market risk then they are likely to respond by holding a large share of their financial wealth in safe assets.

- It is important to note that a significant part of the gain of a switch towards funding stems from giving people discretion about the scale and timing of contributions towards their own personal pension pot. There is a significant value to the flexibility this brings – something which is absent in most unfunded social security systems where contributions are typically a given proportion of earnings. One important implication of this is that there may be substantial gains to be had by increasing the flexibility in the timing of contributions within an existing unfunded, PAYGO pension system.

- A key finding is that longer-run gains from a switch towards greater reliance upon funding, and away from an unfunded system where pensions are linked to salaries, do *not* go disproportionately to the better off. In fact our stylized model is one in which the gains that go to the cohorts that do benefit from reform go disproportionately to the less well off. The losses that are suffered by cohorts that do not benefit from a switch to funding also are suffered disproportionately by the better off. We find no tendency for reform to have adverse distributional consequences – quite the contrary. To an extent this is a somewhat artificial result since we model the PAYGO, unfunded pension system as one in which pensions are tied to final salaries. If pensions were completely flat rate the distributional consequences of reform would be different, and less benign. In fact the current Japanese system has a flat-rate element and an earnings-related element. But we doubt that the flat-rate element is so large that a switch to funding of the sort analyzed in this chapter would have significantly adverse distributional consequences. If it did seem this was likely to be a problem one could choose to preserve the flat-rate element while scaling back the earnings-related element.

NOTES

1. The source for demographic projections and for projected life expectancy rates used in this chapter is the National Institute of Population and Social Security Research.
2. We should interpret capital widely to include housing as well as factories, machines and infrastructure.
3. Japanese Ministry of Health, Labor, and Welfare, *Basic Survey on Wage Structure*, Tokyo.
4. In fact Hubbard et al. set different values of ρ, σ_w and σ_y for those with no high school, high school and college education. The implied unconditional standard deviation of the shocks to log income for these three groups are 0.64, 0.51 and 0.44, respectively.

REFERENCES

Auerbach, A. and L. Kotlikoff (1987), *Dynamic Fiscal Policy*, Cambridge: Cambridge University Press.

Benninga, S. (1990), 'Leverage, time preference, and the equity premium puzzle', *Journal of Monetary Economics*, **25** (1), 49–58.

Brown, J., O. Mitchell and J. Poterba (1999), 'The role of real annuities and indexed bonds in an individual accounts retirement program', NBER Working Paper no. 7005, National Bureau of Economic Research, pp. 148–69, Cambridge, MA.

Cooley, T. and E. Prescott (1995), 'Economic growth and business cycles', in T. Cooley (ed.), *Frontiers of Business Cycle Research*, Princeton, NJ: Princeton University Press.

Deaton, A. (1991), 'Saving and liquidity constraints', *Econometrica*, **59**, 1221–48.

Grossman, S. and R. Shiller (1981), 'The determinants of the variability of stock market prices'. *American Economic Review*, **71** (2), 245–76.

Hall, R. (1980), 'Intertemporal substitution in consumption', NBER Working Paper no. 720, National Bureau of Economic Research, July.

Hansen, P. and K. Singleton (1983), 'Stochastic consumption, risk aversion and the temporal behaviour of asset returns', *Journal of Political Economy*, **91** (2), 230–51.

Horioka, C. (2001), 'Are the Japanese selfish, dynastic or altruistic?', NBER Discussion Paper 8577, November.

Hubbard, G., J. Skinner and S. Zeldes (1995), 'Precautionary saving and social insurance', *Journal of Political Economy*, **103**, 360–99.

Hurd, M. (1989), 'Mortality risks and bequests', *Econometrica*, **57**, 779–813.

Imrohoroglu, A., S. Imrohoroglu and Douglas Joines (1999), 'A dynamic stochastic general equilibrium analysis of social security', in T. Kehoe and E. Prescott (eds), *The Discipline of Applied General Equilibrium*, New York: Springer-Verlag, pp. 301–34.

Kato, R. (1998), 'Transition to an aging Japan: public pensions, savings and capital taxation', *Journal of Japanese and International Economies*, **12**, 204–31.

Kato, R. (2000), 'Government deficits in an aging Japan', Shiga University Working Paper.

Kocherlakota, N.R. (1990), 'On the "discount" factor in growth economies', *Journal of Monetary Economics*, **25** (1), 43–47.

Mankiw, G. (1985), 'Consumer durables and the real interest rate', *Review of Economics and Statistics*, **67** (3), August, 353–62.

Mankiw, G., J. Rotemberg and L. Summers (1985), 'Intertemporal substitution in macroeconomics', *Quarterly Journal of Economics*, **100**, February, 34–61.

Miles, D. and A. Timmermann (1999), 'Risk sharing and transition costs in the reform of pension systems in Europe', *Economic Policy*, October, 253–86.

Mitchell, O., J. Poterba and M. Warshawsky (1997), 'New evidence on the money's worth of individual annuities', NBER Working Paper no. 6002, National Bureau of Economic Research.

Zeldes, S. (1989), 'Optimal consumption with stochastic income', *Quarterly Journal of Economics*, **104**, 275–98.

5. Effects of the old-age pension system for active employees on the labor supply of elderly male workers

Fumio Ohtake and Hisaki Yamaga

1. INTRODUCTION

Declining birth rates and an ageing population are expected to reduce the labor force in Japan in the early twenty-first century. To mitigate the effects of this decline in the workforce, it is essential to raise the labor force participation rates of women and of elderly persons. Iwamoto (1998) estimates that if there is no change in the labor supply within each age cohort, the labor force in Japan will decline by 6 310 000 between 2000 and 2020. A forecast using a macroeconometric model also suggests a decline in the workforce of six million.

Because a decline in the birth rate results in a decrease in the total population, the non-working population will also decrease. If the dependency rate (which indicates the number of insured persons supporting each pensioner) remains unchanged, the decline in the labor force may well be acceptable. There is also the possibility of changes in industrial structure and the possibility that technical innovation will help support the labor force. Nevertheless, it is worth increasing the workforce by raising the labor force participation rates of women and of elderly people, who are currently underutilized because of various institutional restrictions. Summarizing the results of recent studies, Iwamoto (1998) forecasts that a doubling of the staff at nursery schools would lead to new jobs for about 300 000 to 600 000 women and that the abolition of the partial pension would result in new jobs for about 300 000 elderly men (between 60 and 64 years).

The partial pension is the remuneration-related component of the pension. In the employee pension system in Japan, the pension comprises two components: a remuneration-related part (the partial pension) and a fixed part (the 'basic pension'). The age at which payment of the fixed component begins is to be increased by one year-of-age from (the current) 60 years of age to 65 years of age every three years from 2001 to 2013. Thus, in 2013 those aged between 60 and 64 will receive only the remuneration-related component (the partial pension). The age at which payment of the remuneration-related component commences will also be raised from 60 to 65 during the 2013–25 period, again by one year-of-age every three years. In 2013, a reduced pension for those aged 60 to 64 will also be introduced.

The labor supply of elderly people has been affected by the old-age pension system for active employees. This system was introduced in 1965; while retirement had formerly been a requirement for pension payment, the system paid a reduced pension to employed persons depending on their wage levels. Prior to 1995, this pension system restrained employment substantially, because reduced pensions for those in their early sixties had the same effect as higher taxes on wages (Abe 2001; Iwamoto 2000). In 1995, reductions in the active employees' pensions were revised in an attempt to reduce the system's work disincentives. It is important to analyze the impact of the revised pension system on the labor supply of elderly people. This is because, while those in their late sixties (65 to 69 years) currently receive full pensions, from 2002 they will be covered by a system that is similar to the old-age pension system for active employees currently applying only to those aged 60 to 64 years.

To date, no studies have analyzed changes in the employment-controlling effect of the pension system for active employees caused by the revision in 1995. This chapter analyzes the impact of the 1995 revision of the pension system on labor supply by using data from the 'Employment of Older Persons' surveys carried out by the former Ministry of Labor.

The issue addressed by this study is the extent to which the old-age pension system for active employees has controlled the labor supply of those between 60 and 64, who are now eligible for an employee pension. Previous studies have analyzed the impact of the changes in 1986 and 1989.

Section 2 reports on the employment situation of elderly men in Japan and, in particular, looks at recent studies on the relationship between the pension system for active employees and employment rates among those in their early sixties. Section 3 examines the possibility that the pension system discourages the elderly from working by applying the difference-in-differences method, which involves using differences between the pension system for people in their early sixties and the system for those in their late sixties. Section 4 concludes.

2.   LABOR FORCE PARTICIPATION RATES OF ELDERLY MEN

The labor force participation rate of elderly men in Japan is high by international standards. Figure 5.1 compares rates of labor force participation

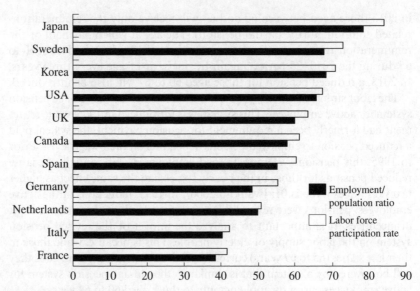

Source: Organization for Economic Cooperation and Development, *Employment Outlook*, Paris: OECD, 2001.

Figure 5.1   Labor force participation rate, 2000 (males, age 55–64)

and employment for men aged 55 to 64, and shows that elderly Japanese men have high rates of both. The labor force participation rate of Japanese men aged 60 to 64 was 72.6 percent in 2000. Figure 5.2 shows the trend for the employment rate of males aged 55 to 59. The rate remained at roughly 90 percent from 1960 to 1990, but began to rise in the 1990s, reaching 94.2 percent in 2000. The employment rate for those in their early sixties continued to decline from 1970 to the late 1980s, increased thereafter until 1993, and decreased slightly in subsequent years. The figure for those aged over 65 showed a similar trend: the employment rate decreased until the late 1980s, then increased until 1992, since when it has declined.

Labor force participation rates of those aged 60 and over continued to fall in the 1970s and 1980s due to reinforcement of the public pension system and declines in self-employment and among farmers (Seike 1993). The second explanation is confirmed by the trend in the employment/population ratios shown in Figure 5.3: the ratios were at similar levels throughout the 1970s and 1980s.

Abe (2001) gives four possible explanations for increased labor force participation rates during the second half of the 1980s and during the first half of the 1990s: (1) an extended retirement age and the spillover effects of this

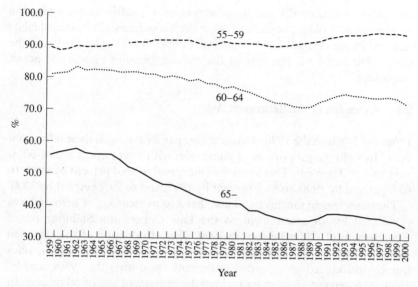

Figure 5.2   Labor force participation rates by age group (male)

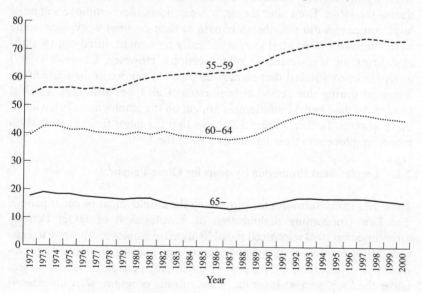

Figure 5.3   Employment/population ratio by age group (male)

on elderly persons; (2) the introduction of subsidies encouraging the employment of older people, and other similar policies; (3) increased labor demand in the period of the 'economic bubble' from the late 1980s to the early 1990s; and (4) changes in the old-age pension system for active employees.

2.1.   Extension of the Retirement Age

From the 1980s to the 1990s Japanese companies extended their retirement ages.[1] In 1980 the proportion of companies with a retirement age of 60 or over was 39.7 percent. This figure had increased to 55.4 percent by 1985, to 63.9 percent by 1990, to 85.8 percent by 1995, and to 99.2 percent by 2000.

The main reason for this trend was that a retirement age of below 60 was prohibited by an amendment to the Law Concerning Stabilization of Employment of Older Persons in 1990. The introduction of the extended retirement age varied considerably according to firm size. Large companies quickly introduced an extended retirement age during the 1980s, and by 1990, 90.6 percent of them had adopted a retirement age of 60 or over. In small businesses, the extension of the retirement age took place mainly during the 1990s. Even after the age was extended, older employees at most large companies did not always remain at their original workplace: some were offered a preferential system for early retirement, hired out to affiliated firms, or transferred to other sections. However, Chuma's (1997) analysis clearly showed that employees' years of service in their late fifties increased during this period at businesses of all types and sizes, which is thought to have had a considerable impact on the employment behavior of these workers. In fact, Figure 5.3 shows that the labor force participation rate of employees in their late fifties rose in the 1990s.

2.2.   Employment Promotion Systems for Older People[2]

Japan has many subsidies for promoting the employment of older people. The Law Concerning Stabilization of Employment of Older Persons amendment in 1994 reinforced the obligation on employers to strive to continue hiring employees of up to 65 years of age, and also prohibited a retirement age of less than 60. As part of an employment stabilization project under the Employment Insurance Law, subsidy programs were introduced to increase employment opportunities for the elderly. These subsidies included: (i) a subsidy for continued employment (a subsidy to companies that introduce a continued employment system for workers aged 61 and over); (ii) a subsidy for the employment of older workers (a subsidy to companies that hire at least a given number of older people as a percentage of their total employment); (iii) a subsidy for creating an environment for hiring older workers (a subsidy for companies that introduce equipment facilitating the employment of older workers); and (iv) a subsidy to support employees' preparations for old-age employment (a subsidy to companies that offer paid holidays to employees who want to learn skills to prepare for employment in old age). These subsidies promoted the employment of older people. Mitani (2001) confirmed that companies with a better working environment for the elderly hire a larger number of older people.

2.3. Increase in Labor Demand

In analyzing the employment behavior of the elderly, Ogawa (1998a, b) developed a new approach to assuming the potential amount of public pension receivable (the 'original pension amount'), and thereby eliminated the simultaneity bias that arises between employment and pension payments received due to the measures designed to reduce old-age pensions for active employees. In this analysis, he showed that an increase in the employment rate of older people between the late 1980s and early 1990s was greatly affected by higher wage incomes. Mitani (2001) also confirmed that employment rates among the elderly react strongly to wage levels and unemployment rates. Since 1998 the aggregate unemployment rate in Japan has increased sharply to about 10 percent. It is assumed that the reduction in labor force participation rates after 1998 among those in their early sixties has been greatly affected by this reduced labor demand.

2.4. Old-age Pension System for Active Employees

The old-age pension system for active employees relaxes the retirement requirement for pension payment and pays reduced pensions to low-wage workers aged 60 to 64. Historical changes to the system are shown in Table 5.1. The system is intended to increase incentives to work. However, a study has suggested that by having the same effect as imposing high payroll tax rates on wages above a certain level, the system promotes short-hour employment and thereby inhibits the labor supply.[3] More specifically, for workers whose wage income exceeded a given amount, pension cuts were sufficient to leave them worse off than previously. To cope with this problem, in 1989 the wage ('monthly standard remuneration') brackets applied to pension reductions were increased in number from three to seven, and the 1995 reforms treated pension reductions like negative income in order to prevent wage increases from reducing overall take-home pay (see Table 5.2). Before the 1995 reforms, the brackets applying to pension reductions depended only on monthly earnings. However, in the reformed system the

Table 5.1   Changes in the old-age pension system for active employees

Year of the revision	Provision for active employees over 65	Provision for active employees 60–65
1965	*Start of old-age pension system for active employees over 65* Retirement had been required for receiving the pension benefit as of that year. New system launched at 80% of pension benefit	
1969		*Start of old-age pension system for active employees between 60 and 65* Before this reform, full retirement was required for receiving pension benefit. Old-age pension system for active employees aged between 60 and 65 introduced with earnings test. Maximum earnings for receiving pension benefit was ¥16 000. According to level of earnings, amount of pension benefit reduced to 80, 60, 40 or 20% of potential amount
1973		Maximum earnings for receiving pension benefit raised to ¥50 000
1975		Maximum earnings for receiving pension benefit raised to ¥74 000. According to level of earnings, amount of pension benefit reduced to 80, 50 or 20% of potential amount
1976	Full amount of potential benefit paid for workers earning less than ¥114 000. Those earning more than ¥114 000 received 80% of potential amount of benefit	Maximum earnings for receiving pension benefit raised to ¥114 000
1978		Maximum earnings for receiving pension benefit raised to ¥134 000
1979		Maximum earnings for receiving pension benefit raised to ¥146 000
1980		Maximum earnings for receiving pension benefit raised to ¥155 000

Table 5.1 (continued)

Year of the revision	Provision for active employees over 65	Provision for active employees 60–65
1985	Earnings test eliminated for elderly aged over 65	Maximum earnings for receiving pension benefit raised to ¥210 000
1989		Maximum earnings for receiving pension benefit raised to ¥250 000. According to level of earnings, amount of pension benefit reduced to 80, 70, 60, 50, 40, 30, or 20% of potential amount
1994		New earnings test introduced in April 1995, which deducted ¥1 benefit for every ¥2 earned

Table 5.2   Old-age pension system for active employees (¥1000)

1986.4–		1989.12–		1995.4–	
Monthly earnings	Pension amount	Monthly earnings	Pension amount	Monthly earnings	Pension amount
~95	0.8*B	~95	0.8*B	~(220–0.8*B)	0.8*B
95~155	0.5*B	95~114	0.7*B	(220–0.8*B)~340	0.8*B–0.5(E-max (0,220–0.8*B))
155~210	0.2*B	114~138	0.6*B	340~	Max{0.8*B–0.5 (340-max(0,220- 0.8*B))–(E-340,0)
210~	0	138~165	0.5*B		
		165~185	0.4*B		
		185~210	0.3*B		
		210~250	0.2*B		
		250~	0		

Note: B is the amount of original pension that the person receives if s/he does not work. E is the amount of monthly earnings.

brackets were made dependent on the sum of earnings and pension. These changes to the old-age pension system were expected to have the effect of promoting the labor supply of workers in their early sixties.

Figures 5.4a and b illustrate the improved pension reduction scheme of the old-age pension system. The horizontal axis represents the monthly

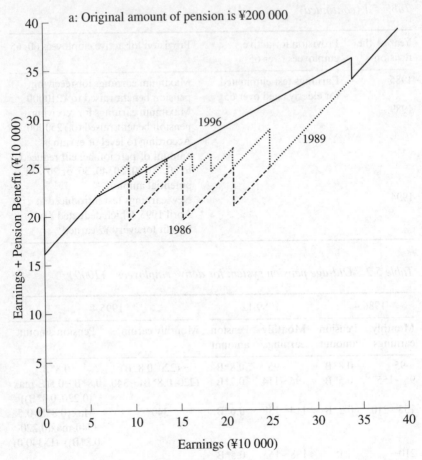

Figure 5.4   Old-age pension for active employees

wage ('monthly standard remuneration') and the vertical axis represents the
sum of pension received and the monthly wage. Figure 5.4a supposes that
the amount of pension that retired workers could receive (the original
pension benefit) is ¥200000 per month. The diagram compares the three
stages of the pension system for active employees: from 1986 to 1989; from
1989 to 1994; and following the 1995 change. As noted above, the change
in 1989 increased the number of wage groups for cutting pensions from
three to seven. Before the 1995 reform, there was a convex kink in the
income schedule at ¥95000 per month. The 1995 reforms eliminated reductions in overall take-home pay (the sum of pension and wages), unless
monthly wages exceeded ¥340000.[4]

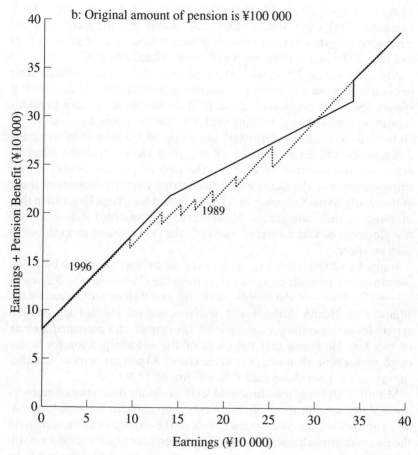

Figure 5.4 (continued)

Figure 5.4b supposes that the amount of the original pension benefit is ¥100000 per month. The figure shows that the convex kink in the 1995 reform moves to the right as the original pension benefit decreases. For the person with an original pension benefit above ¥156250, the 1995 reform changed the location of the convex kink to a point below ¥95000, the point at which the convex kink was located prior to 1995. For the person with an original pension benefit of less than ¥156250, the convex kink was moved to the right by the 1995 reform.

Previous studies have revealed that the old-age pension system for active employees restrains the labor force participation rate and the working hours of employees in their early sixties (Seike 1993; Ogawa 1998a, b; Abe

1998; Iwamoto 2000; and Mitani 2001). The studies of Abe (2001), Iwamoto (2000), and Mitani (2001) also found that the increase in the number of wage brackets for pension reduction from three to seven in 1989 had little effect on the labor supply of workers aged 60 to 64.

Abe (2001) argued that while those in their early sixties suffered large pension reductions as a result of wage increases under the old-age pension system for active employees, those in their late sixties receive pensions regardless of wage levels. Treating the 1989 reforms applied to workers aged 60 to 64 as a 'natural experiment', she analyzed the change by using the difference-in-differences method. If the 1989 change had the effect of increasing the incentive to work, in the case of persons eligible for an employee pension, the increase in the labor force participation rate of those in their early sixties following the change should have been larger than that of those in their late sixties. However, having analyzed data from the 'Employment of Older Persons' surveys, Abe (1998) found no evidence of such an effect.

Iwamoto (2000) estimated a dynamic labor supply model by using pseudo-panel methods on survey data from the Comprehensive Survey of Living Conditions of the People on Health and Welfare (organized by the Ministry of Health, Labour and Welfare), treated the old-age pension system for active employees as a payroll tax system, and estimated the rate of this tax. He found that the effect of the old-age pension for active employees is equivalent to a payroll tax rate of 80 percent or more, and that the tax rate did not change after the reforms of 1989.

Mitani (2001) used a multinomial logit model for the choice of employment status among three alternatives – employment, self-employment, and not working – to analyze the effects of the old-age pension system on the employment behavior of active employees. Like Ogawa (1998a and b), he treated the pension as an income subsidy for those choosing the employment option. Those choosing the option of not working are assumed to receive a full pension. Because those electing employment cannot choose their working hours, the starting wage is used and monthly income is assumed fixed. Having built the model to explain employment behavior, Mitani analyzed the impact of changes to the pension system on employment/not working ratios. As with other studies, Mitani found that the 1989 reforms had little effect on employment behavior. However, he found that the 1995 changes did increase employment/not working ratios. Mitani's results are questionable if the assumption that employees cannot choose their working hours is incorrect. Some of the mechanisms for cutting the old-age pension for active employees are likely to create distortions that promote short-hour employment, but this effect cannot be analyzed.

3. EFFECTS OF THE OLD-AGE PENSION FOR ACTIVE EMPLOYEES ESTIMATED BY THE DIFFERENCE-IN-DIFFERENCES METHOD

This section treats the changes in the old-age pension system for active employees as a 'natural experiment', exploiting the fact that the system treats those aged 60 to 64 and those aged 65 to 69 differently, to investigate whether or not the reforms affected the employment behavior of the elderly. This technique is similar to methods used by Abe (2001), Friedberg (2000), and Gruber and Orszag (2000). First, the history of changes to the pension system is outlined. Since the system for those aged 65 to 69 was not one in which wage increases triggered pension reductions, graphs are used to investigate whether reform of the pension system for those aged 60 to 64 brought about increases in labor force participation rates among those aged 60 to 64 that differed from those aged 65 to 69. Data from the 'Employment of Older Persons' surveys at the three points in time referred to above are then examined using the difference-in-differences method to see if there were variations in labor supply behavior.

Friedberg (2000) applies difference-in-differences and structural model estimation to US data to analyze the impact of earnings tests for pensions on the labor supply of older workers. The earnings test in the US public pension system resembles the test that has been in place in Japan's old-age pension system for active employees since 1995. Friedberg examines the effect on the distribution of earnings of changes induced by pension reforms in the exempt amount for pension payments. He finds that earnings cluster near the exempt amount, and that a change in the exempt amount generates a corresponding change in the location at which earnings cluster. He also carries out policy simulations based on the estimation of a structural model. The simulations show that the abolition of earnings tests would raise aggregate labor supply hours by 5.3 percent. By contrast, an increase in the exempt amount of earnings would lower labor supply.

Gruber and Orszag (2000) analyze the effects of the exempt amount in earnings tests on labor supply and on the behavior of pensioners. They find that the exempt amount does not affect the labor supply of men but does affect that of women, and that more lenient earnings tests raise the rate at which those eligible take up pensions but also reduce the average amount of pensions. Hence the abolition of earnings tests at young ages may lower the living standards of the elderly, and so the authors urge caution with regard to discontinuing tests.

Exploiting differences between the treatment of those aged 60 to 64 years and those aged 65 to 69 by Japan's old-age pension system for active employees, Abe (2001) showed that earnings tests control the labor supply of older people and that the change in the pension system for active employees in 1989 had no impact on the labor supply of those in their early sixties.

3.1. Major Changes in the Old-age Pension System for Active Employees

Table 5.1, above, showed the major changes in the old-age pension system for active employees in Japan. When this system began in 1965, 80 percent of the original pension amount (the amount to be paid when fully retired) was paid to people of at least 65 years of age provided their income from employment had reached a certain level. In 1969 a new system was introduced in which working people of between 60 and 64 years of age received a pension that was reduced according to employment income. In this system, four levels of pension benefit reduction according to employment income were established: 80, 60, 40, and 20 percent of the full pension payable on retirement. No pension was paid to those whose earnings exceeded a particular threshold. This system of reductions tended to reduce the overall incomes (pension plus wage income) of employees aged 60 to 64 as their employment income levels rose to enter the next highest income bracket (see Figures 5.4a and b, above). The upper limit on wage income for pension payments was increased to keep pace with inflation. However, the problematic issue of wage increases leading to lower total income (wages plus pension) was not settled until the introduction of the 1995 reforms. The reform in 1985 stopped pension reductions for those aged 65 and over.

3.2. Graphical Evidence

Figure 5.5 shows differences between the labor force participation rates of those aged 60 to 64 and those aged 65 to 69. Those aged 65 and over are not affected by earnings tests and can therefore be regarded as a control group for checking the effect of changes in the old-age pension for active employees on those aged between 60 and 64. The points in time at which changes in the system occurred (shown by vertical lines) and the labor force participation rate differences between the two age groups do not seem to be correlated. Differences in employment ratios are shown in Figure 5.6 and differences in working hours are shown in Figure 5.7. No obvious correlations are apparent here either.

Differences in labor supply changes between those aged 60 to 64 years and those aged 65 and over are then examined using the difference-in-differences method. Using $x_{60,t}$ for the labor force participation rate of those aged 60 to 64 years in year t and using $x_{65,t}$ for the rate of those aged

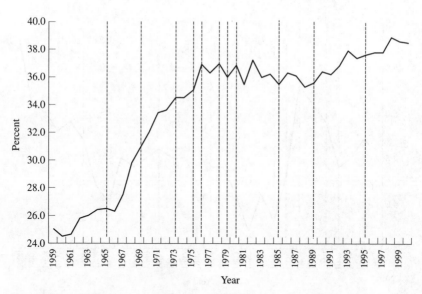

Figure 5.5   Differences in labor force participation rate (male, 60–64 minus 65–)

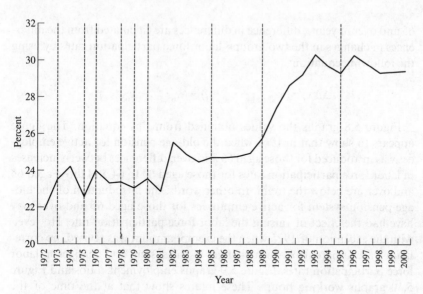

Figure 5.6   Differences in employment/population ratios (male, 60–64 minus 65–)

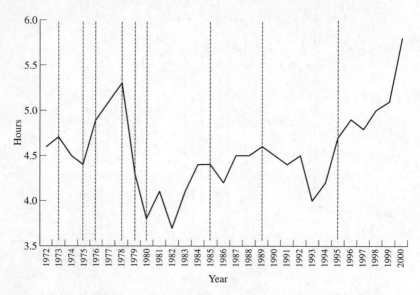

*Figure 5.7   Differences in average weekly working hours (male, 60–64
              minus 65–)*

65 and over in year t, difference in differences are calculated from the differences in changes in the two groups' labor force participation rates by using the following equation:

$$\Delta\Delta x_t = (x_{60,t+1} - x_{60,t-1}) - (x_{65,t+1} - x_{65,t-1}).$$

Figure 5.8 graphs the values obtained from this equation. The figure appears to show that in 1965 when the old-age pension for active employees was introduced for those aged 65 and over, differences between increases in labor force participation rates for those aged 60 to 64 and those aged 65 and over are below the trend. In other words, the introduction of the old-age pension system for active employees for those aged 65 and over may have had the effect of raising the labor force participation rate. However, with the exception of 1975 when the exempt amount was revised, no correlations are apparent between changes in the system and changes in labor force participation rates. Figure 5.9 graphs employment ratios and Figure 5.10 graphs working hours. These figures show that at the time of the change in 1995, employment ratios and working hours increased. However, these increases do not differ greatly from changes in 1999 when there was no revision of the system.

In summary, it seems that changes over time in the pension reduction

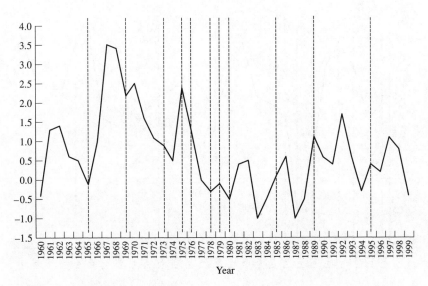

Figure 5.8 Difference in differences in labor force participation (male, Δ60–64 minus Δ65–)

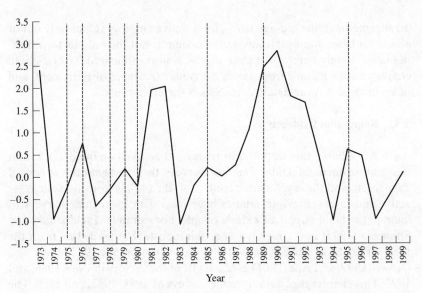

Figure 5.9 Difference in differences in employment/population ratio (male, Δ60–64 minus Δ65–)

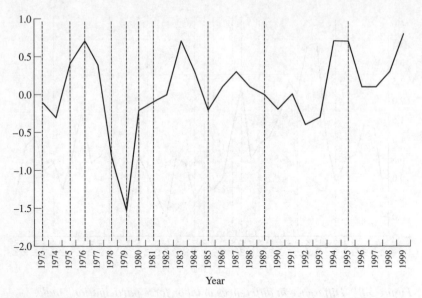

Figure 5.10   Difference in differences in working hours (male, Δ60–64 minus Δ65–)

arrangements in the old-age pension for active employees had only minor effects on labor supply. However, this system is not the only factor affecting labor supply behavior. Labor supply is also influenced by household characteristics, income from assets, previous experience of retirement, and other factors. A more detailed analysis is therefore needed.

3.3.   Regression Evidence

As in Abe (2001), this section uses regression analysis on micro data from the 'Employment of Older Persons' surveys to investigate the effects of changes in, and the employment control of, the old-age pension system for active employees. Previous studies have used data from these surveys to analyze the labor supply of elderly people. For example, Tachibanaki and Shimono (1985) and Amemiya and Shimono (1989) used data from the 1980 survey, Seike and Shimada (1994) used data from the 1983 survey, and Ogawa (1997) and Abe (2001) used data from the surveys in 1983, 1988, and 1992. This chapter uses data from the surveys of 1988, 1992, and 1996. The impact of the changes in April 1995 can be analyzed using the 1996 survey data.[5]

Table 5.3   Changes of labor market status of the elderly

		Changes of employment/elderly ratio (%)			
	Age 55–59	Age 60–64		Age 65–69	
		Beneficiary	Non-beneficiary	Beneficiary	Non-beneficiary
1988	88.04	47.79	69.00	44.84	60.65
1992	92.65	51.84	71.81	50.89	62.55
1996	92.88	54.60	73.11	48.13	58.14

		Changes of average working hour per week of the aged			
	Age 55–59	Age 60–64		Age 65–69	
		Beneficiary	Non-beneficiary	Beneficiary	Non-beneficiary
1988	42.11	32.40	35.74	32.48	33.30
1992	42.69	34.90	37.25	32.92	35.15
1996	42.72	35.52	38.21	32.06	34.81

Source: Surveys on 'Employment of Older Persons'.

Descriptive statistics

In this section, the descriptive statistics from the three 'Employment of Older Persons' surveys are compared and examined. First, Table 5.3 compares employment ratios for men for each age bracket. The employment ratios for those aged 60 and under increased between 1988 and 1996. The ratios for those aged 65 and over rose between 1988 and 1992, but declined in 1996. The employment ratios of those aged 60 to 64, who received old-age (employee) pensions, increased. Regardless of age, those who did not receive a pension had higher employment ratios. The table summarizes the average working hours per week of employees. According to Table 5.3, the working hours of those aged 64 and under increased, while those of pension beneficiaries aged 65 and over hardly changed.

Figures 5.11 and 5.12 present histograms for each survey year of working hours both for male employees who are eligible for the employee pension and for those who are not. For each survey year, the distribution of working hours is concentrated on full-time employment (44 hours/week) and no employment. This is true whether or not persons are eligible for the employee pension. The employment situation of older persons was also affected by the policy of reducing working hours through, for example, amendments to the Labor Standards Law in the 1980s and 1990s. The figures show that in 1996 the percentage of elderly people working 40 hours a week surpassed that of those working 44 hours a week.

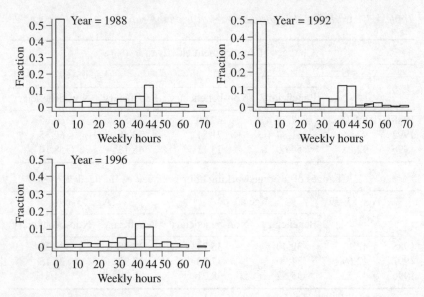

*Figure 5.11   Working hours of persons eligible for the EPI according to
              research years*

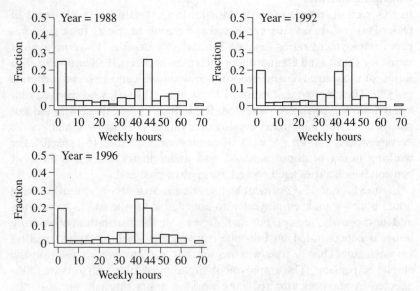

*Figure 5.12   Working hours of persons non-eligible for the EPI according
              to research years*

Changes in labor supply behavior and original pension benefit level

Before the 1995 reform, there was a convex kink in the income schedule at ¥95000 per month. The convex kink in the 1995 reform moves to the right as the person's original pension benefit decreases, as shown in Figure 5.4b, above. For those with a potential benefit of more than ¥156250, the 1995 reform changed the location of the convex kink to a point below ¥95000, at which point the convex kink was located under the system in place before 1995. For those with an original pension benefit of less than ¥156250, the convex kink was moved to the right by the 1995 reform.

If people react to the earnings test, we expect to observe a cluster at the kink.[6] Since the 1995 reform reduced the effective marginal tax rate for the worker with earnings above the convex kink point, the spike at the kink should be smaller in 1996 than in both 1988 and 1992.

Figures 5.13a–c show the earnings distributions for those aged 60 to 64 relative to the first convex kink in 1988, 1992, and 1996 and Figures 5.14a–c show the distributions minus ¥95000. Figure 5.13a illustrates the earnings distribution for persons whose original pension benefit is less than ¥156250, and Figure 5.13b illustrates the distribution for persons whose original pension benefit is more than ¥156250. As expected, the spike at the kink is smaller in 1996 than in 1988 and 1992. In both figures we observe spikes in 1988 and 1992. However, in 1996 the situation changed dramatically. We observe a sharp drop in the 1996 earnings distribution at the kink point in Figure 5.13a.

However, in Figure 5.13b we do not observe a cluster of points around the kink in the 1996 earnings distribution. For workers with an original pension benefit of less than ¥156250 (poor pensioners), the kink point increased following the 1995 reform. Thus, the earnings of poor pensioners increased as the kink increased or remained at its original point. For workers with an original pension benefit of more than ¥156250 (rich pensioners), the kink point decreased following the 1995 reform. A rich pensioner at the kink in the pre-1995 system might not have selected the new kink point in the post-1995 system. In fact, according to Figure 5.14b, most rich pensioners stayed at the original kink, at ¥95000, after the 1995 reform. Rather than showing the new kink point in 1996, Figure 5.14b shows the distribution of earnings from which ¥95000 has been subtracted.

The positive effect of the 1995 reform on the labor supply of elderly people was limited to those with an original pension benefit of less than ¥156250. Since the reform reduced the kink for rich pensioners, these people were hardly affected by the 1995 reform.

Estimation results

Abe (2001) uses data from 1983, 1988, and 1992 to estimate reduced-form equations for labor supply. She also estimates the effects of the changes to the

a: Original pension benefit < ¥156 250

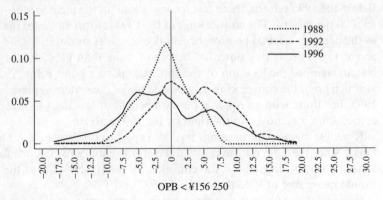

OPB < ¥156 250

b: Original pension benefit > ¥156 250

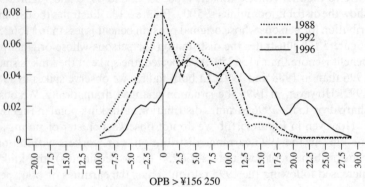

OPB > ¥156 250

c: All sample

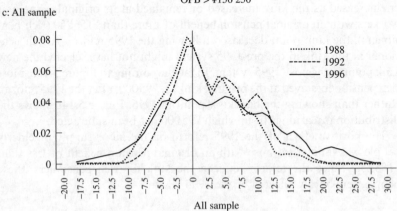

All sample

Figure 5.13   Distribution of earnings minus the kink

a: Original pension benefit < ¥156 250

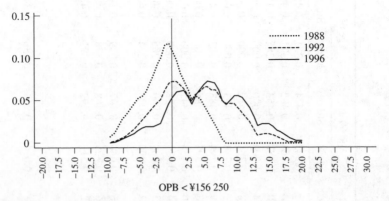

b: Original pension benefit > ¥156 250

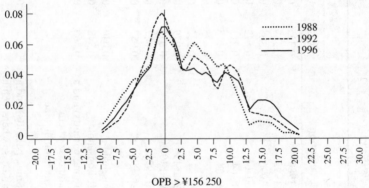

c: All sample

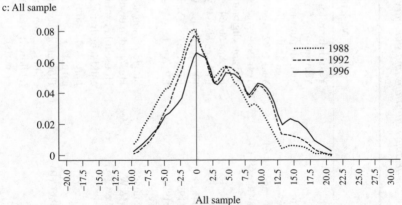

Figure 5.14   Distribution of earnings minus ¥95 000

Table 5.4 Variable definitions and summary statistics

Variable	Variable definition	Age 60		Age 60–64		Age 65–69	
		Mean	Std dev.	Mean	Std dev.	Mean	Std dev.
Year 1988	Year dummy for 1988	0.325	0.468	0.343	0.474	0.301	0.458
Year 1992	Year dummy for 1992	0.369	0.482	0.368	0.482	0.371	0.483
Year 1996	Year dummy for 1996	0.305	0.460	0.288	0.453	0.288	0.453
Age 60–64	Age dummy for 60–64	0.572	0.494	1.000	0.000	0.000	0.000
Year 1992*age 60–64	Year 1992*Age 60–64	0.211	0.408	0.368	0.482	0.000	0.000
Year 1996*age 60–64	Year 1996*Age 60–64	0.165	0.371	0.288	0.453	0.000	0.000
EP	Pension eligibility	0.475	0.499	0.394	0.488	0.583	0.492
EP*Age 60–64	EP*Age 60–64	0.225	0.418	0.394	0.488	0.000	0.000
EP*60–64*1992	EP*Age 60–64*Year 1992	0.079	0.270	0.138	0.345	0.000	0.000
EP*60–64*1996	EP*Age 60–64*Year 1996	0.075	0.264	0.131	0.338	0.000	0.000
EP*65–*1992	EP*Age 65–*Year 1992	0.087	0.283	0.000	0.000	0.205	0.404
EP*65–*1996	EP*Age 65–*Year 1996	0.087	0.282	0.000	0.000	0.204	0.403
Family Type							
Family–Single	Single-person household	0.040	0.196	0.040	0.197	0.039	0.194
Family–H&W	Husband and wife household	0.348	0.476	0.325	0.468	0.378	0.485
Family–P&C(A)	Household containing parent(s) and a child (children), and case where parent(s) is (are) the main income earner(s)	0.460	0.498	0.511	0.499	0.391	0.488
Family–P&C(B)	Household containing parent(s) and a child (children), and case where a child (children) is (are) the main income earner(s)	0.101	0.301	0.074	0.263	0.136	0.343

Family–other	Other household than above categories	0.050	0.217	0.047	0.211	0.053	0.225
Self-employed	Self-employed = 1, else = 0	0.277	0.447	0.251	0.433	0.311	0.463
Health	Health condition is good = 1, else = 0	0.682	0.465	0.724	0.446	0.626	0.483
Experience of mandatory retirement	Experience of mandatory retirement	0.430	0.495	0.411	0.492	0.455	0.498
Original amount of pension	Original amount of pension benefit	7.546	11.255	7.009	12.700	8.247	8.984
Amount of non-EPI pension	Amount of non-EPI pension	4.923	8.017	4.333	7.782	5.714	8.256
Mutual aid pension	Dummy for pension beneficiary of pension for the public service	0.178	0.383	0.160	0.366	0.203	0.402
Mutual aid*1992	Mutual aid pension*Year 1992	0.067	0.250	0.061	0.240	0.749	0.263
Mutual aid*1996	Mutual aid pension*Year 1996	0.048	0.213	0.038	0.191	0.061	0.239
Mutual aid*age 65–	Mutual aid pension*Age 65–	0.121	0.327	0.111	0.314	0.135	0.342
No. of samples		20714		11721		8993	

Notes: EPI = Employees' Pension Insurance; EP = eligible pensioner for EPI.

159

Table 5.5 Estimation results for labor supply function by probit model

	Work = 1		Work as employee = 1		Work as full-time employee = 1	
	Coef.	Std error	Coef.	Std error	Coef.	Std error
Year 1992	0.000	0.061	−0.169	0.131	0.097	0.129
Year 1996	−0.066	0.065	1.432	0.165***	0.555	0.130***
Age 60–64	0.558	0.054***	0.628	0.124***	0.564	0.121***
Year 1992*age 60–64	0.185	0.073**	0.064	0.138	0.007	0.135
Year 1996*age 60–64	0.185	0.079**	−0.637	0.174***	−0.249	0.138*
EP	−0.217	0.061***	−0.245	0.125*	−0.291	0.125**
EP*60–64	−0.688	0.075***	−0.419	0.151***	−0.468	0.150***
EP*60–64*1992	0.030	0.070	−0.087	0.116	−0.098	0.112
EP*60–64*1996	0.123	0.073*	0.663	0.148***	0.529	0.117***
EP*65–*1992	0.207	0.076***	0.242	0.139*	−0.006	0.139
EP*65–*1996	0.154	0.079**	0.206	0.179	0.122	0.142
Family–H&W	0.377	0.051***	0.155	0.079**	0.245	0.071***
Family–P&C(A)	0.430	0.051***	0.200	0.079***	0.261	0.070***
Family–P&C(B)	−0.534	0.057***	−0.421	0.096***	−0.384	0.086***
Family–other	−0.704	0.067***	−0.762	0.099***	−0.715	0.100***
Self-employed	1.065	0.032***	0.866	0.058***	0.034	0.039
Health	0.909	0.022***	0.596	0.034***	0.601	0.031***
Experience of mandatory retirement	−0.391	0.027***	−0.308	0.041***	−0.344	0.034***
Potential amount of pension	0.005	0.002***	−0.002	0.002	−0.006	0.001***
Amount of non-EPI pension	−0.041	0.002***	−0.029	0.003***	−0.030	0.003***
Mutual aid pension	−0.063	0.064	−0.075	0.112	−0.085	0.106
Mutual aid*1992	0.260	0.063***	−0.190	0.095**	−0.275	0.094***

Mutual aid*1996	0.370	0.067***	−0.488	0.118***	−0.146	0.103
Mutual aid*age 65–	0.410	0.055***	0.240	0.076***	0.253	0.071***
Constant	−0.624	0.069***	−0.033	0.141	−0.442	0.135***
Number of observations	20714		10998		10998	
Pseudo R^2	0.2691		0.3037		0.1966	
Log likelihood	−10089.091		−4645.133		−6118.318	

Notes: *** 1% significant, ** 5% significant, * 10% significant.

Table 5.6 Estimation results for labor supply function in working hours

	Work = 1		Work as employee = 1		Work as full-time employee = 1	
	Coef.	Std error	Coef.	Std error	Coef.	Std error
Wage rate/10000	−1.174	0.056***	−0.930	0.068***	−0.495	0.093***
Year 1992	1.619	0.650**	1.267	1.469	−1.194	0.925
Year 1996	1.974	0.711***	1.197	1.435	−1.587	0.907*
Age 60–64	3.329	0.559***	4.361	1.366***	0.771	0.865
Year 1992*age 60–64	−0.538	0.738	−1.044	1.519	0.127	0.955
Year 1996*age 60–64	−0.674	0.811	−1.379	1.482	0.642	0.935
EP	−1.409	0.702**	−1.166	1.474	−0.486	0.946
EP*60–64	−5.210	0.924***	−4.888	1.731***	−0.967	1.127
EP*60–64*1992	2.055	0.817***	1.192	1.209	0.363	0.765
EP*60–64*1996	3.262	0.822***	3.314	1.187***	0.806	0.747
EP*65–*1992	−0.782	0.889	−0.945	1.635	0.722	1.048
EP*65–*1996	−1.883	0.937**	−1.384	1.595	0.573	1.026
Family–H&W	2.599	0.628***	2.187	0.729***	0.305	0.453
Family–P&C(A)	2.920	0.619***	2.469	0.721***	0.748	0.447*
Family–P&C(B)	−4.132	0.742***	−3.406	0.912***	−1.736	0.599***
Family–other	−0.550	0.972	−1.792	1.188	0.860	0.825
Self-employed	−1.225	0.267***	−0.998	0.350***	1.850	0.221***
Health	4.280	0.278***	3.809	0.335***	0.275	0.219
Experience of mandatory retirement	−4.149	0.307***	−3.776	0.337***	−1.668	0.205***
Potential amount of pension	−0.034	0.013***	−0.047	0.013***	−0.010	0.008
Amount of non-EPI pension	−0.240	0.029***	−0.200	0.032***	−0.083	0.020***
Mutual aid pension	−2.615	0.750***	−1.495	1.174	0.086	0.717

Mutual aid*1992	1.226	0.745*	0.391	1.060	−0.039	0.647
Mutual aid*1996	−0.025	0.807	−1.021	1.095	−0.449	0.679
Mutual aid*age 65–	2.953	0.675***	2.733	0.786***	1.234	0.491**
Constant	32.841	0.818***	33.685	1.524***	43.519	0.961***
Number of sample	12719		7742		5701	
Adj. R²	0.146		0.140		0.061	
F	88.14		51.31		15.71	

Notes: *** 1% significant, ** 5% significant, * 10% significant.

163

Table 5.7 Estimation results for labor supply function in log of working hours

	Work = 1		Work as employee = 1		Work as full-time employee = 1	
	Coef.	Std error	Coef.	Std error	Coef.	Std error
Wage rate	−0.277	0.006***	−0.242	0.008***	−0.025	0.003***
Year 1992	0.180	0.027***	0.175	0.062***	−0.020	0.021
Year 1996	0.227	0.030***	0.200	0.061***	−0.026	0.021
Age 60–64	0.162	0.023***	0.211	0.057***	0.021	0.020
Year 1992*age 60–64	−0.036	0.031	−0.072	0.064	0.001	0.022
Year 1996*age 60–64	−0.036	0.034	−0.074	0.062	0.009	0.021
EP	0.008	0.035	0.047	0.065	−0.003	0.022
EP*60–64	−0.359	0.039***	−0.281	0.073***	−0.035	0.025
EP*60–64*1992	0.119	0.034***	0.036	0.051	0.012	0.017
EP*60–64*1996	0.174	0.034***	0.122	0.050**	0.027	0.017
EP*65–*1992	−0.070	0.037*	−0.089	0.069	0.016	0.024
EP*65–*1996	−0.145	0.039***	−0.112	0.067*	0.009	0.023
Family–H&W	0.170	0.026***	0.144	0.031***	0.012	0.010
Family–P&C(A)	0.168	0.026***	0.143	0.030***	0.022	0.010**
Family–P&C(B)	−0.232	0.031***	−0.152	0.038***	−0.045	0.014***
Family–other	−0.099	0.041**	−0.127	0.050**	0.019	0.019
Self-employed	−0.149	0.012***	−0.141	0.015***	0.032	0.005***
Health	0.209	0.012***	0.186	0.014***	0.010	0.005**
Experience of mandatory retirement	−0.194	0.013***	−0.160	0.014***	−0.040	0.005***
Potential amount of Pension	−0.032	0.010***	−0.049	0.011***	−0.006	0.004*
Amount of non-EPI pension	−0.063	0.007***	−0.050	0.008***	−0.014	0.003***
Mutual aid pension	−0.153	0.031***	−0.082	0.050*	0.007	0.016

Mutual aid*1992	0.050	0.031	0.007	0.044	−0.005	0.015
Mutual aid*1996	−0.027	0.033	−0.091	0.046**	−0.018	0.015
Mutual aid*age 65–	0.101	0.028***	0.059	0.033*	0.024	0.011**
Constant	5.569	0.060***	5.302	0.089***	3.965	0.032***
Number of sample	12719		7742		5701	
Adj. R²	0.236		0.205		0.068	
F	157.9		80.96		17.62	

Notes: *** 1% significant, ** 5% significant, * 10% significant.

Table 5.8   Changes in coefficient of pension eligibility between age groups

Panel A: Difference in differences from the probit models (calculated from Table 5.4)

	Model	Year	88–92	92–96	88–96
Age group	Work	60–64	0.718	0.093	0.811
		65–69	0.207	−0.053	0.154
		differences	0.511	0.146	0.657
	Work as employee	60–64	0.332	0.750	1.082
		65–69	0.242	−0.036	0.206
		differences	0.090	0.786	0.876
	Work as full-time employee	60–64	0.370	0.627	0.997
		65–69	−0.006	0.128	0.122
		differences	0.376	0.499	0.875

Panel B: Difference in differences from the working hours models (calculated from Table 5.5)

	Model	Year	88–92	92–96	88–96
Age group	Work	60–64	7.265	1.207	8.472
		65–69	−0.782	−1.101	−1.883
		differences	8.047	2.308	10.355
	Work as employee	60–64	6.080	2.122	8.202
		65–69	−0.945	−0.439	−1.384
		differences	7.025	2.561	9.586
	Work as full-time employee	60–64	1.330	0.443	1.773
		65–69	0.722	−0.149	0.573
		differences	0.608	0.592	1.200

Panel C: Difference in differences from the log of working hours models (calculated from Table 5.6)

	Model	Year	88–92	92–96	88–96
Age group	Work	60–64	0.478	0.055	0.533
		65–69	−0.070	−0.075	−0.145
		differences	0.548	0.130	0.678
	Work as employee	60–64	0.317	0.086	0.403
		65–69	−0.089	−0.023	−0.112
		differences	0.406	0.109	0.515
	Work as full-time employee	60–64	0.047	0.015	0.062
		65–69	0.016	−0.007	0.009
		differences	0.031	0.022	0.053

system in 1989 by adding a dummy variable for employee pension eligibility, a 60 to 64 years of age dummy variable, and a dummy variable for 1992. She also uses interaction terms between these dummy variables and the explanatory variables. This chapter uses Abe's method and data from 1988, 1992, and 1996 to examine the impact of the changes in 1992 and 1995.

The econometric models used follow:

$$\text{Prob(work} = 1) = \alpha_1 \text{ (year dummy)} + \alpha_2 \text{ (year dummy * age 60–64)} + \alpha_3 \text{ (pension eligibility)} + \alpha_4 \text{ (pension eligibility * age 60–64)} + \alpha_5 \text{ (pension eligibility * age 60–64 year dummy)} + \alpha_6 \text{(pension eligibility * age 65 over * year dummy)} + X\alpha + \varepsilon.$$

$$\text{(Weekly working hours)} = \beta_1 \text{ (year dummy)} + \beta_2 \text{ (year dummy * age 60–64)} + \beta_3 \text{ (pension eligibility)} + \beta_4 \text{(pension eligibility * age 60–64)} + \beta_5 \text{ (pension eligibility * age 60–64 * year dummy)} + \beta_6 \text{ (pension eligibility * age 65 over * year dummy)} + X\beta + \varepsilon.$$

The dummies for pension eligibility and for 60 to 64 years of age, and the year dummy are included to estimate the impact of the old-age pension for active employees on labor supply. Because the old-age pension system for active employees was not changed for those aged 65 and over, this age group can be considered a control group. Hence, persons aged 60 to 64 eligible for a pension can be regarded as a treatment group. Therefore, the coefficients of the interaction terms involving the pension eligibility, year, and age group dummy variables reveal the effects of changes to the pension system by the difference-in-differences method. As already noted, during the sample period the system was reformed twice: in 1989 and again in 1995. In particular, the changes in 1995 were intended to limit some of the labor-supply controlling effects of previous systems

Other explanatory variables used are household characteristics, experience of retirement at retirement age, health conditions, amount of pension, and mutual aid pension received. The samples are of men aged 60 to 69 years. Table 5.4 shows the definition of the variables and descriptive statistics.

Table 5.5 summarizes the estimation results of a probit model that uses 'whether employed or not' as the dependent variable. Table 5.6 (Table 5.7) summarizes the results of a model in which the dependent variable is the working hours (log of working hours) of those in the sample that are employed. First, pension eligibility has a significant disincentive effect on both the employment and working hours of those aged 60 to 64. However, there was no negative effect of pension eligibility on the probability of being in employment in 1996. Second, according to Table 5.8, which compares changes in the impact of pension eligibility on labor supply between age groups over time, while the change in 1989 had positive effects on both employment and working hours, the 1995 reform did not affect working hours but did affect employment.

The estimation results in this section show that the old-age pension system for active employees adversely affected the motivation of those aged 60 to 64 years to work, and that this effect decreased slightly following the changes made in 1995 especially for elderly people with small original pension benefits.

4.   CONCLUSION

This chapter has analyzed the impact of the old-age pension system for active employees on the employment behavior of older people using the difference-in-differences method and by estimating dynamic labor supply models. The difference-in-differences results and the estimated dynamic labor supply models both showed that the pension system has disincentive effects on the labor supply of those aged 60 to 64. The results revealed that the changes to the pension system in 1995 affected the choice of whether to work but did not affect working hours. These effects were limited to elderly people with an original pension benefit of less than ¥156250.

The results summarized above suggest that any change in the exempt amount of the old-age pension system would only increase the labor supply of older people to a very limited extent. To achieve greater effects of stimulating labor supply, earnings tests for the payment of public pensions should be abolished. The problem with the old-age pension system for active employees is not that it merely hinders the labor supply of older people, but also that it produces distortions in modes of employment. For instance, to avoid the earnings test, some elderly people will choose to work part-time or become self-employed. An actuarially fairer system for early payment of a reduced pension should be introduced and earnings tests for the old-age pension for active employees should be abolished.

NOTES

1.   This section owes much to Mitani (2001), which provides a useful summary of developments related to the extension of the retirement age from the 1980s to the 1990s.
2.   This section is based on Abe (1998) and Mitani (2001).
3.   Seike (1993) made the first attempt to analyze the effect on work disincentives of the old-age pension for active employees.

4. The change in 2000 eliminated reductions in overall take-home pay for a monthly wage of ¥340000.
5. Mitani (2001) uses the same data sets as those used in this chapter.
6. Using 1983 data, Seike (1993) found that there was a cluster at the kink for eligible pensioners but not for the non-eligible elderly.

REFERENCES

Abe, Yukiko (2001), 'Employees' pension benefits and the labour supply of older Japanese workers, 1980s–1990s', in Seiritsu Ogura, Toshiaki Tachibanaki and David Wise (eds), *Aging issues in the United States and Japan*, Chapter 9, Chicago: University of Chicago Press, 273–305.

Amemiya, Takeshi and Keiko Shimono (1989), 'An application of nested logit models to the labor supply of the elderly', *Economic Studies Quarterly*, **40**, 14–22.

Chuma, Hiroyuki (1997), 'The changes of economic condition and the increasing trend in the length of job tenure', in Hiroyuki Chuma and Terukazu Suruga (eds), *The Changes of Employment Practice and Female Labor*, Tokyo: University of Tokyo Press, pp. 47–80.

Friedberg, Leora (2000), 'The labor supply effects of the social security earning test', *Review of Economics and Statistics*, **82** (1), 48–63.

Gruber, Jonathan and Peter Orszag (2000), 'Does the social security earnings test affect labor supply and benefits receipt?', NBER Working Paper No. 7923, National Bureau of Economic Research.

Iwamoto, Yasushi (1998), 'Japan's labor force in the year 2020' (in Japanese), *Keizai Kenkyu* (Economic Review), **49** (4), 297–307.

Iwamoto, Yasushi (2000), 'The social security earnings test and labor supply of the elderly: evidence from Japanese repeated cross-section data' (in Japanese), *Kikan Shakaihosho Kenkyu* (Quarterly Journal of Social Security Research), **35** (4), 364–76.

Mitani, Naoki (2001), 'Employment policy for the elderly and labor demand', in Takenori Inoki and Fumio Ohtake (eds), *Koyoseisaku no Kenzaibunseki* (An economic analysis of employment policies in Japan), Tokyo: University of Tokyo Press, pp. 339–88.

Ogawa, Hiroshi (1997), 'The effects of social security on the labor supply of the elderly', *Research on the Social Security Reform on Retirement Behavior*, Tokyo: Japan Institute of Labor.

Ogawa, Hiroshi (1998a), 'The effect of household structure on labor participation behavior of Elderly Males' (in Japanese), *Keizai Kenkyu* (Economic Review), **49** (3), 245–58.

Ogawa, Hiroshi (1998b), 'Empirical study of the labor participation behavior of the elderly: the effect of the social security system' (in Japanese), *Nihon Rodo Kenkyu Zasshi* (Monthly Journal of the Japan Institute of Labour), **40** (11), 52–64.

Seike, Atsushi (1993), *Labor Market in Aging Society*, Tokyo: Toyokeizai Shinposha.

Seike, Atsushi and Haruo Shimada (1994), 'Social security benefits and the labor supply of the elderly in Japan', in Yukio Noguchi and David Wise (eds), *Aging in the United States and Japan: Economic Trends*, Chicago: University of Chicago Press, 43–61.

Tachibanaki, T. and K. Shimono (1985), 'Labor supply of the elderly: their desires and realities about full-time jobs, part-time jobs, self-employment or retirement', *Keizai Kenkyu* (Economic Review), **36**, 239–50.

6. Strengthening employment-based pensions*

Robert L. Clark and Olivia S. Mitchell**

1. INTRODUCTION

The Japanese population is ageing more rapidly than any other, and very low fertility rates going forward mean that this nation's population will start shrinking within the next few years.[1] International retirement system experts would do well to examine developments in Japanese retirement policies, so as to assess how employer-sponsored pensions fare in such a rapidly ageing society. Demographic change in Japan also places pressure on plan sponsors to efficiently manage pension funds and to offer cost-effective pensions that workers value. Government policy makers must monitor and revise national pension systems and develop appropriate regulations and tax policies for employer pension plans. Coordination of public and private retirement programs will be essential in the coming decades.

Two important questions are addressed in the present analysis: how is the Japanese pension market for funded employment-based pensions evolving, and what additional steps are needed to strengthen public and private retirement plans? The Japanese pension system is one of the largest in the world, second only to that of the US pension market. Institutional public and employer pension assets in Japan have been estimated to be around US$3 trillion (Cerulli 1999; Conrad 2001), of which some US$0.6 trillion are in private plans (Sakamoto 2001a). But economic news has not been favorable for Japanese pension plans of late. Financial stagnation has sharply reduced asset values, lowered returns on bonds and other fixed income assets, and raised unemployment rates.[2] In addition, the weak economy is undermining firms' commitment to traditional lifetime employment contracts as deferred compensation promises (Seike 1997).

To modernize the pension environment in Japan, a number of regulatory changes were recently passed. These changes, intended to restructure and provide new opportunities for employer-sponsored retirement plans, followed closely on the heels of modifications in the Japanese pay-as-you-go social security system which is made up of the Employees' Pension Insurance and the National Pension, described in more detail later. Furthermore, publicly traded firms in Japan must now comply with new and more transparent accounting standards. These standards will also shape pension restructuring, as firms are required to provide new information regarding retirement plan liabilities and assets. To permit an assessment of these patterns, we begin with a review of the status of the Japanese pension system at the end of the twentieth century. Our analysis considers changes in both public and private pension plans and how these programs are interrelated. Next, we turn to a summary and evaluation of the major changes in the employer-provided pension arena emerging from the 2001 legislation. We show that several important unanswered design questions still remain before Japanese employment-based pensions can be effectively modernized. Additional regulations will be required before recently enacted reforms will fully achieve the objective of enhancing retirement security. We also discuss some of the lessons that might be gleaned from recent changes in pension plans in the United States.

2. THE JAPANESE PENSION SYSTEM AT THE END OF THE TWENTIETH CENTURY

There are about 67 million economically active persons in Japan. Virtually all workers are included in the national social security system. In addition, about 39 million of these workers are covered by some form of employer-sponsored pension plan (Miyatake 2000). This section explores how the Japanese retirement system works and outlines the major changes in Japanese retirement policy over the recent past. We trace potential employer as well as employee responses within the context of the current economic situation, population ageing and broader changes in human resource policies in Japan. Employer pensions are developed within the framework of social security rules and benefits. Changes in mandatory benefit programs, such as lower replacement rates and higher retirement ages, will influence employer and employee preferences concerning private retirement plans. Thus, our analysis begins with a review of the continuing evolution of social security in Japan.

2.1. An Overview of the Japanese Publicly Provided Retirement Program

The Japanese national social security system is composed of two parts, both of which are mainly financed on a pay-as-you-go-basis (see Figure 6.1). The first pillar is the National Pension (NP), which provides a flat benefit to all persons who contribute to the system.[3] The NP was established in 1959 to provide benefits to self-employed workers, farmers, their dependent spouses, the unemployed, and students. These groups are required to make monthly contributions to the NP (¥13300 per month in 1999; US$111).[4] Since 1986, employed individuals and their spouses have participated in the NP system through their own and their employers' mandatory contributions to the Employees' Pension Insurance (EPI). Each year, the EPI system transfers to the NP account sufficient funds to pay for the flat benefit of covered employees and their spouses.[5]

The NP flat benefit is equal to a specified quantity of yen per month, multiplied by the number of 'covered' months (how long the worker contributed to the system). In 1999, a retiree with full benefit from the NP would receive a monthly benefit of ¥67017 (US$558). Prior to the 1986 reform, the full NP benefit was payable at age 65 after 25 years of service; reduced benefits could also be taken as early as age 60, and the benefit amount could be increased if the worker delayed acceptance until age 70 (Clark 1991).[6] These benefits are indexed to the cost of living after retirement. The 1986 reforms made a full benefit conditional on 40 years of contributions.

The second pillar of the public pension system takes the form of an earnings-related defined benefit (DB) plan called the Employees' Pension Insurance program. The EPI was established in 1941 to cover employed persons. Prior to 1986, the EPI benefit formula was 1.0 percent of pay per year of service, linked after retirement to the cost of living index. Subsequently, the benefit formula has been reduced to 0.75 times average indexed (or revalued) earnings, not including bonuses, times the number of covered years. The reduction in the benefit formula was to be phased in over 20 years, and the new lower level will apply to all persons born in 1946 or thereafter, reflecting the larger number of covered working years of younger cohorts. Currently, the tax rate used to finance the EPI is 17.35 percent of covered earnings, divided equally between the employer and the employee. This contribution is used to finance the flat NP benefit for the worker and his or her spouse plus the earnings-related EPI benefit described above.

Using the current benefit formula, a worker with 40 years of coverage would receive an earnings-related benefit of 30 percent of average real earnings. The flat benefit for a married worker and spouse provides a total replacement rate of over 50 percent for most retirees. For example, consider a retired employee with average earnings (approximately ¥340000 or US$2833 per month) who had 40 years of coverage and whose spouse was a full-time housewife. This couple would receive a flat benefit of ¥67017 (US$558) per month for both the husband and the wife, or a total basic

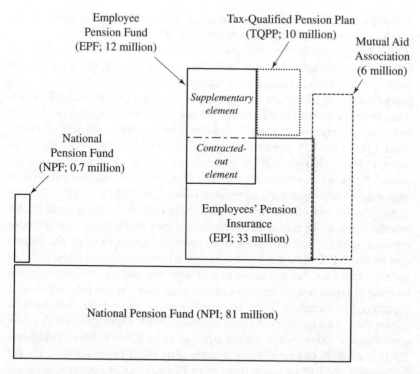

Source: Derived from Conrad (2001) and Sakamoto (2001b).

Figure 6.1   Schematic view of Japanese retirement programs pre-2001
(number of members)

benefit of ¥134000 (US$1117) per month. In addition, the retiree would receive ¥104000 (US$866) per month from the earnings-related EPI benefit. Thus, the combined publicly supported benefit for the family would be about ¥238000 or US$1983 (Miyatake 2000). Reforms implemented in 1994 gradually boosted the eligibility age for the NP flat benefit from age 60 to 65; however, eligibility for EPI benefits was maintained at age 60 throughout the 1990s.

If those benefit promises had been maintained in the face of Japan's rapid pace of ageing, additional tax revenue would have been required to cover promises made under NP and EPI rules (Ministry of Health, Labor, and Welfare 1999). For instance, government review groups projected that EPI tax rates would have to increase from 17.35 to 34.5 percent of covered earnings by 2025, and contributions to the NP were projected to have to rise by about 100 percent. As a result, a comprehensive review of benefit formulas, eligibility conditions, retirement ages, and financing options was conducted, resulting in the reform law of 2000.

One key aspect of the 2000 public pension reforms was that they cut future social security benefits in various ways. First, the EPI benefit formula was further curtailed by about 5 percent, from 0.75 to 0.7125 percent per year of service. Second, the indexation of EPI and NP retirement benefits for beneficiaries aged 65 and older was switched from wage indexation to price indexation. Third, for future workers, the normal retirement age for the EPI pension was raised from 60 to 65 for both men and women. These changes will be gradually phased in over time for new retirees.[7] It has been estimated that the 2000 reforms reduced benefits in aggregate by approximately 20 percent (Takayama 2001).

Another aspect of the 2000 reforms was that they also altered future revenue streams. In particular, general revenues flowing into the NP were boosted, with the subsidy rising from one-third to one-half of the annual cost of the NP. Unlike the United States, where an earmarked payroll tax entirely finances the government old-age benefits at present, general revenue in Japan will be used to support even more of the total retirement system cost than before. There has been considerable debate over the most appropriate way to support these subsidies, with some analysts favoring consumption taxes, while others oppose them (Hatta 2001; Takayama 2001). The 2000 public pension reforms also hiked the maximum age for inclusion in the EPI program from 65 to 70 and extended covered earnings to include bonuses. Thus, future retirees will have substantially lower benefits than had previously been expected, even as they must pay higher taxes during their working years.

As a result of these changes, the projected tax rate increase slated for the EPI was moderated; instead of doubling from 17.35 to 34.5 percent, it is now expected to grow to 27.8 percent of covered earnings based on recent projections.[8] Of course, this is still a substantial increase in payroll taxes required to support the social security system, and with the government subsidy, the total cost of the retirement system is larger still. Clearly Japan will continue to wrestle with the difficult issue of whether the public will agree to pay these higher taxes in the future, or whether it instead will reduce the public pension promise further (Clark and Ogawa 1996).

2.2. Japanese Company Pension Plans

In the presence of these changes in the EPI and NP, employers and employees must consider how they want employer pensions to evolve. Should mandatory retirement ages be increased to match the new normal retirement ages in the EPI and NP? Should normal retirement ages for employer pensions also be increased? If social security benefits are being reduced, can employer pension benefits be expanded to keep retirement income at previous levels, or will current economic conditions mean that changes in employer pension plans will exacerbate the adverse effects of cuts in social security on retirement income? Given legislated changes in social security, the future of retirement income will be determined in large measure by how employer pensions are changed.

There are three main types of company retirement plans in Japan: unfunded severance benefit plans, the employee pension funds (EPFs), and the tax-qualified pension plans (TQPPs). More than 90 percent of all Japanese employees have severance pay plans that relate termination benefits to years of service and earnings. These are financed from corporate operating revenue (they are book-reserved, for funding purposes). Severance benefits are typically paid as lump sums when workers leave their career employers. The average male retiree from a major corporation receives a severance payment of about ¥25 million (US$208 000) at retirement, equivalent to about 38 months of earnings (Seike 1997).

The average size of severance payments from a large corporation has increased over time (from ¥13 million in 1974, or US$108 000 in today's terms), but it has declined relative to annual earnings. Average monthly earnings rose 3.5 times between 1974 and 1996 (from ¥88 000 to ¥305 000; US$733 to US$2542), while retirement payments less than doubled (Seike 1997). One reason for this decline is the change in formulas used to determine severance pay and a reduction in the proportion of total compensation included in the determination of the benefit. Another reason is that the prevalence of severance plans is declining, as more firms shift from lump-sum payments to pension plans paying annuities. In 1974, 43 percent of large companies had only lump-sum retirement plans and no additional pension plan. By 1996, only 5 percent of all firms relied solely on the severance pay plans for retirement benefits (Seike 1997).

Turning now to more conventional company pension plans, about half of all full-time employees participate in an EPF or a TQPP. There were 1849 EPFs in 1999 covering over 12 million employees (Miyatake 2000), a figure that represents 37 percent of all EPI participants (Employees' Pension Fund Association 1996). By contrast, there were more than 91 000 TQPPs covering over 10 million workers. In the past, Japanese companies were allowed to offer only DB plans of these two types, but 2001 legislation has expanded options for plan choice.

EPF plans were introduced in 1966 to enable firms to provide earnings-related benefits to retired workers over and above the government earnings-related pension. They were established mainly by larger employers with 500 or more employees.[9] These plans were permitted to partially 'contract out' from paying contributions to the government pension system, in exchange for which they committed to provide benefits worth 130 percent of the EPI benefit. Historically, the EPFs have paid 3.2 to 3.8 percent of payroll to finance the contracted-out component of the EPI (Employees' Pension Fund Association 1996). EPF benefits based on the contracted-out or 'substitutional' EPI component may be paid in the form of a life annuity, while supplemental benefits may be lump sum. Approximately 40 percent of beneficiaries opted to take a lump-sum distribution for the supplementary benefits in 1997 (Chunhong 2000). EPFs have been regulated by the Ministry of Health, Labor, and Welfare and have had to meet more reporting and funding standards than other types of Japanese pension plans.

TQPPs were first established in 1962, and they have been adopted by many small and medium-sized firms as well as some larger firms. Companies must have at least 15 employees to establish a TQPP. Most TQPPs are financed entirely from employer contributions though, in theory, employees are permitted to contribute to these plans. Despite their name (tax-qualified pension plans), they are legally subject to an annual asset tax levied on the value of the pension portfolio, worth about 1.173 percent of assets. Most retirees under these plans can elect ten-year certain payouts, but most select a lump-sum option. The TQPPs have been supervised by the Ministry of Finance, historically, which has led to an entirely different set of regulations than those that govern the EPFs.

The growth of EPF pension plans in Japan has produced a DB plan asset pool (EPF plus TQPP) estimated at about US$0.6 trillion, much smaller than the US private sector asset base (Johnson 2001; Sakamoto 2001a). It must also be emphasized that any pension asset estimates are not directly comparable with those from other countries, since Japanese pension plans have traditionally marked assets at book value instead of market value; EPF assets have been marked to market only since 1997. Furthermore, Japanese asset values are currently quite depressed, and pension investment performance has been quite poor of late. The government suggested that pension investment rate of return (ROR) be targeted at 5.5 percent annually and the Corporate Income Tax Law requires that the assumed ROR be at least 5 percent; nevertheless, actual investment returns have been far lower. This is in part because of pension fund managerial conservatism, which is a legacy of the old regulatory 5:3:3:2 rule requiring that plans hold at least 50 percent in secure assets such as long-term government bonds. These rules also limited other investments: caps were 30 percent on domestic stocks, 30 percent in foreign-currency assets and 20 percent in real estate (Gordon 1999). Recent evidence suggests that the EPF plans continue to allocate their portfolios in roughly this manner (Sekine 2001).

Limited evidence indicates that Japanese pensions are currently quite underfunded, at least according to Western standards.[10] Chunhong (2000) and Goldman Sachs (1999) estimate that the total amount of underfunding in private corporate sector pension plans is between 40 and 60 trillion yen (404 to 485 billion US dollars). A 1996 study of 24 Japanese firms listed on the New York Stock Exchange shows that pension assets were worth only 40 percent of liabilities (Gordon 1999). According to data from the Employee Pension Fund Association (Sakamoto 2001a), half of all EPF plans in 1999 had less than 90 percent of the assets needed to cover liabilities, but these calculations do not adopt US-type standards (Cerulli 2001).[11]

Severance pay plans tend to be not funded, and this liability represents yet another 324 to 404 billion US dollars (Goldman Sachs 1999). Such extensive underfunding poses risks for existing DB plans, and it also makes the transition to new DB or defined contribution (DC) plans more difficult.

3. INTRODUCTION OF DC AND NEW DB PLANS

Financial deregulation has been in full swing since the mid-1990s. The major impetus driving this effort was the desire to move toward a system where banks, insurers, securities firms, investment advisors and foreign money managers would compete on a more level playing field (Cargill et al. 1997). For the first time, foreign money managers were permitted entry, companies began (slowly) to adopt international accounting standards and insurance regulation was relaxed (Patrikis 1998).

Accompanying this effort to modernize Japan's financial environment came a change in the rules governing employer-sponsored pensions. The changes were intended to make more flexible the heavily regulated system that previously stifled creativity and short-changed the country's savers (MacIntyre 1998). Nevertheless, this has been a gradual process. For instance, in 1999, the government eliminated the requirement that EPFs liquidate their entire holdings when changing investment managers, and it further eliminated the practice of requiring fixed brokerage commissions on stock trades. Subsequently, investment advisory firms were permitted to manage pension assets, whereas only trust banks and insurers had been allowed to do so previously. Life insurers gained entry to the mutual fund business, and the state-owned postal savings and life insurance bureaus (Yucho and Kampo) received permission to hire specialist investment managers to handle over ¥300 trillion in postal saving system assets (US$2.5 trillion) (Asia Agenda International 2001). As Lincoln and Litan (1998) have noted, it was hoped that 'by allowing Japanese pension funds greater investment freedom – specifically, broader authority to purchase equities, domestic and foreign – the Big Bang [would] help ease the pressure on Japanese corporations to fund their pension plans with current earnings'.

3.1.   The Pension Reform Bill of 2001

The Japanese government took a further step toward modernizing its pension sector in June of 2001 with legislation that alters plan design choices and aspects of existing plans (see Table 6.1). In many ways, this bill continues and extends the process of financial sector reforms implemented during the late 1990s as they apply to pensions.[12]

The pension reform bill contained features pertaining to both DC and DB plans. Focusing first on the defined contribution set, the key elements were (William M. Mercer 2001):

- Companies are permitted to offer DC pensions as of October of 2001.
- A corporate DC plan may be financed by tax-deductible employer contributions. (Employee contributions into such plans are not permitted.) If the plan sponsor has no other pension plan, annual tax-qualified DC contributions are capped at ¥432000 (US$3472); however if another tax-qualified plan is available, the taxable annual maximum DC contribution is reduced to ¥216000 (US$1736).
- A worker whose company offers no other pension may alternatively be offered a DC plan into which he can contribute out of pre-tax earnings up to an annual limit of ¥180000 (US$1447). No employer contributions are permitted in this case. The self-employed may set up DC plans into which they can contribute ¥816000 (US$7700).
- Employer DC plan contributions vest in three years and are portable if the worker changes companies.
- Participants must be provided with at least three investment choices for their DC monies, one of which must be principal-guaranteed. Participants will be able to change investment allocations every three months.
- DC pension payouts may be taken as a lump sum or annuity as early as age 60, and payouts must commence by age 70. A 60-year old must have at least 10 years of participation; the service requirement falls to age 65 after which only one month of service is required.
- Companies must obtain employee permission before instituting a DC plan, and must obtain authorization from at least half of all employees before terminating an old DB plan and moving to a DC plan.

The pension reform bill of June 2001 also contained elements relevant to corporate sponsors of DB plans:

Table 6.1   The Japanese retirement provision system: old and new structures

---

The Pre-2001 Environment[1]
Non-earnings-related publicly-run retirement plan
   National Pension Insurance (NPI)
      20 million self-employed members (type 1)
      39 million private sector employees, civil servants, etc. (type 2)
      12 million insured dependents (type 3)
Earnings-related employer-sponsored partly private, partly public pension plans
   Employee Pension Insurance (EPI)
      33 million members; covers all type 2 members in private sector
   Employee pension plans (EPF)
      12 million members; substitute for some EPI benefits and contributions
   Tax-qualified pension plans (TQPP)
      10 million members
   Lump-sum severance pay plans
      Covers 80% of enterprises (Japan Institute of Labor 2000)
   Mutual aid associations
      6 million members, set up separately from EPI benefits and contributions
      (certain sectors)
Personal provision
   Personal pension plans
   Private saving and family support

Changes Under 2001 Reforms[2]
Tier 1: Non-earnings-related publicly-run retirement plan
   National Pension Scheme (NP): no change
Tier 2: Earnings-related employer-sponsored partly private, partly public pension
plans
   Employee Pension Insurance (EPI): no change
   Employee pension plans (EPF): firms with DB may buy out of substitutional
   EPI component; new DC plans as well as DB plans to be permitted, possibly
   cash balance plans
   Tax-qualified pension plans (TQPP): to be phased out over 10 years
   Mutual aid associations: no change
Tier 3: Personal provision
   New individual pension to be permitted
   Personal pension plans: no change
   Private saving and family support: no change

Sources: 1. Derived from Conrad (2001); 2. Derived from Sakamoto (2001a).

- Companies offering TQPPs will be required to terminate them within a decade (Sakamoto 2001a).
- Employers offering EPF plans will be permitted to divest themselves of the contracted-out 'substitutional' element of their EPF plan (Sakamoto 2001a). This will permit plan sponsors to gain relief from paying that portion of the government earnings-related pension by transferring a lump sum of assets to the government. However, participants in the newly constituted DB plans will no longer be granted an exemption from the asset tax that had been imposed only on TQPPs. The specific rules governing this restructuring of old EPF plans remain to be clarified. The Pension Fund Investment Fund will manage these assets and be responsible for paying the previously contracted-out benefits (Cerulli 2001).

In addition to permitting new DC and DB plans, the 2001 law alters important aspects of the pension regulatory environment.[13]

The most evident change is that the new Ministry of Health, Labor, and Welfare (MHLW) will now supervise and regulate all DB plans as well as all new DC plans. In the past, the Ministry of Finance had supervised TQPP; however, now these plans must be terminated within ten years, and all new plans will be under the regulatory control of the MHLW. How these regulatory and supervisory tasks are to be managed at MHLW has not yet been clarified.

It appears that the severance pay plans mentioned above will be unaffected by this most recent pension law change; if so, they will remain book reserve and unfunded. However, the restructuring of pension plans in response to the 2001 legislation along with the continued evolution of other types of compensation may encourage firms to alter or eliminate their severance pay plans.

3.2.   DC Pensions in Japan: Unsettled Issues

The new legislation on DC plans in Japan differs from that governing US 401(k) plans, which are DC pensions named after the section of the US tax code that established them.[14] In evaluating the 2001 law changes, we have organized our comments about the emerging Japanese DC model according to the four main functions of a pension plan: collecting contributions, recordkeeping and reporting, managing investments, and paying benefits.

Issues pertaining to contributions and membership

Which kinds of workers will be allowed to participate in new DC plans?   In practice, there may be administrative cost reasons to limit entry to workers under (or over) a cutoff age; or to restrict membership to new employees; or to limit participation to full-time workers. In the past, most part-time Japanese employees have not participated in company plans, leaving those workers with low coverage rates.[15]

Rules for DC plan participation in Japan are still being developed: whether these workers will now be included in company pensions, as the labor force becomes more flexible, will be interesting to watch. It is notable that Pasona, the first firm to adopt a DC pension plan in Japan, is a temporary employment agency that offers its part-time employees access to a portable pension program along with full-time workers (Pasona, Inc.). The 2001 regulations specify that the maximum age for employee participation in DC plans must be age 60.

Can the tax-qualified cap on employer contributions be increased, and will employees be allowed to contribute additional funds?   When pension reform legislation was being developed, many analysts and industry leaders expected that the level of tax-qualified contributions permitted in Japanese DC plans would be similar to those in the US 401(k) environment. However, the low employer contribution ceilings in the 2001 bill reflected the government's reluctance to allow more compensation to be protected from tax at a time when the economy was depressed and tax revenues were relatively low, producing fiscal deficits. The tax-qualified employer DC contributions under the new Japanese law are capped at an annual US$3472, about 6 percent of annual salary (Cerulli 1999).[16]

Additionally, no matching employee contributions are permitted to these plans in Japan. By contrast, in the United States, employee contributions to a 401(k) plan may total $10500 per year, a legal limit slated to rise to $15000 in 2006. In addition, US employers can match employee contributions: the combined employer and employee DC cap is now $35000, and it will rise to $40000 by 2006 (Portman and Cardin 2001). New regulations allowing employee contributions in Japan would likely enhance the appeal of the DC model.

To help assess what a maximum contribution of about US$3500 might generate over work lives of various lengths for Japanese workers, we have prepared Table 6.2. This indicates the approximate accumulation value and an implied annuity payout of a DC plan over ten, 20 and 30 years of contributions. For example, after 30 years of investing the maximum contribution in a relatively safe asset such as might be permitted in the new Japanese DC environment, the worker could amass almost US$122000 (assuming a relatively conservative 1 percent real return). The annuity value of such an accumulation might be worth at most about US$8300 per year for men, or about 14 percent of current average earnings.[17] The benefits are much

Table 6.2   Estimated real value of Japanese DC account accumulation and annual benefit if annuitized

Years of saving	Retirement accumulation ($)	Annuitized single life value ($)	
		Men	Women
10	36618	2497	1904
20	77067	5255	4008
30	121747	8301	6331

Notes: Assumes maximum contribution of US$3500 (real) per year; 1% real rate of return on assets pre- and post-retirement; no mortality prior to retirement; no investment fees or insurance loading; single-life annuity; and EPF (sex-specific) tables after retirement at age 65.

Source: Authors' computations.

smaller for shorter contribution periods: for instance after ten years of saving, the annual payout would come to at most $2500 or about 4 percent of current average earnings.

One factor that might make DC plan establishment more appealing in Japan is the possibility that companies could fund a new such plan by contributing a tax-free lump sum recognizing workers' past service. It has been suggested that this would be equivalent to the annual maximum DC contribution level multiplied by each worker's years of service, plus a credit of the guaranteed rate of return promised by the DB plan – traditionally 5.5 percent (Cerulli 2001). While this might jump-start the formation of DC plans, coming up with the lump sum might be difficult for firms that severely underfunded DB plans. A related issue is that the government has signaled a willingness to permit firms to terminate an old DB plan and move surplus assets into the new DC plan. We discuss this possibility below in more detail.

Issues pertaining to recordkeeping
One lesson from the US market is that recordkeeping requires a substantial investment in information technology and a clean system of tracking individual participants (Mitchell 1998). While Japan has no system of unique taxpayer identification numbers, it has recently adopted a system of social security numbers to assist in the management of retirement accounts. In the past, the lack of unique identification numbers has made it difficult to both collect taxes and track employee accounts (Anderson 1999). The fact that the new DC plans will be very small at the outset also exacerbates the start-

up administrative and recordkeeping cost problems. If frequent fund transfers are permitted, this will also make it more costly to provide plan reporting and recordkeeping.

As a result, some have expressed concern that the likely small initial size of Japanese DC accounts will render the business unprofitable. For instance, Ruffell (2001) argues that 'U.S. experience shows that recordkeeping has proven in the main a distinctly unprofitable enterprise'. Unless economies of scale and scope are perceived, this line of business in Japan will likely not prove very profitable in the short term. Thus Cerulli (1999) estimates that until DC accounts amount to at least US$80 billion, recordkeepers will not break even. On the other hand, Sumitomo predicts that it will take only three years to cover start-up costs, and Fidelity has suggested that its expertise in the 401(k) market should help that firm arrive at breakeven sooner (Anderson 1999).

Issues pertaining to investment management of DC plans

Who will manage the money?   There is substantial controversy about who will manage the money in the new Japanese DC framework. Some analysts estimate that 75 percent of new funds flowing into these plans will be principal-guaranteed products (Anderson 1999); others note that '[i]n the short term, there will be a preference for capital guaranteed-type products and that will favour in the short-term domestic players and not foreign players' (Johnson 2001).

Additionally, Western experts suggest that

> [DC plans require] a population willing to take advantage of newly available financial instruments. But the Japanese public remains distinctively risk averse in its investment decisions, keeping a high share of its savings in the form of bank accounts and insurance policies. It is not at all clear that many people will broaden their savings portfolios to include asset-backed securities, foreign mutual funds, derivatives, foreign bank accounts, and other investment opportunities. In the absence of an eager household sector, financial deregulation could leave the Japanese financial system under the continued domination of banks, which may end up as the primary holders of the new financial instruments. (Lincoln and Litan 1998)

Based on the US experience, it would not be surprising if, during the early phases, DC plan participants tended to select fairly conservative investment holdings; on the other hand, they will be more likely to move to a more diversified portfolio, after learning more about the options. This process will be influenced by the investment choices selected by plan sponsors, who select the types of options made available in their fiduciary role.

How will investors be educated about risk and return?   An interesting set of issues not yet settled in the changing Japanese pension environment is how plan sponsors and managers will handle a whole new set of responsibilities that heretofore they have not had to worry about. For example, plan sponsors must now ensure that contributions are actually invested; they must choose participant investment options; and they must also select and evaluate money managers. In the future, they will have to educate participants about risk and return.[18]

Eventually, they must see that benefits are paid. Some argue that DC plans are, in fact, 'un-Japanese' and that it will be difficult to educate workers on how to manage their portfolios since they are not accustomed to taking this responsibility. However, as one expert notes, 'Japan has a math-literate population that will quickly grasp investment concepts . . . the empowerment of the individual could be surprisingly strong where they can participate in the market, and believe it to be a fair and well-regulated arena' (Global Custodian 1998).

A related but not well-appreciated point is that the Japanese government is slowly altering its position on guaranteeing bank savings deposits. In particular, instead of providing a 100 percent guarantee as in the past, the government has indicated that only the first US$85000 of assets will be protected at some point in the future (this would amount to only 30 percent of Japanese bank deposits) (Anderson 1999). Eliminating the full guarantee for all benefits is being phased in, and this change might powerfully alter DC plan participants' views of the principal-guaranteed investment option mandated for the plan.

Will the new defined contribution plans be subject to tax on inside buildup? Japan has a tradition of exempting contributions into pension plans but taxing the asset value of the TQPP pension fund. The tax of 1.173 percent on the value of TQPP assets was suspended until 2003, in view of the very low returns being earned by pension fund assets over the last decade. It is not known at present whether the suspension will be continued or the tax reimposed. Inevitably, imposition of such a high tax on Japanese pension funds that are invested in assets with extraordinarily low returns will discourage new pension formation.

Issues pertaining to payouts

How will portability and vesting be handled?   At this juncture, little is known about how the new Japanese DC pension system will function in terms of vesting and portability. In the DC context, vesting refers to workers' claims on plan accumulations if they leave their employers prior to retirement. US employer contributions must be vested after five years, and the majority of 401(k) plans allow vesting earlier than that (one-third allow immediate vesting) (Mitchell 2003). Job-changing workers in the United States are permitted to preserve their tax-qualified vested accumulations by moving the funds into either a new employer plan or into a 'rollover' account handled by a licensed investment manager (McGill et al. 1996). The new regulations in Japan allow workers who change jobs to move all vested accumulations from one DC plan into another offered by the new employer. If the new employer does not offer such a plan, the worker can leave the funds with the old employer's plan, or he/she may move them to the National Pension Fund Association. The new Japanese pension laws require that all employer contributions be vested after three years. While portability is specifically recognized in the regulations, the mechanism for exchanging pension assets across firms is as yet unclear.

What about other types of payouts?   In addition to rollover payouts, a set of rules must be written to govern pension payouts at retirement. It appears that the minimum age at which workers will be permitted to access the funds (known as the preservation age in some circles) will be 60 for the new Japanese DC plans. This is interesting since the national pension system's normal retirement age is slated to rise to 65. The difference in the retirement ages under the two systems may create potentially unexpected incentives. As an illustration, retirees in Australia may access their entire DC accounts at 60 and spend down the entire amounts prior to eligibility for a means-tested national benefit at 65 (Bateman et al. 2002). However, in Japan, some employers and older workers may anticipate that the company DC plan will support retirement consumption between age 60 and the age at which they are eligible to receive social security benefits.

This also illustrates the important interaction between the preservation age and how the funds can be accessed. In the United States, many 401(k) plans provide lump-sum payouts and only about one-quarter offer an annuity option (Mitchell 2003). Allowing job changers to access their entire DC accumulations may undermine the plan's purpose as a retirement saving vehicle. An immediate spend-down is discouraged in the United States; although 401(k) plan participants may receive their entire account in a lump sum if they wish, someone over age 70 must pay income tax on the entire lump sum, and a retiree younger than 59½ pays income tax as well as a 20 percent penalty on the sum. Another concern is that people may not buy inflation-indexed annuities with their DC accumulations, leaving them vulnerable to inflation and longevity risk (J. Brown et al. 2001).

3.3. DB Pensions in Japan: Unsettled Issues

Just as several questions remain that, until they are clarified, will retard the development of DC plans in Japan, similar questions arise concerning the continued use of DB plans. These issues are organized according to the four main functions of a pension plan: collecting contributions, recordkeeping and reporting, managing investments, and paying benefits.

Issues pertaining to membership and contributions

What types of plans will be permitted?   Under the new pension law and regulations, there will clearly be a continued commitment to traditional DB plans in Japan, although many of these will now lack the contracting-out substitutional element previously found in the EPFs. There is also widespread belief that cash-balance or hybrid schemes will be allowed, although the method for establishment of such plans remains to be developed. Given the very low 'safe' asset returns in Japan currently, it appears that hybrid plans could offer guaranteed rates of return only just over 1 percent (Cerulli 2001). The lower the guaranteed rate of return, the less appealing are cash balance plans. Unless foreign investment is pushed strongly as part of the funds portfolio, the low returns on domestic Japanese assets will make it more difficult to offer higher returns. Legally, hybrid plans will be DB plans, just as they are in the United States (Feinberg 2001a).

Who will establish these new DB plans?   A company that previously sponsored a DB plan might consider moving to a new DB plan depending on the type of plan it offered and its funding status:

- If a firm previously offered a TQPP, it must now terminate the plan within ten years. As noted above, plan sponsors are typically smaller (15 employees and up), and they have tended to pay mainly lump-sum benefits due to tax preferences. It appears that underfunding is a substantial problem in this sector, which may be a constraint if firms with TQPPs seek to set up new DB or DC plans.
- If a firm previously provided an EPF with the substitutional element, it may be entitled to buy out of the substitutional or contracted-out portion of the EPF plan by presenting the government with a satisfactory asset transfer to cover the buy-back. After this transfer is made, an EPF plan might or might not have sufficient assets to continue as a reformulated DB plan (without the contracted-out portion), or to move toward a DC plan. Alternatively, the former-EPF plan may be allowed to amortize unfunded liabilities over a

20-year period after covering its obligation for the substitutional amount. Final regulations on these issues are still evolving. (Sakamoto 2001b)

One key factor affecting the decision to offer a new DB plan is how the company's employees would react to the change. According to Japanese labor law, at least 50 percent of all employees must agree to convert a company pension from a DB to a DC plan. As an alternative, however, some firms have been allowed to terminate their old DB plan without obtaining the 50 percent permission and have issued a lump-sum cash payout to discharge their old plan obligations. EPF plans can only be terminated with the approval of 75 percent of their trustees (Sakamoto 2001b). At some future date, such companies may start up a new plan (defined benefit or defined contribution). In other words, a firm's plan choice under the new rules will be influenced by the extent of underfunding in its old DB plan as well as workers' agreement. If the plan has assets insufficient to cover the substitutional component of the EPF, it would be less likely to adopt a new plan.

A related issue is how the old EPF plan obligations are to be calculated when determining the assets sufficient to permit divestiture of the contracted-out portion. Regulations are still in flux regarding the buyout price for the EPF substitutional benefit. One approach might require valuing workers' and retirees' accumulated benefit obligations (ABOs) and setting aside assets sufficient to cover that portion of plan benefits. In this event, the choice of a discount rate becomes of paramount importance. Using a high rate shrinks future liabilities and makes it easier to set aside assets adequate to achieve the buy-back. Another possibility suggested by Japanese pension experts is that a firm might have to ante up a lump-sum equivalent to foregone contributions relative to the substitutional element in the EPF plan, plus very likely a low rate of return.

Will employee contributions be permitted? The old EPF plans did permit employers and employees to share the financing of the substitutional component of the plan benefits. Similarly the TQPPs were permitted to have employee contributions although, in most cases, employers contributed the entire amounts (Conrad 2001). It is not yet clear whether the new DB plans will be permitted to take employee contributions on a voluntary or mandatory basis.

Will the new DB plans be subject to tax on inside buildup? As noted above, the 1.173 percent of assets tax on TQPP pensions is in suspension currently, but the plan is to reinstate the tax in 2003. Old DB plans may have little in the way of assets to tax. The asset tax may become important when the new DB plans amass some assets.

Issues pertaining to recordkeeping

Will recordkeeping and reporting change for those employers remaining with conventional DB plans alone? According to available information, publicly traded firms providing DB plans in Japan must move to implement international accounting standards. This will require recognizing pension liabilities using more realistic discount rates and presumably will also lead to market valuation in measuring pension assets (Choy 1999).

How will recordkeeping change if cash balance plans are permitted? If cash balance or hybrid plans are accounted for as DB plans, as they are in the United States, this will require the recordkeeping and reporting mentioned above, as well as the need to track and report on contributions made on individual workers' behalf, plus investment returns and individual accumulations.

Issues pertaining to investment management of DB plans

How might DB investment change? As part of the Big Bang financial liberalization process, DB plan managers will no longer be required to assume that assets will return 5.5 percent per annum when projecting future pension costs. To the extent that plan sponsors do assume more realistic (and likely far lower) returns consistent with long-term Japanese patterns, this will reduce the chance that the newly-formed DB plans will become seriously underfunded. In addition, adopting modern investment strategies could also boost investment performance and enhance DB plan appeal, an avenue that institutional investors have already begun to explore. The Employees' Pension Fund Association in Tokyo, which oversees EPF pension management, recently introduced concepts of risk management to its member managers. Noboru Terada, a member of the Investment Expert Committee of the Government Pension Investment Fund, has expressed strong interest in indexing so as to hold down fees (Feinberg 2001b). Terada has also pushed for a clearer statement of pension fiduciary responsibility, along the lines of the US ERISA law (Global Custodian 1998).

Will investment patterns become more diversified? To the extent that domestic asset returns remain depressed, it will remain difficult for DB plan sponsors to meet investment targets and to avoid underfunding. For this reason, DB plans are increasingly investing outside Japan. For instance, in

1998, Sony indicated that it would move a substantial component of its pension assets outside Japan in the hopes of reaping better rewards (Global Custodian 1998). Further, Honda Motor Co. has invested almost half its US$4.6 billion pension fund outside Japan (MacDonald 1998).

Issues pertaining to payouts

How will annuities be handled? When the EPFs were integrated with the government earnings-related pension, the plan sponsor was responsible for base nominal benefits but not for the inflation–indexation component of the EPI benefit. Whether the de-integration of DB plan benefits will alter this policy has not yet been clarified.

4. PENSION PLAN DEVELOPMENTS IN THE UNITED STATES

For the past 25 years, employer pension plans in the United States have been moving away from traditional DB plans, toward DC and various types of hybrid plans, especially cash balance plans. These developments have been in response to changes in government regulations that increased the cost of DB plans, new tax policies that permitted pre-tax employee contributions to 401(k) plans, changes in the composition of the labor force, and fluctuations in the rate of economic growth. This section provides a brief history of the continuing evolution of occupational pensions in the United States. These developments and their causes can be compared to the current situation in Japan with the hope that analysis of US trends can provide some insights into the possible development of Japanese pension plans in the coming decade.

4.1. Developments in US DB Pensions

Historically, pensions in the United States were primarily final pay, DB plans that provided early retirement subsidies to many employees. These plans were especially prominent among large, unionized employers, and in the public sector. Since the mid-1970s, there has been a dramatic and continuing movement away from the use of DB plans and toward greater adoption of DC plans. More than 80 percent of pension participants were covered by a DB plan in 1979, but by the mid-1990s, coverage by such plans had declined to only 50 percent of pension participants (PBGC 1999). The rapid growth of DC plans is attributed to changes in government regulation that increased the cost of DB plans relative to DC ones, especially for small plans (Clark and McDermed 1990). As a result, virtually no small employers now offer DB pensions. In addition, regulations permitting the development of 401(k) plans stimulated a rapid growth in these plans that allow pre-tax employer and employee contributions (Papke 1999). DC plans tend to be more portable, and today's employees seem to place a greater emphasis on these individual account plans that can be taken with them when they change jobs.

In the last 15 years, some larger firms transformed their traditional DB plans into so-called hybrid or cash balance pensions. Legally these are classified as DB pensions, but they have many characteristics of DC plans. BankAmerica created the first hybrid pension in 1985. During the 1990s, the number of plan conversions increased and, by 2000, some 400 US companies had adopted a cash balance plan. Today, about 20 percent of the Fortune 500 firms offer cash balance plans (Cerulli 2001).

Companies that establish cash balance pensions offer workers a mix of features taken from both DB and DC designs. Table 6.3 illustrates key features of DB and DC plans and compares them to cash balance provisions. Many contribution and participation features of a cash balance plan are similar to those of traditional DB plans, rather than to most DC plans, which allow employees to make decisions about participation and contribution rates. On the other hand, cash balance plans largely eliminate penalties for workers who terminate employment prior to retirement, which makes them similar to DC plans. The accumulation of accounts and provision of lump-sum benefits at termination facilitate communication and portability like 401(k) plans.

Cash balance plans alleviate some but not all of the financial market risks faced by workers in self-directed DC plans. This is because a worker's account balance is credited with an annual rate of return equal to some specific rate such as the T-bill rate, selected usually by the employer. This reduces the employee's exposure to investment risk in a DC plan. The plan sponsor does retain investment risk in cash balance plans, but the investment return promised workers is typically set so earnings on plan assets are anticipated to cover the guarantee. The worker still retains some residual investment risk in a cash balance plan, since benchmark rates used for crediting of returns to accounts will change over time. Nevertheless, the expectation would be that these will be less volatile than stock market returns. The participant also faces the risk that the plan sponsor might change the benchmark crediting rate over time.

Cash balance plans also have other differences from traditional DB pensions. One key feature is that they are more age-neutral than traditional DB plans in their retirement incentives. This arises because they tend not to have early retirement subsidies, as depicted in Figure 6.2. This illustrates the

Table 6.3 *Features of US employer-sponsored retirement plans*

Plan feature	DB plan	DC plan	Cash balance plan	Cash balance tendency
Employer contributes	Virtually always	Sometimes	Virtually always	DB
Employee contributes	Very rarely	Virtually always	Very rarely	DB
Participation	Automatic	Employee choice	Automatic	DB
Contribution level	Automatic	Employee choice	Automatic	DB
PBGC Insurance	Yes but capped	Not needed	Yes but capped	DB
Early departure penalty	Yes	No	No	DC
Benefits easily portable	No	Yes	Yes	DC
Annual communication	Benefit at end of career	Current balance	Current balance	DC
Retirement incentives	Occur at specific ages	Neutral	Most are neutral	DC
Accrual of benefits	Loaded to career end	Level over career	Level or back loaded	Mixed
Financial market risks	Employer bears	Employee bears	Shared	Mixed
Longevity insurance	Typically yes	Typically no	Not often taken	Mixed

Source: Clark, Haley, and Schieber (2001).

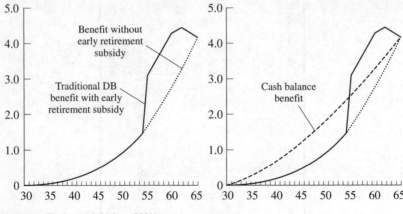

Source: Clark and Schieber (2001).

Figure 6.2   *Value of accrued pension benefit as a multiple of annual wage*
at various ages for a new hire at age 30 with a starting wage of
$40000 per year

typical backloaded accrual pattern common to conventional DB pensions, and the much smoother accrual pattern pertinent to the typical cash balance plan. Another difference is that US cash balance plans must offer an annuity as a benefit option since they are legally DB plans; most also offer lump-sum benefits. Anecdotal evidence suggests that the overwhelming majority of workers takes lump-sum benefits when offered the choice under these plans.

4.2.   Changing Views on Retirement Plan Design

A decade of US economic expansion, accompanied by a slower rate of growth in the labor force, has had a powerful impact on many companies' human resource policies. Previously, older workers were encouraged to retire so they could be replaced by lower-cost younger workers. More recently, employers have sought new methods to retain senior employees as hiring young workers became difficult. The composition of the labor force has also changed, prompting employers to accommodate the preferences of a more diverse and more mobile workforce.

These changes in the US labor market environment are manifested in changes in pension plan offerings and plan design. One development is that some firms have altered their DB plans to stop encouraging workers to retire in their fifties and early sixties. Research shows that eliminating early retirement subsidies in a traditional DB plan greatly curtails retirement benefits for many employees, whereas converting to a cash balance plans can mitigate this benefit change (Clark and Schieber 2001).

Another development is that companies are changing the entire structure and composition of employee compensation (K. Brown et al. 2000). Thus, converting a defined benefit into a cash balance plan is also sometimes accompanied by changes in retiree health insurance provisions, or changes in contribution rates to supplemental retirement accounts. Companies have also reduced pension costs and then used cost savings to offer more competitive non-pension compensation. Many US employers have focused on retaining productive senior employees, so that changes in pay and benefits reflect this new perspective.

A further explanation for the US trend to DC and cash balance plans is that workers often have difficulty understanding the value provided in DB plans. As a result, they may not value the expenses associated with traditional DB pensions (Clark and Munzenmaier 2001). Financial concerns have also influenced employer decisions to shift from traditional DB to cash balance plans. This is because cash balance benefit accruals are smoother and more predictable throughout workers' careers, as compared to accruals in traditional DB plans. This sometimes stabilizes the stream of employer contributions needed to cover cash balance plans.

In some instances, US employees have argued that their employer may have used a cash balance conversion to limit or reduce the employer's expenditures on pension benefits. However, the evidence indicates that the results are more disparate. Some companies have lower costs after plan conversion, while others increase retirement expenditures; furthermore, many companies have essentially the same retirement costs before and afterward (K. Brown et al. 2000). It has been claimed that some firms shifted to a cash balance plan when the traditional DB plans were overfunded. This conjecture is widely believed; however, the data show that many traditional DB plans that were not converted to cash balance plans were just as well-funded as those that were converted (Clark et al. 2001).

4.3. Worker Preferences for Retirement Plan Type

Limited evidence indicates that workers prefer some of the characteristics in Table 6.3 that hybrid plans share with DC plans. Foremost among these is the element of individual accounts. It has been found that workers better understand having their own individual account balances, as compared to assessing the value of future benefits under a traditional DB plan (Third Millennium 1999; Clark and Munzenmaier 2001).

Another important feature of retirement plans with individual accounts is that the vested account balance is immediately available to a worker if he/she leaves the firm at any age. In other words, the current value of the pension is the same whether the worker remains with the firm or quits. In contrast, traditional DB plans tend to be backloaded, as discussed above, paying greater benefits to someone who remains with the firm until at least the age of early retirement. The portability feature of cash balance plans and DC plans is important to the increasingly diverse labor force in the United States. Young workers in today's labor force are less likely to believe that they will work for the same firm for 30 or 40 years. Instead, expectations are that they will change jobs several times and, as a result, they are more likely to demand retirement plans that have portable benefits.

4.4. Implications for Japanese Pension Plans

What implications might these US developments over the past three decades have for Japanese pension plans in the twenty-first century? What are the parallels that could lead to predictions about how Japanese plans will evolve? First, it seems clear that, in the United States, the emergence of DC plans was driven, in part, by changes in regulations and tax policy. In the 1970s, the US government adopted regulatory policies that sharply increased the cost of DB plans relative to DC plans, especially among small firms. In addition, changes in tax laws in the 1980s allowed the development of new types of DC plans based on employee contributions, the 401(k) plans. New changes in tax and regulatory policy may stimulate similar changes in Japan. However, as we have noted, the caps on employer contributions to DC plans in Japan are much more restrictive than in the United States, and current regulations do not allow both employer and employee contributions to the same plans.

Second, changes in the composition of the US labor force have increased the demand for more portable pensions. Worker preferences for individual accounts, the option of lump-sum distributions based on accruals to date, less backloading of benefits, and easier-to-understand pension plans have also played a major role in the movement toward DC and hybrid pension plans. As the Japanese system of industrial relations continues to evolve, these issues may become increasingly important to Japanese workers. In such a context, the growth of DC plans will proceed more rapidly.

Third, the recent period of rapid US economic growth, in conjunction with a slowly growing labor force, has induced employers to develop human resource policies that retain older workers. Traditional DB plans embody important early retirement incentives, put in place during an era when employers were attempting to encourage early retirement. The Japanese labor force is also ageing very rapidly, and the government is prodding companies to raise retirement ages. While the economic stagnation in Japan implies that companies are relatively uninterested in retaining older employees, the long-term demographic shift may stimulate modifications in pension policies along the lines seen in the United States.

The importance of these factors in Japan will help determine the growth of DC and cash balance plans during the next decade. The US experience clearly illustrates that, under certain conditions, the transition from a system of mainly DB pensions to one relying heavily on DC plans can be quite rapid.

5. DISCUSSION AND CONCLUSIONS

During the 2001 Japanese pension reform debate, plan sponsors, financial analysts and many Japanese government officials indicated interest in reforming the nation's pension system. The 2001 legislation will surely spur the formation of new plans and the termination of some old ones. Despite the fact that a full set of regulations is not yet fully specified, some companies are already taking the initiative. Two large financial firms, Nomura Securities Co. and Nikko Securities Co., recently announced they will be withdrawing from their multi-employer DB association known as the Japan Securities Dealers Employees Pension Fund, to set up DC plans (Singer 2001). This is consistent with Ruffell's view (2001) that many companies wish to relieve themselves of the old DB plans:

> The unfunded pension liabilities of corporate Japan defy measurement and they are growing daily – an awful domestic equity market, compounded by the truly woeful historic performance of the trust banks which manage the overwhelming bulk of institutional funds in Japan, has ensured that Japanese corporations have done nothing but contribute year after year into their defined benefit plans. For all the talk about Japan's societal need for defined benefit plans, an exodus of Japanese corporations fleeing a debilitating defined benefit framework for a less onerous defined contribution system can be taken as a given.

Plan redesign is taking place against the context of important, if slow, changes in the Japanese labor market. Large employers are less committed to and less able to guarantee lifetime employment, unemployment is rising, and pension benefits are changing along with the rest of compensation. In 1999, Nissan Motors laid off 21 000 workers in an attempt to cut costs. Some companies, including Sumitomo Chemical, have even reduced retiree benefits; others curtailed prospective benefits by raising the retirement age from 60 to 65 (Anderson 1999). These changes signal massive changes in the Japanese labor market, previously marked by lifetime employment and extraordinarily low levels of joblessness.

Even with the economic troubles plaguing Japan's macroeconomy, companies will still need to supply pensions, and employees will still demand pensions, for the same reasons they wanted them in the past. It also seems clear that as new accounting standards increase corporate and pension system transparency, Japanese firms will be increasingly interested in capping liabilities for pension benefits and severance pay. An alternative to reducing pension costs could be to flatten age/earnings profiles, and evidence suggests this is in fact starting to occur in Japan (Seike 1997).

Informed opinion in Japan is extraordinarily divided regarding the likelihood of the DC plan model taking off in Japan. Some experts are very positive, arguing that the 'scope of the DC market . . . [is] between U.S. $193–770B' (Cornell nd). By contrast, the US 401(k) market today amounts to over US$2.3 trillion. Another positive view is Johnson's (2001), which suggests that the total pension asset pool to be created by the new pension law is larger still, at US$777 billion. The bet here is that DC assets will grow faster in Japan than current wisdom has it. Some 16 percent of 128 listed Japanese firms surveyed indicated they were actively considering introducing a DC plan, and only 18 percent indicated they had no intention of changing their plan type (Dow Jones 1999).

A less optimistic assessment comes from Cerulli, which projects the DC market at only US$48 billion over the next five years (Anderson 1999). In fact, this influential research group has stated that 'DC plans remain the biggest mirage in the Japanese asset management industry' (Cerulli 2001), because of their low contribution ceiling and the persistent underfunding problem makes it difficult for firms to exit their DB plans. And of course the adoption of a DC plan, either solo or as a second-tier plan on top of a DB pension, will not alone solve the enormous underfunding problem associated with DB plans in Japan. As noted by Matsuura (2000), 'the shift is likely to take several decades'.

Some experts argue that instead of setting up DC plans, Japanese companies will move to cash balance plans because

> [They are] better suited (than defined contribution plans) for Japanese society . . . Many Japanese people like saving by using banks or the post office authority rather than investments such as bonds or equities, so many people will support cash balance plans (which don't require investment decisions by the employee) rather than defined contribution plans. (Feinberg 2001a)

Others concur, and Feinberg noted further that: 'cash balance plans are between defined benefit and defined contribution plans and look better suited to the beginners' (Feinberg 2001a). In addition, experts estimate that they may offer a guaranteed rate of return below the 4–5 percent currently assumed in DB plans, which should enhance their appeal to plan sponsors (Feinberg 2001a).

On the surface, it may appear that the key factors that have spurred growth in the US cash-balance and DC arena over the last decade are not central to Japanese conditions today. Labor demand is far from robust; workers still do not change employers very frequently; traditional DB plans are underfunded; asset returns are low; and the new DC pensions do not have a particularly favorable tax environment. And as we have shown, many questions remain to be answered, particularly regarding the DC plan blueprint. Nevertheless, the fact that some major Japanese companies have already adopted DC plans presages greater momentum when the economy picks up again. If liberalized somewhat, the new pension models outlined by the 2001 legislation could provide Japanese savers an opportunity to diversify their investments so as to permit greater return with low risk. The recently enacted Japanese pension law will not turn all Japanese employer-sponsored pensions into 401(k)-style plans overnight, but it will make a contribution to modernizing the structure of Japanese compensation and retirement provision. In sum, the 2001 legislation could well signal the beginning of a 'Big Bang' transformation in pay, benefits, and mobility for the Japanese labor market, and change Japanese workers from 'savers' into 'investors'.

NOTES

* Originally published as 'Strengthening employment-based pensions in Japan', by Robert L. Clark and Olivia S. Mitchell in *Benefits Quarterly*, 2nd Quarter, 2002, 22–43. It is reprinted with permission; copyright International Society of Certified Employee Benefit Specialists, Inc., Brookfield, Wisconsin, USA.
** The authors are grateful for financial support for this research from the Economic and Social Research Institute and the National Bureau of Economic Research. Without implicating them, we have benefited from discussions with many experts, most recently Harald Conrad, Tatsuo Hatta, Charles Yuji Horioka, Milton Isa, Sumio Morita, Shinichi Nishiyama, Naohiro Ogawa, Junichi Sakamoto, Atsushi Seike, Kenji Sekine, William Shipman, Noriyuki Takayama, Masaharu Usuki, and Bill Wilder. Any errors and all opinions remain the authors' own. This study is part of the NBER program on the Economics of Ageing.
1. Japan is currently the most rapidly aging country in the world. This aging reflects a very low total fertility rate of approximately 1.3, and high life expectancy of 77 years for men and 84 years for women. Projections indicate that the proportion of the population aged 65 and older will increase from about 15 percent in 1995 to 27 percent by 2025 and the absolute size of the Japanese population will begin to decline in the five years (Ministry of Health, Labor, and Welfare 1999; Miyatake 2000).
2. For example, the index of the stock market (Nikkei 225 stock index) fell from just under 40000 in the late 1980s to around 15000 during the 1990s. The unemployment rate rose from 2 percent at the beginning of the 1990s to 5.3 percent in September 2001. In addition, average land prices in Tokyo plummeted during this period and interest rates hover near zero.

3. Prior to 1986, the NP covered only persons who were not included in the Employees' Pension Insurance system. Reforms introduced in 1986 expanded the NP to include participants in the EPI and, in essence, the NP became a universal retirement program (Ministry of Health, Labor, and Welfare 1999).
4. Throughout this chapter, yen figures are converted to US dollars in 2001 at a rate of US$1 = ¥120.
5. The amount of monies transferred by the EPI is determined every year by the number of insured employees paying into the EPI (aged 20 to 59 years) and the number of their dependent spouses (aged 20 to 59 years).
6. Benefits taken at age 60 are 70 percent of the age 65 benefit. If the initial acceptance of benefits is delayed until age 70, the benefit is 142 percent of the age 65 benefit (Sakamoto 2001b).
7. The higher normal retirement age will be phased in over the next two decades. Persons born after 2 April 1961 will be eligible for full benefits for both the flat benefit and earnings-related benefit at age 65.
8. If the government were to try to adjust benefits to the level of revenue supplied by the current 17.35 percent payroll tax, we estimate that benefits would have to decline by more than one-third. This estimate is based on the simple calculation that if a specified benefit level requires 27.8 percent of covered earnings (0.278 times the wage base provides sufficient revenues for an average benefit), then a tax rate of 17.35 percent of covered earnings would provide sufficient income for benefits that were 62 percent of the initial benefit level (17.35/27.8 = 0.62).
9. An individual company with at least 500 employees can establish an EPF. Allied companies can organize an EPF provided that they have 800 employees. Multi-company EPFs can be established provided that the plan sponsor has 3000 participants. (Employees' Pension Fund Association 1996).
10. Underfunding in the pension context refers to a gap between the pension plan assets and accrued liabilities. In the DB context, under US private sector pension law, a plan would be underfunded if its assets valued at current market prices were less than the accumulated benefit obligation (ABO); see McGill et al. (1996).
11. More specifically, 0.8 percent of EPF plans had assets that were less than 60 percent of liabilities, 8.8 percent of plans were between 60 and 70 percent, 21.6 percent of plans were between 70 and 80 percent, 19.8 percent were between 80 and 90 percent, and 18.0 percent of all EPFs had funding between 90 and 100 percent of assets (Sakamoto 2001a).
12. Cerulli (1999, 2000) has a useful discussion of the various players in the Japanese financial market and why they supported earlier versions of DC pension legislation in Japan.
13. The Financial Services Agency will supervise the function of financial institutions that are managing the assets of pension funds.
14. For more on 401(k) plans in the US context see McGill et al. (1996).
15. This is similar to the United States, where part-time employees have much lower pension coverage rates than full-time employees.
16. A firm that offers another tax-qualified plan is limited to an employer maximum DC of only US$1736 per year. A self-employed worker may contribute US$7700 to a tax-qualified plan, and an employee lacking any company plan may contribute up to US$1447 on a tax-qualified basis.
17. This computation uses the Japanese EPF annuitant table and assumes no loads and no administrative costs; see McCarthy and Mitchell (2000).
18. Pension plans with individual accounts that require employees to make contribution and investment decisions necessitate that workers have a certain degree of financial literacy. Important issues for discussion include the extent of worker knowledge of financial markets, their understanding of the investment process, and the role of companies in the provision of such education. These issues are also receiving considerable attention in the United States (Clark and d'Ambrosio 2001).

REFERENCES

Anderson, Jenny (1999), 'Ready to rumble', *Institutional Investor Online*, 1 November, http://www.iimagazine.com/channel/definedcontributions/199911010360.html, viewed 5 August 2001.

Asia Agenda International (2001), 'Big Bang's burning pension fuse', *Japan Pensions Industry Database*, http://www.asiagenda.com/timer.html, viewed 4 August 2001.

Bateman, Hazel, Geoffrey Kingston and John Piggott (2002), *Forced Saving: Mandating Private Retirement Income*, Cambridge: Cambridge University Press.

Brown, Jeffrey, Olivia S. Mitchell, James Poterba and Mark Warshawsky (2001), *The Role of Annuity Markets in Financing Retirement*, Cambridge, MA: MIT Press.

Brown, Kyle, Gordon Goodfellow, Tomeka Hill, Richard Joss, Richard Luss, Lex Miller and Sylvester Schieber (2000), *The Unfolding of a Predictable Surprise*, Bethesda, MD: Watson Wyatt Worldwide.

Cargill, Thomas, Michael Hutchison and Takatoshi Ito (1997), 'Japan's "Big Bang" financial deregulation: implications for regulatory and supervisory policy', *Japan Information Access Project*, June, http://www.nmjc.org/jiap/dereg/papers/deregcon/hutchison.html, viewed 4 August 2001.

Cerulli Associates (1999), *Trends in the Japanese Asset Management Marketplace*, The Cerulli Report, Boston, MA: Cerulli Associates, Inc.

Cerulli Associates (2001), *Japanese Asset Management*, The Cerulli Report, Boston, MA: Cerulli Associates, Inc.

Choy, John (1999), 'Japan securities industry: from Big Bang to E-Boom', *Japan Economic Institute Report*, 22A, 11 June.

Chunhong, Chan (2000), 'An overview of Japan pension system and pension reform', unpublished paper, Tokyo: NLI Research Institute.

Clark, Robert (1991), *Retirement Systems in Japan*, Homewood, IL: Irwin (Pension Research Council).

Clark, Robert and Madeleine d'Ambrosio (2001), 'Financial education and retirement savings', unpublished paper, North Carolina State University.

Clark, Robert, John Haley and Sylvester Schieber (2001), 'Adopting hybrid pension plans: financial and communication issues', *Benefits Quarterly*, **17** (1), 7–18.

Clark, Robert and Ann McDermed (1990), *The Choice of a Pension Plan in a Changing Regulatory Environment*, Washington, DC: American Enterprise Institute.

Clark, Robert and Fred Munzenmaier (2001), 'Impact of replacing a defined benefit pension with a defined contribution plan or a cash balance plan', *North American Actuarial Journal*, 4th Quarter, **9** (4), 6–14.

Clark, Robert and Naohiro Ogawa (1996), 'Public attitudes and concerns about population aging in Japan', *Ageing and Society*, **14** (4), 190–208.

Clark, Robert and Sylvester Schieber (2001), 'Taking the subsidy out of early retirement: the story behind the conversion to hybrid pensions', in Olivia Mitchell, Zvi Bodie, Brett Hammond and Steve Zeldes (eds), *Innovations in Financing Retirement*, Philadelphia, PA: University of Pennsylvania Press, pp. 149–74.

Conrad, Harald (2001), *The Japanese Social Security System in Transition: An Evaluation of Current Pension Reforms*, Tokyo: German Institute for Japanese Studies.

Cornell, Andrew (nd), 'Japan opens up $3Tn pensions market', *Financial Review*, http://afr.com/handheld/2001/067/27/FFXH2FWAFOC.html, viewed 4 August 2001.

Dow Jones (1999), 'Japan companies seen favoring DC pensions', *Dow Jones News Wire*, New York, 28 April.

Employees' Pension Fund Association (1996), *Pension Schemes in Japan*, Tokyo: Pension Fund Association.

Feinberg, Phyllis (2001a), 'Japan prepares for dawn of its cash balance era', *Pensions and Investments*, 9 July, 1.

Feinberg, Phyllis (2001b), 'Risk budgeting, indexing catch on in Japan', *Pensions and Investments*, 25 June, 14.

Foreign Press Center (2001), 'Defined contribution pension plan to begin in October', Japan Brief, FPC 0128, Embassy Newsletter, http://www.embjapan.dk/info/Japan%20Brief%etc2001/jb250601.html, viewed 4 August 2001.

Global Custodian (1998), 'In Perry's wake', Spring, http://www.assetpub.com/gcspring98/perry_right.html, viewed 5 August 2001.

Goldman Sachs (1999), 'Unfunded liabilities of Japanese corporate pensions', *Pension Group Services Report*, 20 May.

Gordon, Bill (1999), 'A critical evaluation of Japanese accounting changes since 1997', University of Sheffield dissertation for Masters in Advanced Japanese Studies, http://wgordon.web.wesleyan.edu/papers.jacc2.html, viewed 5 August 2001.

Hatta, Tatsuo (2001), Personal Communication with the authors, Tokyo, July.

Japan Institute of Labor (2000), *Japanese Working Life Profile: 2000 Labor Statistics*, Tokyo.

Johnson, Simon (2001), 'Hard run for Japan's pension money', *Financial Review*, 27 June, http://afr.com/personalfinance/2001/06/27/FFX3AEXAFOC.html, viewed 4 August 2001.

Lincoln, Edward J. and Robert E. Litan (1998), 'The "Big Bang"? An ambivalent Japan deregulates its financial markets', *Brookings Review*, **16** (1) (Winter), 37–40, http://www.brook.edu/press/review/win98/linwi98.html, viewed 4 August 2001.

MacDonald, James (1998), 'Japan's pension funds hike foreign investing: managers gear up for accounts', *Pensions and Investments*, 16 November, 16.

MacIntyre, Donald (1998), 'Bang, you're liberalized: Japan's big move to free its financial markets is marred by a wave of bad news and investor jitters', *Time*, 13 April, http://www.time.com/time/magazine/1998/int/980413/japan.html, viewed 4 August 2001.

Matsuura, Tamie (2000), 'The tax treatment of the DC plan, from company and individual perspectives', *NLI Research*, no. 138, June.

McCarthy, David and Olivia S. Mitchell (2000), 'Assessing the impact of mortality assumptions on annuity valuation', Pension Research Council Working Paper, Wharton School.

McGill, Dan, Kyle N. Brown, John J. Haley and Sylvester J. Schieber (1996), *Fundamentals of Private Pensions*, 7th edn, Philadelphia, PA: University of Pennsylvania Press, Pension Research Council.

Ministry of Health, Labor, and Welfare (1999), *Outline of Social Insurance in Japan*, Tokyo: Ministry of Health, Labor, and Welfare.

Mitchell, Olivia S. (1998), 'Administrative costs of public and private pension plans', in Martin Feldstein (ed.), *Privatizing Social Security*, NBER, Chicago: University of Chicago Press, pp. 403–56.

Mitchell, Olivia S. (2001), 'Managing pensions in the twenty-first century: global lessons and implications for Japan', presented at the 1999 CIRJE Conference on Social Security Reform in Advanced Countries, University of Tokyo (Revised).

Mitchell, Olivia S. (2003), 'New trends in pension benefit and retirement provisions', in O.S. Mitchell, D. Blitzstein, M. Gordon and J. Mazo (eds), *Benefits for the New Workplace*, Philadelphia, PA: University of Pennsylvania, Pension Research Council, pp. 1–20.

Miyatake, Go (2000), *Social Security in Japan*, Tokyo: Foreign Press Center.

Ogawa, Naohiro (2001), Personal communication with the authors.

Papke, Leslie (1999), 'Are 401(k) plans replacing other employer-provided pensions? Evidence from panel data', *Journal of Human Resources*, **34** (2), 346–68.

Pasona, Inc. (2001), 'Pasona launches 401kNet internet finance site with To-Shin Shijo', http://www.pasona.co.jp/english/jeu/03.html, viewed 4 August 2001.

Patrikis, Ernest (1998), 'Japan's Big Bang financial reforms', First Vice President, Federal Reserve Bank of New York, Speech at the Brooklyn Law School, 27 April, http://www.ny.frb.org/pihome/news/speeches/ep980427.html, viewed 4 August 2001.

Pension Benefit Guaranty Corporation (1999), *Pension Insurance Data Book, 1998*, Washington, DC: PBGC.

Portman, Rob and Ben Cardin (2001), The Comprehensive Retirement Security and Pension Reform Act (HR 10), http://www.house.gov/portman/pensiondetailed.htm, viewed 4 August 2001.

Ruffell, Charles (2001), 'DC in Japan: the sun might be setting on the skeptics', *Plan Sponsor*, 21 June, http://www.plansponsor.com/eprise/main/PlanSponsor/News/Opinions/carjapan401k, viewed 4 August 2001.

Sakamoto, Junichi (2000), 'Pension reform and funding options', paper presented at the 13th International Conference of Social Security Actuaries and Statisticians, Quebec, October.

Sakamoto, Junichi (2001a), Personal communication with authors, Tokyo, July.

Sakamoto, Junichi (2001b), Personal communication with authors, e-mail, August.

Seike, Atsushi (1997), *New Trends in Japan's Labor Market.* Tokyo: Foreign Press Center.

Sekine, Kenji (2001), Personal communication with authors, email, August.

Singer, Jason (2001), 'Nikko, like Nomura, to exit pension fund', *Asian Wall St. Journal*, 16 July, 1.

Takayama, Noriyuki (2001), 'Reform of public and private pensions in Japan', paper presented to Ninth Annual Colloquium of Superannuation Researchers, University of New South Wales, Sydney, Australia.

Third Millennium (1999), *Public Attitudes Toward Cash Balance Retirement Plans*, www.thirdmil.org/media/releases/991013_cashbalance.html, viewed 4 August 2001.

William M. Mercer, Inc. (2001), 'Defined contribution plan legislation passed in Diet', *Global Market Alert*, Late Breaking Information for Multinational Employers, 28 June, http://www.wmmercer.com/global/english/resource_news_market_topic_01_09_html, viewed 4 August 2001.

7. Retirement provision: accumulations, security, and insurance

John Piggott, Sachi Purcal and Matthew Williams

1. INTRODUCTION

Throughout the twentieth century, governments increasingly have taken responsibility for financial provision of the elderly. At the end of the century, however, a steady retreat from this position can be observed throughout the world. Population ageing, combined with electoral pressure for smaller government, has led to lower benefit entitlements for those relying on publicly funded social security; this is sometimes accompanied by calls for mandated retirement financing to (at least partly) replace public provision.

Retirement provision is an active policy issue in almost every developed country, and in many cases, reforms have already been enacted. Some of these are parametric, involving changes to the parameters of traditional social security systems: increases in contribution rates, benefit cuts, changes in the retirement age, or in survivorship provisions. Others, however, involve structural reform.

Structural reform, as the name implies, involves more fundamental policy change, for example, the privatization of social security (debated, but not enacted, in the United States), or the development of a mandated employer or employee contribution to a pension fund, as in Australia and Chile. The UK reforms might be seen as combining elements of both. The United States, while fighting shy of structural reform of social security, has nevertheless moved to encourage greater private participation in retirement financing through tax concessions to 401(k) pension plans, which are essentially defined contribution (DC) partially preserved retirement saving plans. The advent of 401(k)s has dramatically changed the structure of retirement provision in that country.

Similar reforms are under consideration in Japan. In recent times, there has been active debate surrounding the introduction of tax preference for DC 401(k) type plans, which may or may not involve employee contributions. The critical features of these plans are that to qualify for tax preference, accumulations must be at least partially preserved until late in the life cycle; and that the beneficiary bears investment risk.

In one or another of its many guises, the most fundamental question in DC-based retirement provision is: how much is enough for adequate retirement financing? In any predominantly accumulation-based scheme, the contribution rate required to produce an adequate retirement income stream is a central continuing issue. It will depend on many factors, including the length and nature of participation in the workforce, the pattern and size of earnings on accumulated funds, taxation of retirement saving, choice of retirement benefit, target replacement rate, longevity, and operation of government transfer and subsidy systems. The problem is distinct from the more conventional financial problem of stochastic returns over time of a once-and-for-all stake, because the nature of pension accumulations is that the investor's contribution is made through time, and may itself be subject to stochastic variation from labor market fluctuations.

Germane to this is the question of how funds should be invested and how they should be protected. Attention should also be paid to the question of life insurance and to the portfolio choice which might underlie income streams purchased to finance the post-retirement years. In a DC environment, the choice of investment strategy can be critical in determining the outcome of an accumulation program. Financial engineering of various kinds can have an impact on the rate of contribution required for a given specification of retirement accumulation distribution. Techniques such as age-phasing and portfolio insurance can help mould the nature of the financial risk confronted by the worker, and can help to make the most of a given contribution plan.

These strategies have considerable potential for benefiting individuals in all retirement saving frameworks where investment risk is borne by the worker. They may, however, be of special importance in Japan, where traditionally savers have operated within a highly capital-protected environment. All have the effect of modifying the distribution of outcomes that can be anticipated under given assumptions about the investment innovations process. They may therefore have a role to play in persuading life-cycle savers in Japan to invest in risky assets.

In common with most other developed economies, Japan has a comprehensive social security system which provides Japanese workers with some financial security in old age. We ask the following hypothetical question: if instead of social security contributions, the same contributions had been invested in Japanese securities, what would the outcome have been? By

considering different time periods and a small menu of alternative strategies, the importance of risk in choosing investment strategies is demonstrated.

The above exercise is of course carried out with the benefit of hindsight.
We therefore go on to ask the following question: suppose the year was
1970, and we had no certain knowledge of the future. All we had was expectations about returns and volatilities of different asset classes. What would
the expected distribution of outcomes at the end of 1999 look like under
alternative strategies, viewed from 1970, given that these parameters are set
to reflect the actual (but then unknown) outcome?

In this way, we try to take some preliminary steps towards understanding how Japanese retirement provision works, and how the performance of
the Japanese economy and financial system over the last 30 years might
impact on perceptions of investment risk in the context of lifelong financial security. Of course, current pension reform proposals in Japan do not
envisage 'privatization' of social security, and our analysis should not be
seen as taking a position on any such proposal. Nor do we take account of
the widespread defined benefit (DB) occupational pension plans in Japan.
But in thinking about DC-based retirement saving, it is convenient to take
the existing retirement provision system as an initial benchmark.

The results are preliminary in at least three significant ways. Japanese
institutional features, such as taxation, prudential supervision, and other
regulation are largely ignored; the simulation methodology is based on the
simplest possible financial markets innovations processes; and labor market
volatility is ignored except to the extent that we incorporate Japanese wages
history.

2. AGEING, SOCIAL SECURITY, AND FINANCIAL MARKETS

In what follows, we consider a hypothetical experiment in which employer
and employee social security contributions made by or on behalf of a
Japanese worker on average earnings are invested in Japanese securities.
The economic and financial data required for this exercise are summarized
in Table 7.1; further details also appear in Appendix 7A. Average growth,
volatility, and the range of extreme year-on-year changes are reported. The
data that we use are all monthly series. Wages, prices, and the bill rate are
not very volatile, but the Nikkei index is. In this example, we ignore the
potential benefits from international diversification.

In Figure 7.1, we chart the Nikkei's history in the last 30 years. The lower
of the two lines is the Nikkei index, while the upper line is the Nikkei

Table 7.1   Summary of economic and financial market experience,
1970–2000 (continuously compounding rates, %)

	Wages[1]	Prices[2]	Nikkei (real)[3]	Nikkei (nom)[3]	Bill rate[4]
Mean	5.9	3.9	4.1	8.2	4.7
Volatility	2.2	2.5	26.5	25.4	0.9
Range	(−1.9, 29.1)	(−1.1, 24.7)	(−40.9, 95.1)	(−38.6, 106.6)	(0.5, 12.2)

Sources:
1. CEIC Database, *Japanese Nominal Wage Index*, All Industries, Monthly, January 1970–June 2000.
2. CEIC Database, *Japanese Consumer Price Index*, Monthly, January 1970–June 2000.
3. Gary Burtless, *Real Total Return of Japan Stock, 1970–2000*, Washington, DC: Brookings Institution, 2001.
4. CEIC Database, *Japanese Three Month Bank of Japan Bill Rate*, Monthly, January 1970–June 2000.

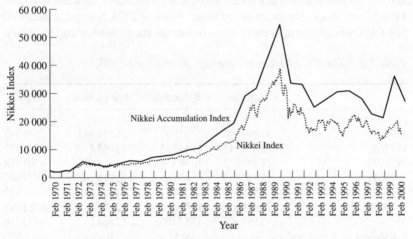

Figure 7.1   The Nikkei index, 1970–2000

accumulation index, which adjusts for dividend reinvestment. The figure reveals the dramatic shifts in trend that have occurred through subperiods of the 30-year span we examine. In particular, the index climbed dramatically through the 1980s, and fell just as dramatically through the 1990s. Its current value is still less than half its peak a decade earlier. The importance of this is demonstrated in the counterfactual analysis to follow.

We model four alternative investment strategies. The first is an all-equities strategy – all contributions are invested in the Nikkei. The second involves a 'balanced' portfolio, in which contributions are split evenly between stocks and bonds, and the accumulation is rebalanced each period to maintain the constant proportion in risky assets. The third is an 'age-phased' strategy, in which the proportion of the portfolio invested in stocks is gradually reduced over the life cycle. Personal finance experts frequently urge their clients to decrease their exposure to risky assets as they age, although financial economists have a hard time coming up with a theoretical justification for this advice.[1] Finally, in the 'safe' strategy, all contributions and earnings are held in short-term bills. All these four strategies are illustrative, and none would be followed by an optimizing investor.

Table 7.2 reports the outcomes for selected 20- and 25-year horizons, as well as the full 30-year investment span which our data permits. Means and coefficients of variation are reported for all 20- and 25-year horizons encompassed by the data; all prices are in ¥ (2000). The accumulations reported in the table illustrate several points. First, the return on equity investment in Japan over the last 30 years has varied enormously by subperiod. Consider first the 20-year spans. They reveal massive accumulations between 1970 and 1990, nearly twice that experienced from 1980 and 2000. Second, a balanced portfolio, while offering a more modest average accumulation and volatility,

Table 7.2   The DC alternative: the last 30 years, ¥ (2000)

	Equities	Balanced	Age-phased	Safe
20-year horizon				
1970–89	23899896	13520922	16514962	7374332
1972–91	13315942	11142481	12655449	8538752
1974–93	11308942	10793803	12338478	9367838
1976–95	12080003	11497653	12718262	10074697
1978–97	8507964	9784437	11512188	10374622
1980–99	13648401	12996352	12802555	10883199
Mean	12557979	11174800	12664142	9475246
Coefficient of variation	0.34	0.11	0.11	0.12
25-year horizon				
1970–94	14813552	11892208	14855748	11025382
1972–96	14003261	12777422	14953609	11935211
1974–98	10764980	12169019	14505206	12602783
1975–99	18315367	16660259	16667415	13072635
Mean	14018026	13005961	15091500	12069918
Coefficient of variation	0.20	0.14	0.05	0.06
30 year horizon				
1970–99	21587358	19112955	18205550	14397945

Sources: CEIC Database, and authors' calculations; see Appendix 7A for definitions.

nevertheless realizes a wide range of accumulations over a 20-year horizon. Third, the longer, 25-year span sharply reduces the variation in returns in all strategies, except for the balanced strategy. For example, the coefficient of variation on equity accumulations is 0.34 for 20-year time spans, but only 0.20 for 25-year spans. Fourth, had protection against calamitous returns been available, the returns on equity investment would have been much higher. (In one year, equities lost nearly half their value – see Table 7.1.) Finally, the age-phased strategy does best in six of the 11 cases reported.

Table 7.3 compares social security with the outcomes of securities-based accumulations for a worker on average earnings over 20- and 25-year spans to the end of 1999. To do this, price indexed annuity factors were calculated for couples, encompassing one worker retiring at age 65, with 75 percent survivor benefits.[2] These calculations yielded factors of 19.47 for a husband and wife both aged 65, and 21.36 for a husband aged 65 with a wife aged 5 years younger.

Table 7.3   Comparison of social security with DC Benefits, ¥ (2000)

	Social security benefits		Benefits under DC system			
	EPI[1]	EPF[2]	Equities	Balanced	Age-phased	Safe
20 years	1 101 974	1 207 515	702 378	668 822	658 849	560 074
25 years	1 226 680	1 358 606	942 550	857 375	857 743	672 748
30 years	1 418 403	1 576 714	1 108 750	981 662	935 056	739 494

Notes:
Calculations assume that individual is exempt from contributions to the national pension before employment begins. Time period is 1970 to 1999 for 30 years, 1975 to 1999 for 25 years, and 1980 to 1999 for 20 years. Contributions adjusted to earn interest during part of year in which contribution made. Couple assumed to be same age, retiring at 65.
Annuity factor: 19.47 (see text).
Age-phasing patterns:
30 years – 8 yrs 80/20, 7 yrs 60/40, 7 yrs 40/60, 7 yrs 20/80;
25 years – 6 yrs 80/20, 6 yrs 60/40, 6 yrs 40/60, 6 yrs 20/80;
20 years – 5 yrs 80/20, 5 yrs 60/40, 5 yrs 40/60, 4 yrs 20/80.
1. Employees' Pension Insurance.
2. Employee Pension Fund.

Sources: CEIC database, and authors' calculations; see Appendix 7A for definitions.

The life annuities assumed here are valued on a population mortality basis, in line with the idea that, consistent with social security, annuity purchase is mandatory. The difference between the social security benefits reported and the estimated annuity payments provides one possible measure of the government subsidy to retirement provision on the assumptions used here, over and above social security tax revenue.

Our results suggest that whatever investment strategy were adopted, a 30 year history of social security contributions would not be sufficient to deliver adequate retirement income from a DC plan. They also point to the riskiness of financial markets – accumulations vary significantly with the chosen strategy, and with the time period considered.

Of course, the calculations presented here benefit from hindsight. In 1970, the realized wage and price changes, changes in social security contributions and benefits, and movements in the Nikkei, used in the above analysis, were not known. Although suggestive in a number of respects, this analysis cannot offer a rigorous guide to the future. For this, a framework encompassing uncertainty is required, and outcomes presented in probabilistic terms. To make progress in this direction, we begin with a review of relevant theory.

3.   THEORETICAL CONSIDERATIONS

The theoretical underpinnings of the analysis of strategies for lifelong financial security have been developed over the last half century. Beginning with the work of Tobin (1958) and Markowitz (1959), which considered portfolio selection over one period, economists have wrestled with the more general question of multiple period optimal consumption and investment. This brief review divides into three subsections: how to invest, how to protect your investments, and how to insure against non-financial life contingencies.

3.1.   How to Invest

The question of how best to invest your money over your lifetime has been addressed by the intertemporal consumption and portfolio choice literature. Early important papers include Merton (1969, 1971) and Samuelson (1969). Simply stated, the papers address the question of how an investor, wishing to maximize his/her lifetime utility, should invest his/her money as time passes, choosing between a risky and a safe asset at each instant. Merton's (1969) classic solution to the problem assumed stationary lognormal stock returns and constant interest rates. This work has provided a useful benchmark for later researchers, who have sought to add greater realism to these original assumptions.

One aspect of the Merton (1969) solution that has attracted attention is the result that for the family of constant relative risk aversion (CRRA) utility functions, investors will invest a constant proportion of their wealth in the risky asset. This result is in stark contrast to observed investor behavior and the advice of financial planners (Jagannathan and Kocherlakota 1996). How can this result be reconciled with observation? Two approaches have been offered, relating to time-varying investment opportunity (that is, stock returns are no longer stationary lognormal) and accounting for labor market behavior.

Merton (1971) himself considered the question of time-varying investment opportunities. In this more general framework the proportion invested in risky assets is no longer constant, and now depends on the investment horizon of the investor. Other authors have made important contributions to this aspect of the literature (Kim and Omberg 1996; Brennan et al. 1997; Campbell and Viceira 1999, 2000). Of interest also is the work of Wachter (1999), which recognizes the presence of mean reversion and persistence in the returns process.

The papers by Liu (1998) and Detemple et al. (1999) extend this area of research by allowing for variability in the safe rate of interest. Researchers have also sought to address the question of market incompleteness (Chacko and Viceira 1999), the risk of bankruptcy (Sethi 1997), and borrowing constraints (Fleming and Zariphopoulou 1991).

Those papers largely ignore non-tradable assets, especially human capital, in their analysis. This issue was dealt with by Bodie et al. (1992), who showed, for the case of certain future income, that if the value of human capital is added to wealth, then the constant proportion Merton rule has the appearance of a reducing proportion invested in risky assets over one's working life. That is, although the investor invests a constant proportion of his/her human capital augmented wealth over his/her lifetime, as a proportion of wealth (not augmented by human capital) his/her investment in risky assets falls over his/her working life. These authors also point out the importance of a correlation between labor earnings and stock returns – a positive correlation will lead to lower investment in risky assets. Viceira (2001) considers the case of risky labor income not perfectly correlated with stock returns, pointing out the effects of increasing labor income risk on savings and portfolio decisions.

In a general equilibrium setting, Basak (1999) details how the presence of labor income can lead consumption to be smoother than the stock market, explaining an oft-quoted empirical observation.

Another aspect of the optimal consumption and investment literature is the question of how individual investors will behave if their investment in risky assets is affected by a deterioration in background (or undiversifiable) risk. Koo (1995) shows that an increase in the variance of permanent income shocks will reduce the amount invested in risky by CRRA utility investors. Later work by Elmendorf and Kimball (1999) confirms Koo's findings.

3.2.   How to Protect Your Assets

Investments made to DC plans which are invested in equities clearly have fluctuating final accumulations. DB plans, on the other hand, offer fixed promises, with plan sponsors assuming the investment risk. What, then, are some strategies available to add a degree of protection to DC final balances?

Turner (2000) surveys employer-backed minimum guarantees for DC schemes. Here, the employer agrees to contribute more to the fund in difficult times, thus sharing in the investment risk. Khorasanee and Ng (2000) discuss hybrid plans, combining the desirable features of DC and DB plans. These plans also involve the employer sharing investment risk.

Rate of return guarantees can also be implemented for DC plans using derivatives. Bateman (1998) discusses the use of portfolio insurance techniques, such as protective puts and collars, to protect DC accumulations. Bodie and Crane (1999) discuss the use of call option strategies pioneered by Merton et al. (1978). Grossman and Zhou (1996) place portfolio insurance strategies in a general equilibrium setting.

Bodie and Crane also point to the developing market for innovative protective products in securities markets as a means of protecting employee balances. Equity indexed annuities have generated much interest in the United States since their introduction in 1995, and improved versions of such products may make useful contributions to retirement saving programs.

3.3.   Insurance

DB retirement plans often offer valuable ancillary benefits, such as life insurance, to protect a member's dependents. Within the economics literature the question of determining the optimal amount of life insurance within the framework of the intertemporal consumption and portfolio choice problem has been addressed by Richard (1975) and Purcal (1997). This model also includes the optimal purchase of annuities, and can inform the debate on optimal annuity design.

Most of the literature above is, as is much of this financial economics literature, framed in a single agent optimization setting. The papers by Grossman and Zhou (1996) and Basak (1999) are notable exceptions. While intertemporal general equilibrium models (Merton 1990, ch. 16) have demonstrated that the Merton (1969) results can carry over to this richer setting, in general, the formulation of these financial models in a general equilibrium setting is a difficult and unresolved issue. Recent work by Kogan and Uppal (1999) deals with solving consumption and portfolio problems in continuous time in both partial and general equilibrium formulations and may provide a way forward in this area.

3.4. Summary

Recent economic theory has done much to increase our understanding of how individuals might optimally invest their assets over their lifetimes, how they should protect their investments, and how much life insurance and annuities they should buy at different stages of their lives. These disparate strands in the literature provide the theoretical underpinnings of our research, which can be seen as focusing on household retirement in an environment of increasing reliance on self-provision. This work will investigate the role of alternative financial strategies and policy settings.

4.   INVESTING FOR LIFETIME SECURITY: STOCHASTIC COUNTERFACTUALS

While elegant results have been obtained in the finance literature which point to optimal lifetime financial investment strategies, added doses of realism typically render theoretical analysis intractable, and numerical simulation must be used to make further headway. In this chapter we model a simple innovations process over only one stochastic variable – investment returns. The assumed stochastic process follows geometric Brownian motion. The index grows at a trend rate which is continuously disturbed by random shocks. This 'proportional random walk' implies that the volatility of the time path is proportional to the level of the associated index.

Formally, the process can be represented by

$$\frac{dX}{X} = \mu dt + \sigma dW \tag{7.1}$$

where X is the value of the real risky accumulation index, μ is the mean rate of change, and σ^2 is the corresponding variance.

The return index is generated by discrete approximations to the above processes. Drawing on a standard result in mathematical finance, it can be shown that valid approximations to (7.1) are given by:

$$\frac{\Delta X_t}{X_t} = \mu \Delta t + \sigma \sqrt{\Delta t}\, \varepsilon_t \tag{7.2}$$

where $\varepsilon_t \sim N(0, 1)$ and independent, and we measure time units in fortnights ($\Delta t = 1/26$ of a year) so that for an accumulation of 30 years we have 780 periods.

The Merton (1969) result, that standard preference maximization yields a constant proportion in risky rule, provides a starting point for designing investment strategies over the life cycle. Three of the four strategies we model here flow from the simplest possible constant proportions rules: all in risky, all in safe, and a 50–50 split.

The intuition underlying risk constancy is that we seek to optimize by trading off risk at the margin much as we trade off other commodities. We drive slower in wet weather to expose ourselves to constant risk while driving. Equally, so long as risky does not change its riskiness, we should not alter our portfolios.

Our fourth strategy involves age-phasing, which may be thought of as a simple illustration of a sophisticated strategy for lifelong financial security. Superficially, risk constancy would appear inconsistent with the flavor of much popular financial advice, which suggests that exposure to risky assets should decrease with age. It is, however, possible to reconcile the risk constancy result with age-phasing advice.[3]

The two most convincing arguments for age-phasing are well articulated by Bodie et al. (1992). The first essentially extends the risk constancy proposition to include human as well as non-human capital. If human capital is relatively safe, then as the stock of human capital depletes with age, a compensating financial portfolio adjustment should take place to preserve constant exposure to risk overall. This will have the effect of increasing the proportion of safe assets in a financial portfolio with age.

The second argument, less analytically crisp but perhaps more robust, is that people's ability to adjust their behavior to accommodate the consequences of bad luck decreases with age. A family that takes a hit when the household head is in his/her thirties, or even forties, has more margins on which to adjust than one whose head is approaching retirement. Work effort (including secondary labor force participation), job retraining, even family size, are all examples of adjustments that are much more feasible earlier rather than later in the life cycle.

Figure 7.2 maps out the proportion of a gradually accumulating financial portfolio which should be held in risky assets over time by an exemplar individual, given safe human capital.[4] In the early years, until about age 40, the entire portfolio is risky. Were borrowing permitted, the optimizing investor would borrow against his/her human capital to increase exposure to risky assets. As his/her financial portfolio increases in size, and his/her human capital depletes, safe assets enter into the financial portfolio, until at retirement, he/she holds between 35 and 40 percent of the portfolio in

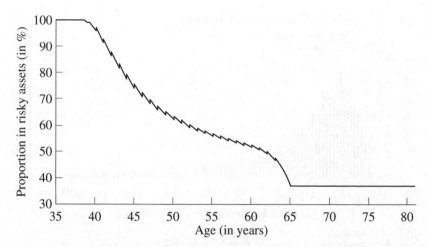

Figure 7.2   Age-phasing: variation in optimal exposure to risky assets with age (safe human capital)

risky assets. It is noteworthy that exposure to risky assets is still significant, even after retirement. This suggests that annuity designs should perhaps include some degree of exposure to risk, as is the case with the variable annuity.

In Figure 7.3, we reproduce the distributions of outcomes in the portfolios where there is some degree of exposure to risk, and point to the safe return as a comparator. Returns and volatilities were set consistent with Japan's experience over the last 30 years. The safe rate of return was set at 4.6 percent, the risky rate at 8.2 percent, and volatility at 25.4 percent. These are the continuously compounding rates of return matching those given in Table 7.1. The contribution rate was set at 15.33 percent. This is the value that, invested in safe assets, gives the accumulation at age 65 that would actually have been realized (see Table 7.2).

The mean accumulation under the all equities regime is highest, at ¥29.83 million; next comes the age-phased portfolio, with ¥22.98 million. The balanced case generates a mean accumulation of ¥22.17 million, with the safe strategy returning ¥17.01 million with certainty. The standard deviations in each case indicate a clean trade-off between risk and return in the four cases we examine, with coefficients of variation of 1.21 for the all-equities portfolio, 0.45 for the age-phased portfolio, and 0.44 for the balanced portfolio.

Inspection of Figure 7.3 suggests that by age-phasing, it is possible to narrow the distribution of outcomes – and thus reduce uncertainty – without a large sacrifice in mean expected return. By contrast, the all-equities

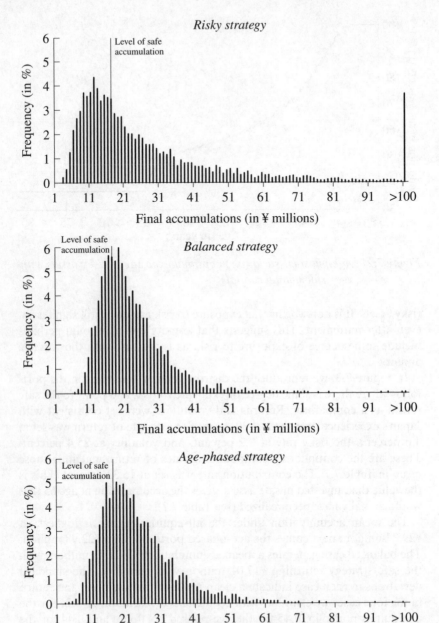

*Figure 7.3   Accumulation distributions under alternative investment
strategies*

portfolio offers the possibility of considerable upside, but at the cost of a high probability of indifferent outcomes. The role of investment strategies of the age-phased type, and financial engineering more generally, is to shape the distribution of outcomes to more closely fit the preferences of the life-cycle investor than would be possible with unsophisticated strategies.

Table 7.4 reports the percentile outcomes from these simulations. Note that while the mean return of the all-equities portfolio is significantly greater than any other, the median is little greater than the safe return. The age-phased strategy offers the highest median return.[5]

Table 7.4   Percentile accumulations for alternative investment strategies (¥ m)

Percentile	Equities	Balanced	Age-phased	Safe
90	59.791	34.404	36.375	17.009
75	33.933	26.379	27.968	17.009
50	19.383	19.940	20.989	17.009
25	11.942	15.459	15.764	17.009
10	8.090	12.442	12.236	17.009

5.   CONCLUSION

This chapter canvasses questions raised by the worldwide trend towards increased individual responsibility for lifelong financial security, and specifically focuses on the implications for Japan. Publicly provided social security, and many occupationally based DB plans have traditionally provided insurance against longevity, investment, and inflation risk, and have also offered life insurance to support dependents. As individuals increasingly rely on their own resources and decision-making to insure against demographic and financial risks, privately based delivery of the underlying investment and insurance services will become critically important.

In this chapter we use Japanese data and social security structures to compare market-based outcomes with public outcomes, using time spans covering the past 30 years. We use a simple stochastic model of investment returns innovations to generate distributions of outcomes under alternative investment strategies. We find that increasing the sophistication of the investment strategy generates outcomes, or distributions of outcomes, which dominate those implied by simple constant-proportions positions.

APPENDIX 7A　　DATA SOURCES FOR ECONOMIC AND FINANCIAL DATA SERIES USED IN JAPAN SOCIAL SECURITY AND INVESTMENT CALCULATIONS

Prices and nominal wages series　Taken from the CEIC database. Figures are for December each year and are the change on the previous December figure. The nominal wage series is seasonally adjusted by averaging the values of the preceding twelve months.

Monthly wages　Average monthly cash earnings of regular employees figures taken from Japan Institute of Labor webpage (http://www.jil.go.jp/ estatis/e0301.htm). The figures for 1994–98 were each taken back to December 1970 using the nominal wages series, and the average of the five figures was around ¥67000 (the exact figures were: ¥66581 based on the 1998 series; ¥66649, 97 series; ¥66879, 96 series; ¥67325, 95 series; ¥67752, 94 series). The series was then constructed using the nominal wages series to get the time series. The estimated figure for December 1999 is ¥364638.

Bonuses　Data from the Ministry of Labor's Monthly Labor Survey on their webpage (http://www.mol.go.jp/info/toukei/english/index.htm) has figures on contractual cash earnings (regular salary) and special cash earnings (bonuses). Analysis of the data shows that bonuses account for just over 20 percent of total average monthly earnings (data for June 1999 to June 2000). So for the model we have estimated regular salary (that is, used as basis for pension contributions and benefits) is 80 percent of average total monthly earnings, and bonuses are 20 percent of total earnings. Thus, in December 1999, average regular monthly salary was ¥291710 and average monthly bonuses were ¥72928.

EPI contribution rate　Taken from *Social Security Programs Throughout the World* (1999), Takayama (1998) and Clark (1991). The series is 12.4 up to 1989, 14.5 percent 1990–93, 16.5 percent 1994–95, 17.35 percent 1996 onwards. Also one percent of bonus is contributed.

Rates of return　Taken from CEIC databases and data supplied by Gary Burtless. The risky rate of return is the change in the Nikkei accumulation index over previous December's figure. The safe rate of return is the Bank of Japan bill rate series with estimates calculated for missing values.

NOTES

1. MacNaughton et al. (2000) develop this point, and cite a number of sources advocating this strategy.
2. Annuity factors were calculated using Japanese Life Table 18 (population mortality), assuming a one percent rate of interest and continuous payments.
3. Kingston et al. (1992) use stochastic simulation to illustrate the efficacy of age-phasing in the Australian context.
4. This assumes an individual maximizing standard power utility function $U = C^{1-\gamma}/(1-\gamma)$, where $\gamma = 1.5$, and follows Merton (1969) and Bodie et al. (1992).
5. This result is of course independent of the historical path of the Nikkei index over the past 30 years, unlike the strong performance of the age-phased strategy in Table 7.2.

REFERENCES

Basak, Suleyman (1999), 'On the fluctuations in consumption and market returns in the presence of labor and human capital: an equilibrium analysis', *Journal of Economic Dynamics and Control*, **23**, 1029–64.

Bateman, Hazel (1998), 'Risk management issues for mandatory private retirement provision: roles for options', *Australian Journal of Management*, **22**, 175–97.

Bodie, Zvi and Dwight B. Crane (1999), 'The design and production of new retirement saving products', *Journal of Portfolio Management*, Winter, 77–82.

Bodie, Zvi, Robert C. Merton and William F. Samuelson (1992), 'Labor supply flexibility and portfolio choice in a life cycle model', *Journal of Economic Dynamics and Control*, **16**, 427–49.

Brennan, Michael J., Eduardo S. Schwartz and Ronald Lagnado (1997), 'Strategic asset allocation', *Journal of Economic Dynamics and Control*, **21**, 1377–403.

Campbell, John Y. and Luis M. Viceira (1999), 'Consumption and portfolio decisions when expected returns are time varying', *Quarterly Journal of Economics*, **114**, 433–95.

Campbell, John Y. and Luis Viceira (2001), 'Who should buy long-term bonds?', *American Economic Review*, **91**, 99–127.

CEIC Database (2000), DX Data, Sydney.

Chacko, George and Luis Viceira (1999), 'Dynamic consumption and portfolio choice with stochastic volatility in incomplete markets', Working Paper, Harvard Business School, Cambridge, MA.

Clark, Robert L. (1991), *Retirement Systems in Japan*, Boston, MA: Irwin (Pension Research Council).

Detemple, Jerome, Rene Garcia and Marcel Rindisbacher (1999), 'A Monte Carlo method for optimal portfolios', Working Paper, Rotman School of Management, University of Toronto, Canada.

Elmendorf, Douglas W. and Miles S. Kimball (2000), 'Taxation of labor income and the demand for risky assets', *International Economic Review*, **41**, 801–33.

Fleming, Wendell H. and Thaleia Zariphopoulou (1991), 'An optimal investment/consumption model with borrowing', *Mathematics of Operation Research*, **16**, 802–22.

Grossman, Sanford and Zhongquan Zhou (1996), 'Equilibrium analysis of portfolio insurance', *Journal of Finance*, **51**, 1379–403.

Jagannathan, Ravi and Narayana R. Kocherlakota (1996), 'Why should older people invest less in stocks than younger people?', *Federal Reserve Bank of Minneapolis, Quarterly Review*, **20**, 11–23.

Khorasanee, M. Saki and Ho Kuen Ng (2000), 'A retirement plan based on fixed accumulation and variable accrual', *North American Actuarial Journal*, **4**, 63–79.

Kim, Tong Suk and Edward Omberg (1996), 'Dynamic nonmyopic portfolio behavior', *Review of Financial Studies*, **9**, 141–61.

Kingston, Geoffrey, John Piggott and Hazel Bateman (1992), 'Customized investment strategies for accumulation superannuation', in Kevin Davis and Ian Harper (eds), *Superannuation and the Australian Financial System*, London: Allen & Unwin, pp. 139–56.

Kogan, Leonid and Raman Uppal (1999), 'Risk aversion and optimal portfolio policies in partial and general equilibrium economies', Working Paper, Sloan School of Management, Massachusetts Institute of Technology, Cambridge, MA.

Koo, Hyeng-Keun (1995), 'Consumption and portfolio selection with labor income I: Evaluation of human capital', Unpublished paper, Washington University, St Louis, MO.

Liu, Jin (1998), 'Portfolio selection in stochastic environments', Working Paper, Graduate School of Business, Stanford University, Stanford, CA.

MacNaughton, Tracey, John Piggott and Sachi Purcal (2000), 'Growing old gracefully: age-phasing, targets, and saving rules', *Journal of Private Portfolio Management*, **2**, 20–24.

Markowitz, Harry M. (1959), *Portfolio Selection: Efficient Diversification of Investment*, Chichester: John Wiley & Sons.

Merton, Robert C. (1969), 'Lifetime portfolio selection under uncertainty: the continuous-time case', *Review of Economics and Statistics*, **51**, 247–57.

Merton, Robert C. (1971), 'Optimal consumption and portfolio rules in a continuous-time model', *Journal of Economic Theory*, **3**, 373–413.

Merton, Robert C. (1990), *Continuous-time Finance*, Oxford: Basil Blackwell.

Merton, Robert C., Myron S. Scholes and Matthew L. Gladstein (1978), 'The returns and risks of alternative call option portfolio investment strategies', *Journal of Business*, **51**, 183–242.

Purcal, Sachi (1997), 'Optimal portfolio selection and financial planning', Working Paper, University of New South Wales, Sydney.

Richard, Scott F. (1975), 'Optimal consumption, portfolio and life insurance rules for an uncertain lived individual in a continuous time model', *Journal of Financial Economics*, **2**, 187–203.

Samuelson, Paul A. (1969), 'Lifetime portfolio selection by dynamic stochastic programming', *Review of Economics and Statistics*, **51**, 239–46.

Sethi, Suresh P. (1997), *Optimal Consumption and Investment with Bankruptcy*, Dordrecht: Kluwer Academic.

Social Security Administration (1999), *Social Security Programs Throughout the World*, Washington, DC: United States Government Printing Office.

Takayama, Noriyuki (1998), *The Morning After in Japan: Its Declining Population, Too Generous Pensions and a Weakened Economy*, Tokyo: Maruzen Co. Ltd.

Tobin, James (1958), 'Liquidity preference as behavior towards risk', *Review of Economic Studies*, **25**, February, 68–85.

Turner, John (2000), 'The best of both worlds?', *The Actuary*, August, 20–21.

Viceira, Luis M. (2001), 'Optimal portfolio choice for long-horizon investors with nontradeable labor income', *Journal of Finance*, **56** (2), April, 433–70.

Wachter, Jessica (1999), 'Portfolio and consumption decisions under mean-reverting returns: an exact solution for complete markets', Working Paper, Harvard University, Cambridge, MA.

8. Issues in Japanese health policy and medical expenditure*

Yasushi Iwamoto

1. INTRODUCTION

Japanese citizens are worried about the rising burden of medical costs. Frequent reports of medical malpractice and accidents indicate, however, that the quality of medical services does not match the rising bill. This chapter discusses how Japanese policy makers could control the cost and quality of medical services. To this end, the chapter first examines the past behavior of the national medical-care expenditure and its future path. Possible reforms to slash medical costs and improve the quality of medical care are then proposed.

Per capita real medical expenditure is driven by two factors; a change in the population structure and the so-called 'natural increase' (a change in input due to technological change). Section 2 shows that about 30 percent of the past growth was due to population ageing and the remaining 70 percent to technological change. The section also surveys the effect of population ageing on future medical-care expenditure and finds that medical expenditure will increase by around 20 percent in 20 years due to population ageing.

Section 3 focuses on a reform of health insurance for the elderly and presents some policy recommendations. Once the government started working on a fundamental reform of public health insurance, it was a very long time until such a plan for the elderly was formulated. After twice failing to meet a deadline, the government and ruling parties finally reached an agreement on health-care reform in November 2001. The agreed plan, however, has not resolved some fundamental problems. One of the most serious is that virtually no organization in the health-care market evaluates the quality of medical services or helps to improve it. It has not been clarified whether the rising medical costs are the result of waste or of necessity. Reforms should attempt to make insurers play a more active role in the health-care market as informed agents of patients. Since the public sector has been dominating the health insurance business, dramatic outsourcing of the health insurance business to the private sector should be promoted.

2.   THE EFFECT OF AGEING ON MEDICAL COSTS

2.1.   Past Experiences

The national medical expenditure in 2000 was ¥30 trillion, and each citizen spent an average of ¥239 thousand a year on medical care. As shown in Figure 8.1, the ratio of medical expenditure to GDP increased in the 1990s and reached 6.3 percent in 1999.[1] Since the share of medical expenditure for the elderly has been growing, many people think that the ageing of the population is a major reason for the increasing medical costs. However, focusing only on population ageing will result in overlooking another important source of the growth of medical costs. Even if the ratio of the elderly to the total population remains stable, an overall growth of medical expenditure, including the non-elderly, is possible.

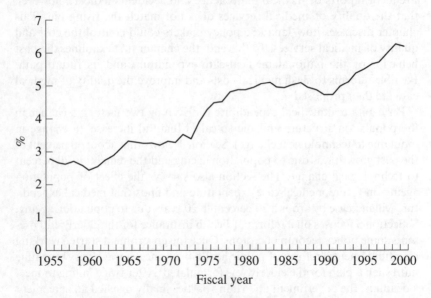

Figure 8.1   Total medical costs (ratio to GDP)

To determine the importance of the role of population ageing on the increase in medical costs, Table 8.1 summarizes information from the Ministry of Health, Labor, and Welfare and shows that real per capita medical expenditure grew at a rate of 4.5 percent per annum from 1980 to 1999. The contribution of population ageing is obtained by changing only the population structure and keeping the medical cost for each age group constant. The annual growth rate that is attributed to the change in the

Table 8.1   Sources of increase in medical costs (%)

Year	Growth rate			Sources	
	Medical costs	Medical costs per capita	Real medical costs per capita	Population ageing	Others (natural increase)
1980	9.4	8.6	8.6	1.0	7.5
1981	7.4	6.7	5.0	1.0	3.8
1982	7.7	7.0	7.0	1.2	5.7
1983	4.9	4.2	5.5	1.2	4.3
1984	3.8	3.2	5.2	1.2	4.0
1985	6.1	5.4	4.2	1.2	3.0
1986	6.6	6.1	5.4	1.2	4.1
1987	5.9	5.4	5.4	1.2	4.1
1988	3.8	3.4	2.9	1.3	1.6
1989	5.2	4.8	4.0	1.3	2.7
1990	4.5	4.2	3.2	1.6	1.5
1991	5.9	5.6	5.6	1.5	4.0
1992	7.6	7.3	4.8	1.6	3.0
1993	3.8	3.5	3.5	1.5	2.0
1994	5.9	5.7	3.8	1.5	2.1
1995	4.5	4.1	3.4	1.6	1.7
1996	5.8	5.6	4.8	1.7	3.0
1997	1.9	1.7	1.3	1.8	−0.5
1998	2.6	2.3	3.6	1.8	1.8
1999	3.7	3.5	3.5	1.6	1.9
2000	−1.9	−2.1	−2.3	1.7	−4.0
1980–1999*	5.4	4.9	4.5	1.4	3.1

Notes: * Simple average of growth rates of each year. Since the reduction in medical costs in 2000 was due to the shift of some long-term care spending from health insurance payments to long-term care insurance payments, the average excludes the year 2000.

Source: Ministry of Health, Labor, and Welfare, *National Medical Care Expenditure*.

population structure was 1.4 percent from 1980 to 1997. Population ageing increased the real per capita medical cost by 27 percent during this period. Therefore, about 30 percent of the medical cost growth is due to population ageing. The 'residual' growth (3.1 percent per annum) is attributed to a change in medical technology.

Table 8.1 reveals the following three points. First, population ageing is not entirely responsible for the rising medical costs. Second, population ageing in Japan is a bigger factor than is population ageing in other developed countries, as pointed out by Niki (1995). For example, Newhouse (1992) and Cutler (1997) indicated that the contribution of the change in the population structure in the United States was much smaller.[2] Third, the impact of ageing is more significant in a later period. Since population ageing in Japan is expected to accelerate in the near future, attention needs to be paid to the consequences.

Figure 8.2 shows the per capita medical expenditure by age group (0–14, 15–44, 45–64, 65 and over) in different years. The medical costs of those aged 15–44 for each year is normalized to be one. The medical costs of those aged 65 and over exhibit a higher growth than those of other age groups; from 4.6 times as big as those of people aged 45–64 in 1977 to 8.3 times in 1999. A sharp increase was observed between 1980 and 1985.[3]

2.2. Future Projections

If the elderly continue to incur higher medical costs than the non-elderly, the increasing ageing population will raise the per capita medical costs of the entire population.

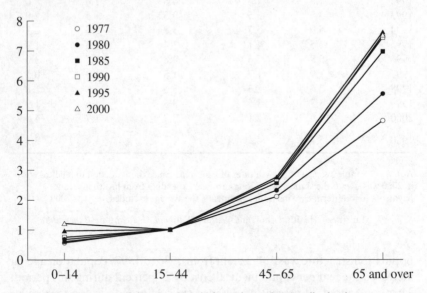

Note: The medical cost of those aged 15–44 for each year is normalized to be one.

Source: Ministry of Labor, Health, and Welfare, *National Medical Care Expenditure*, various issues.

Figure 8.2   Medical costs by age group

The Ministry of Health, Labor, and Welfare periodically provides a projection of future medical costs. However, the methodology used by the ministry includes a dubious procedure, that is, they extrapolate the recent *nominal* growth rate. The predicted medical costs in 2025 varied wildly among predictions. For example, according to the 1994 projection, the cost in 2025 would be ¥141 trillion, but the 2001 projection indicated that it would be ¥81 trillion. This dramatic decline of nominal costs reflects the recent low nominal growth of medical expenditure, which is in turn due to the disinflation and deflation of the Japanese economy.

Since economists prefer a projection based on *real* costs, many alternative studies of estimating real medical costs have been conducted (for example, Ogura and Irifune 1990; Ogura 1994; Niki 1995; Iwamoto et al. 1997; Nishimura 1997; and Tokita et al. 1997). To estimate the real expenditure, it is necessary to predict what the inflation rate and technological change will be in the future.[4] A conservative approach to predicting the future inflation rate of medical services is to assume that it will be the same as the overall inflation rate. A more difficult problem is how to predict the future growth of medical service input. A naive assumption is that the real medical service input is proportional to the real income. When we combine these assumptions, the nominal medical costs for an average person are proportional to the nominal income. The effect of an ageing population is then isolated as follows. Take the recent data of medical costs of various age groups and change only the population data to the projected future value (the government projection is commonly used). The total medical costs are the product of the per capita medical cost and the medical costs of an average person. Since the growth rate of the latter is equal to the income growth rate, the growth rate of the former reflects the change in the ratio of total medical expenditure to the income. When we focus on this ratio, we do not have to specify either the inflation rate or the income growth rate.

Table 8.2 summarizes the existing research, which calculated the future medical costs using the above-mentioned approach. These studies show a similar pattern. For projections in the early twenty-first century, Ogura and Irifune (1990) estimated that the national medical expenditure would grow by 13.6 percent from 2001 to 2021. Niki's (1995) projections showed 18.5 percent from 2000 to 2025. The growth between 2000 and 2020 was estimated as 22.7 percent by Nishimura (1997) and 19 percent by Tokita et al. (1997). A rough consensus is that national medical expenditure will grow by about 20 percent in the first 20 years of the twenty-first century.

Table 8.2   Projections of future medical costs

Ogura and Irifune (1990)				
Fiscal year	Total medical costs (trillion yen, in 1986 price)		Medical costs per capita (yen, in 1986 price)	
1986	15.23	(100)	125196	(100)
2001	19.59	(128)	151572	(121)
2021	22.26	(146)	179397	(143)
Ogura (1994)				
Fiscal year	Total medical costs (trillion yen, in 1989 price)		Medical costs per capita (yen, in 1989 price)	
1989	17.49	(100)	142075	(100)
2004	22.77	(130)	178765	(121)
2024	25.41	(145)		
Niki (1995)				
Fiscal year	Total medical costs (trillion yen, in 1990 price)		Medical costs per capita (yen, in 1990 price)	
1990	20.61	(100)	166720	(100)
2000	24.55	(119)	192720	(116)
2010	27.31	(133)	209420	(126)
2025	29.10	(141)	231280	(139)
Iwamoto, Takeshita and Bessho (1997)				
Fiscal year	Total medical costs (trillion yen, in 1992 price)		Medical costs per capita (yen, in 1992 price)	
(A)				
1992	21.13	(100)	169826	(100)
2010	27.64	(131)	211968	(121)
2025	29.52	(140)	234623	(138)
(B)				
2010	27.63	(131)	216508	(127)
2025	29.54	(140)	244288	(144)
Nishimura (1997)				
Fiscal year	Total medical costs (trillion yen, in 1994 price)		Medical costs per capita (yen, in 1994 price)	
1994	25.00	(100)	199818	(100)
2000	27.86	(111)	218707	(109)
2005	30.24	(121)	233792	(117)
2010	32.03	(128)	245634	(122)
2015	33.30	(133)	256089	(128)
2020	34.18	(137)	266313	(133)
2025	34.19	(137)	271768	(135)

Table 8.2 (*continued*)

2030	33.72	(135)	274209	(137)
2035	33.15	(133)	274668	(137)
2040	33.63	(135)	286725	(143)

Tokita et al. (1997)

Fiscal year	Total medical costs (trillion yen, in 1993 price)		Medical costs per capita (yen, in 1993 price)	
1993	20.17	(100)	161440	(100)
2000	22.51	(112)	177395	(110)
2005	23.86	(118)	186868	(116)
2010	25.08	(124)	196516	(122)
2015	26.44	(131)	209104	(130)
2020	26.79	(133)	215817	(134)
2025	26.39	(131)	218256	(135)

Notes:
Numbers in parentheses are normalized so that the base year has 100.
Medical costs per capita of Ogura and Irifune (1990), Ogura (1994), Nishimura (1997), Tokita et al. (1997), total medical costs of Niki (1995) and Iwamoto, Takeshita and Bessho (1997), and case (B) of Iwamoto, Takeshita, and Bessho (1997) are the author's calculation. Ogura and Irifune (1990) and Ogura (1994) relied on their own population projections. Case (B) of Iwamoto, Takeshita and Bessho (1997) relied on the official population projection for January 1997. Other studies employed the official population projection for September 1992.

3. DEBATES ON A COMPREHENSIVE REFORM OF HEALTH INSURANCE FOR THE ELDERLY

3.1. Reform Debates Entangled

Since the growth rate of medical expenditure exceeded that of the national income, the financial situation of the health insurance system has steadily worsened. The necessity for a comprehensive reform of the system has been recognized since the Medical Insurance Council of the former Ministry of Health and Welfare started discussions in March 1995. The toughest problem to be tackled is how to finance the medical costs of the elderly, who spend much more and contribute less than other sectors of the population.

Under the current system, workers and their families are enrolled in Employees' Health Insurance (EHI), and retired workers and their families belong to the National Health Insurance (NHI), which is mainly for the self-employed and the elderly. If the NHI tried to maintain an independent budget, its financial situation would seriously worsen. The government, then, is forced to subsidize the NHI. When the Health Service for the Elderly (*Roken* in Japanese) was established in 1983, the financing scheme of the medical costs of the elderly was fundamentally changed. First of all, the *Roken* is in a unique position because it is responsible for the provision of benefits only, while other health insurance subsystems are responsible for both the provision of benefits and the collection of insurance premiums. After the establishment of the *Roken*, the elderly remained enrollees of existing systems, for which they pay a premium, but they receive benefits from the *Roken*. The *Roken* itself does not collect premiums. Medical costs are financed from transfers from other health insurance groups. Roughly speaking, the amount each subsystem pays to the *Roken* is in proportion to the number of their enrollees.[5] The medical costs of the elderly are effectively supported by all the public health insurance subsystems. However, the EHI is unhappy about subsidizing the *Roken*. The increased share of medical costs of the elderly has caused a substantial increase in transfers from other insurance groups, thus depleting the financial resources of the EHI.

From 1995, when the former Ministry of Health and Welfare started work on a reform plan for public health insurance, the formulation of a concrete reform plan of health insurance for the elderly was a long-drawn-out procedure. When the out-of-pocket payment for employees and the elderly was raised in September 1997, the government could not provide a plan of fundamental reform and promised to deliver one by FY 2001. After heated debates, the government was unable to reach a conclusion, and subsequently postponed the reform until FY 2002.

To meet the new deadline, policy makers had to finalize a plan in 2001. In the report published in March 2001, the Ministry of Health, Labor, and Welfare presented four possible plans for a comprehensive reform of health insurance for the elderly: (i) to establish an independent health insurance group for the elderly with heavy governmental subsidization; (ii) to move retired workers into the EHI; (iii) to introduce a risk adjustment scheme among health insurance groups; and (iv) to amalgamate public health insurance subsystems and launch a new single insurance group for the total population.

The Ministry of Health, Labor, and Welfare proposed a reform plan in September 2001. According to this plan, the eligible age to qualify for the *Roken* would be raised from 70 to 75. A 10 percent coinsurance rate would be applied to elderly participants aged 75 and over (20 percent for those aged 70–74). Fifty percent of medical expenses would be subsidized by the national budget, compared with the current figure of 30 percent. The coinsurance rate for the employees would be raised from 20 to 30 percent. The ministry also proposed to introduce a cap system that would keep the growth rate of medical costs for the elderly within the growth rate of the per capita GDP (if the medical costs grew higher, the health insurance would automatically lower the price that would be paid). The Ministry of Finance and the Council on Economic and Fiscal Policy each advocated a cap system that would keep the *total* medical cost growth within the rate of economic growth.[6]

On 29 November 2001, the government and ruling parties finally reached an agreement concerning the reform plan. While the increase in the eligible age for the *Roken* was in accordance with the Ministry of Health, Labor, and Welfare plan, the hike in out-of-pocket expenses for the elderly was met with criticism. A 10 percent coinsurance rate would be applied to those aged 70 and over (20 percent for the high-income households).[7] The idea of the cap system, which was unpopular with doctors, was dropped from the plan.

3.2. What Went Wrong?

The agreed reform plan is a mismatch of compromises. It partially incorporates the first contender of the March 2001 report by increasing the subsidies from the national budget. It also partially incorporates the second contender by transferring retired workers aged 70–74 and their dependents to the *Taishokusha Iryo*, which is effectively part of the health insurance scheme for employees.[8] The agreed reform plan does not provide a final answer as to how the medical costs of the elderly will be financed. Nor does it solve the problem of increasing medical costs. Therefore, further reform will be needed within a few years if medical costs continue to grow.

The long delay in the overhaul of the health-care system is a result of addressing the problems in the wrong order. Since the total medical expenditure is not likely to be changed substantially by the current reform plan, reducing somebody's burden will increase somebody else's. The finance of health insurance is essentially a zero-sum game. While a cap system would automatically cut expenses, its effect on the quality of medical service is ambiguous. Since Japan has virtually no workable quality evaluation system, there is no guarantee that the cap system will cut back only inefficient medical treatment. Moreover, it will be impossible to check whether the quality of the medical services will stay the same or decline. The problem that should be addressed first is how to make the provision system more transparent and efficient. Until people are convinced of the quality of medical services, a satisfactory fundamental reform of health insurance will not be realized.

There is no difference between consumer demand for better and cheaper services in the health-care market and that in other markets. In the market

economy, consumer choice usually puts pressure on providers, thus resulting in an improvement in quality and a reduction of prices. However, due
to asymmetric information, consumer sovereignty has not been well established in the area of health care. A possible solution would be to have a pro-
fessional third party acting as an informed agent for patients. An example
is managed care, where an insurer plays a more active role than in traditional insurance policies.[9]

A naive application of managed care would not be workable in Japan
because a dominant part of health insurance is operated by the public
sector, which is not seen as the driving force of the market mechanism.
Japanese regulators have basically given up measuring quality, and instead
they have targeted the ratio of medical expenditure to national income. As
a result, attempts to improve the quality of services in Japan lag far behind
those of the United States, where private companies run the health insurance business. The Japanese government has just started promoting
evidence-based medicine, which has already been incorporated into
medical practices outside Japan.

3.3. The Japanese Way of Promoting Managed Care

Providers of medical services have had no experience of strong market
forces under the public health insurance system.[10] Therefore, Japanese
health policy should outsource a substantial part of the public health insurance business to the private sector and make the role of insurers more
active. Such action has been initiated not by the Ministry of Health, Labor,
and Welfare but by the Regulatory Reform Council (*Sogo Kisei Kaikaku
Kaigi*), which ranked health care as one of the six most important areas of
promoting regulatory reforms in 2001. Based on Council's plan, the
Reform Work Schedule (*Kaikaku Kotei Hyo*, designed by the Council on
Economic and Fiscal Policy, September 2001) contains important items for
facilitating the activities of insurers. Insurers will be able to conduct an *ex
post* review of medical practice, whereas current legislation forces them to
delegate that responsibility to special public agencies (*Shiharai Kikin* and
Kokuho Rengokai). Insurers will also be able to make direct contact with
medical service providers and apply a different payment schedule from that
determined by the public health insurance.

When the reforms advocated by the Reform Work Schedule are realized,
insurers will be given an opportunity to play a more active role in the
health-care market. In particular, the design of a payment schedule will
play an important role in improving medical practice. The introduction of
a prospective payment system (PPS) has been advocated in the reform
of the payment schedule because the insurer will evaluate the quality of

providers and give them incentives through a reward based upon outcome rather than input.

In 1990, the public health insurance first introduced a PPS into the in-patient fee of the elderly. The PPS was later gradually introduced into other areas. What will be the consequence of the PPS? If medical service provid-ers seek profit, the introduction of the PPS will result in a lower service input. Its effect on quality would be ambiguous, since the original fee-for-service payment distorts the behavior of providers. An early study of the consequences of the introduction of the PPS in 1990 was Takagi (1993), which provides a case study of a hospital. A comparison before and after the introduction of the PPS indicated that the hospital had substantially reduced the utilization of drugs and screening. In terms of the numbers of deaths at the hospital, the quality of medical services did not show a sig-nificant decline.

An important difference from the US Medicare PPS is that Japanese pro-viders choose the PPS or a fee-for-service schedule. While the choice cannot be made on a case-by-case basis, the providers will choose the PPS if the expected revenue under the PPS is higher than that under the fee-for-service schedule. Kawai and Maruyama (2000) focused on the introduction of PPS to outpatient care for chronic diseases of the elderly and for infant children in April 1996, and they found that providers respond to incentives given by the PPS. A hospital that expected a lower average medical cost under the fee-for-service schedule would choose PPS. Since policy makers intended to involve many medical-care providers in the PPS, the payments under the PPS became generous for hospitals that spend less on patients. Therefore, the PPS was not helpful in reducing medical costs. The mandatory applica-tion of PPS has to be considered as a policy option.

4. CONCLUDING REMARKS

To determine whether and how medical costs can be cut without a de-terioration in quality, we need to have a satisfactory system to evaluate the quality of medical care. Thus creation of a workable evaluation system should be given top priority.

A market-oriented approach, that is, competition through a choice by informed agents of patients, will help to improve the efficiency of health-care provision. The public operation of health insurance has deprived vital activities of the involvement of the private sector. The introduction of managed care into a world governed by publicly operated universal health insurance will require a different strategy from that needed in a world dom-inated by private health insurance. Therefore, a naive imitation of US experiences may not be workable, and Japanese policy makers will have to design a system that fits the Japanese situation. The provision and financing of health care varies among countries. The ongoing Japanese experience will help us understand the interaction of the market and institutions more thoroughly.

In policy debates, the question of whether we have to pre-fund the health insurance against the expected rise of future medical expenses has been totally ignored; however, some academics have raised the issue (Nishimura 1997; Suzuki 2000; and Iwamoto 2002). Since we have more problems to address than problems resolved, continued effort will be necessary to pursue a better health policy.

NOTES

*   An earlier version of this chapter was presented at the Second International Forum of the Collaboration Projects held in Tokyo on 18–20 March 2001. I would like to thank Robert Dekle for his helpful comments.
1.   Medical-care expenditure decreased slightly in 2000 due to the introduction of public long-term care insurance. Before then a significant number of people with disabilities had replaced medical services provided by health insurance for long-term care services. However, other data sources indicate that the upward trend of medical-care costs has not qualitatively changed since 2000. Although resources devoted to both medical and long-term care should be a focus of health policy for the elderly, issues in long-term care costs are beyond the scope of this chapter.
2.   Newhouse (1992) estimated that 15 percent of the growth between 1950 and 1987 was explained by population ageing. Cutler (1997) pointed out that population ageing explained only 2 percent of the growth from 1940 to 1990.
3.   The elderly aged 70 and over had received free medical care from 1973 to 1983. In 1983, a fixed, albeit tiny, amount of out-of-pocket payment for the elderly was introduced. If the total medical cost is affected by out-of-pocket expenses, the increased cost associated with the increased burden in this period is puzzling. However, evidence from other reforms of the out-of-pocket payment rule supports the conventional wisdom that the medical cost responds negatively to out-of-pocket expenses (see Iwamoto and Kishida 2001). It is therefore likely that other technological factors have a significant effect on the growth of medical costs for the elderly.
4.   More than 90 percent of national medical-care expenditure is paid by public health insurance with its officially determined fee schedule. The estimation of the inflation rate of medical services (shown in Table 8.1) is based mainly on the change in this payment schedule.
5.   The exact formula for transfers is rather complicated.
6.   This suggests that the health insurance reform was an extraordinarily complicated event, because it is highly unusual for the Ministry of Finance to propose its own reform plan concerning a policy that is the responsibility of another ministry.
7.   This hike was realized in October 2002. A 30 percent coinsurance rate for employees was applied in April 2003.
8.   The *Taishokusha Iryo* currently consists of retired workers aged under 69 and their dependents.
9.   Glied (2000) surveys issues in managed care.
10.   Medical expenses vary widely among regions. The prefecture with the highest per capita medical costs spent 1.53 times as much as the one with the lowest cost in 1999, even after

adjusting for the difference in the population structure. The large regional variations have been considered as evidence that Japanese medical practices are not standardized. A recent report of the regional variations has pointed out that the excess capacity of medical institutions drives medical costs up by inducing a demand for medical care (Chiikisa Kenkyukai 2001).

REFERENCES

Chiikisa Kenkyukai (ed.) (2001), *Iryohi no Chiikisa* (Regional variations in medical expenditure), Tokyo: Toyokei Shinposha (in Japanese).

Cutler, David M. (1997), 'Public policy for health care', in Alan J. Auerbach (ed.), *Fiscal Policy: Lessons from Economic Research*, Cambridge, MA: MIT Press, pp. 157–98.

Glied, Sherry (2000), 'Managed care', in Anthony J. Culyer and Joseph P. Newhouse (eds), *Handbook of Health Economics*, Vol. 1A, Amsterdam: Elsevier, pp. 707–53.

Iwamoto, Yasushi (2002), 'Koreisha Iryo Hoken Seido no Kaikaku' (Reform of health insurance for the elderly), *Nihon Keizai Kenkyu*, No. 44, March, 1–21 (in Japanese).

Iwamoto, Yasushi and Kensaku Kishida (2001), 'An estimation of the price elasticity of medical care: evidence from Japanese policy reforms during 40 years', mimeo.

Iwamoto, Yasushi, Satoshi Takeshita and Masashi Bessho (1997), 'Iryo Hoken Zaisei to Kohi Futan' (Public health insurance and government subsidies), *Finansharu Rebyu*, No. 43, November, 174–201 (in Japanese).

Kawai, Hiroki and Shiko Maruyama (2000), 'Hokatsu Barai Sei Donyu ga Iryohi to Shinryo Mitsudo ni Oyoboshita Eikyo ni Kansuru Bunseki: Rojin Mansei Shikkan Gairai narabini Nyuyouji Gairai ni Kanshite' (An analysis of the effect of the inclusive payment system on costs and intensity of care: the cases of elderly and infant outpatients), *Iryo Keizai Kenkyu*, **7**, 37–64 (in Japanese).

Newhouse, Joseph P. (1992), 'Medical care costs: how much welfare loss?', *Journal of Economic Perspectives*, **6** (3), Summer, 3–21.

Niki, Ryu (1995), *Nihon no Iryohi: Kokusai Hikaku no Shiten kara* (Medical care in Japan: from a comparative perspective), Tokyo: Igaku Shoin (in Japanese).

Nishimura, Shuzo (1997), 'Choki Tsumitate Gata Iryo Hoken Seido no Kanosei ni Tsuite' (On the possibility of fully-funded social health insurance), *Iryo Keizai Kenkyu*, **4**, December, 13–34 (in Japanese).

Ogura, Seiritsu (1994), 'The cost of aging: public finance perspectives for Japan', in Yukio Noguchi and David A. Wise (eds), *Aging in the United States and Japan*, Chicago: University of Chicago Press, pp. 139–73.

Ogura, Seiritsu and Tsuyoshi Irifune (1990), 'Waga Kuni no Jinko no Koreika to Kaku Kouteki Iryo Hoken no Shushi ni Tuite' (Population aging and the financing of public health insurance),' *Finansharu Rebyu*, No. 17, August, 51–77 (in Japanese).

Suzuki, Wataru (2000), 'Iryo Hoken ni Okeru Sedai Kan Fukohei to Tsumitatekin wo Motsu Fea na Zaisei Hosiki heno Iko' (A proposal for removing intergenerational inequity from the Japanese health insurance system), *Nihon Keizai Kenkyu*, March, 88–104 (in Japanese).

Takagi, Yasuo (1993), 'Rojin Byoin ni Okeru Kaigo Ryoku Kyoka to Hiyo Manpawa no Henka: Waga Kuni no Rojin Choki Kea no Genjo to Iryo Shisetsu no Henbo' (Introduction of an inclusive per-diem reimbursement system for geriatric care and its effects in reducing the costs of medication and diagnostic tests and improving the patient's ADL),' *Kikan Shakai Hosho Kenkyu*, **28** (4), March, 395–404 (in Japanese).

Tokita, Tadahiko, Tetsuro Chino, Hideaki Ritaki, Izumi Yamamoto and Mitsuyoshi Miyagi (1997), 'The present and future national medical expenditure in Japan', *Keizai Bunseki*, No. 152, September.

9. Conjoint analysis and effect of child-care policies on fertility

Yasushi Ohkusa*

1. INTRODUCTION

The rapid ageing of the population and reduction in the number of children have changed the status of children from private goods of families to public goods, in the sense that they are contributors to the labor supply, tax revenue and social welfare costs. Such a significant positive externality of children has lowered the private rate of return below the public one, and this situation calls for public intervention. This implies a need for change in child-care policy, from a welfare policy that primarily targets the poor to a positive public policy for the whole economy.

However, there has been little research on this issue.[1] There are significant differences among regions that may lead to the imposition of drastic political changes. Observational data are limited, and cross-sectional data do not give a time-series perspective and may suffer from selection bias. Conducting a social experiment on fertility would be the best solution. However, such experiments are very expensive in terms of money and time. Moreover, they involve serious ethical problems that are likely to make their realization impossible. Instead of social experiments, questionnaires on hypothetical situations are used in surveys at different times; these incur lower costs but are less accurate.

Tsukahara (1995) is the pioneer in this field in Japan; however, his research ignores the effects of variables such as age, income and the actual number of children. In this sense, the responses to the questionnaire do not necessarily bear any relationship to the actual situation of the individuals involved. Although it is doubtful whether the study has political implications for policy evaluation, it estimated that the number of children would rise by 6.8 percent if there was 100 percent income support during the child-care period, in comparison with no income support. Further, if the financial benefits for bearing children were doubled, then the number of children was estimated to increase by 1.7–2.1 percent. Thus, the estimated impact of Tsukahara's paper on such policies is very limited.

Shigeno and Ohkusa (2000) analyzed data from the 'Supplement of the Survey of Living Standards in Japan', which investigated the duration and level of income support for child-care leave, lump-sum payment for delivery, and fees for day care if the ideal number of children were born. The results showed that if the period of child-care leave was extended from one to two years, the number of children would rise by 0.37; if there was full income support during that leave, the number of children would rise by about 0.5; if there was a lump-sum payment of ¥1 million for delivery, the number of children would rise by 0.48; and if there was a low fee of about ¥10 000 per month, there would be an increase of one child. The limitation of this survey is that the ideal and planned numbers of children were separate issues, and the willingness-to-pay method was used with the respondents. In these situations, it is difficult for respondents to make appropriate responses.[2]

This chapter examines fertility in Japan by using conjoint analysis, that is, a survey that asks about the respondent's behavior under hypothetical conditions. Because it replicates actual decision making and appropriate economic theory, it is preferable to the willingness-to-pay method, which specifies conditions for undertaking certain behavior. Moreover, this method can account for individual effects by changing certain conditions. Therefore, conjoint analysis is a better method for policy evaluation.

2. DATA

The data used were obtained from research conducted under the direction of Professor Toshiaki Tachibanaki. The respondents were married females who were 20–49 years of age. The sample was chosen randomly through a two-step stratified method. The survey was conducted in October and November 2000. Of the 5000 questionnaires sent to respondents, 1493 (29.9 percent) replies were obtained.

In this survey, in addition to age, family structure, income, assets and employment history, the questionnaire asked sample individuals about the number of children that they would like under a range of hypothetical situations. These situations were defined according to four dimensions: (i) the length of child-care leave: one year (the actual situation), one and a half years and two years; (ii) the replacement rate of income support during child-care leave: 20 percent (the actual situation), 50 and 75 percent; (iii) the conditions for entry to day care for children: 'easy', 'waiting list' and 'very difficult'; and (iv) the financial benefit for caring for children: ¥5000 (the actual situation), ¥50 000 and ¥100 000. Since the conditions for entry to day care vary among regions, family structure and/or job status, and more-over, that recognition by respondents is not uniform, the actual situation could not be determined uniquely.

These four dimensions and the three conditions in each dimension made 81 hypothetical cases. In order to reduce the burden, each respondent was assigned ten hypothetical cases. Moreover, five patterns of ten hypothetical cases were used in the survey and thus the survey covered 50 hypothetical cases, which were assigned randomly to respondents. Table 9.1 presents a summary of descriptive statistics.

3. BRIEF EXPLANATION OF CONJOINT ANALYSIS

In this research, conjoint analysis is one of the most reliable techniques for dealing with individual effects by using a questionnaire survey. The conjoint analysis questionnaire concerns hypothetical choices. Thus, the researchers can analyze choice by reference to the scenarios, and the individual proper-ties in the statistical models can fully control for individual effects.

To evaluate the benefit of a new medicine or a new technology in the field of health economics, researchers have conventionally employed the willingness-to-pay (Tolley et al. 1994) or standard gamble, time trade-off and rating scale methods. However, these methods suffer from various theoretical problems. For instance, the price obtained by willingness to pay obviously differs from the utility level. The other three methods also display this shortcoming, which does not reflect the utility level. Under the theoretical concept of ordinal utility, utility cannot be compared or aggre-gated among individuals. Compared with willingness to pay, conjoint anal-ysis has the advantage that respondents react as the price is given and make no prior assumptions about their choices. Furthermore, the statistical model using conjoint analysis can experiment with policy simulations by changing the values of the explanatory variables.

Conjoint analysis has conventionally been widely used in the fields of environment and traffic economics. In health economics, conjoint analysis has recently been applied in the evaluation of new medical treatment tech-nology (Ryan and Hughes 1997; Van der Pol and Cairns 1997; Bryan et al. 1998; Farrar and Ryan 1999; Ryan 1999; Ryan et al. 1999). For example, it has been applied in the study of fertilization (Ryan 1999), dentistry correc-tion technology (Farrar and Ryan 1994), suspension technology (Ryan and Hughes 1997), blood transfusion technology (Van der Pol and Cairns 1997), and the application of magnetic resonance imaging (MRI) to damage caused by knee injuries (Bryan et al. 1998). Unfortunately, there

Table 9.1 *Summary statistics*

	Average	Std dev.	Maximum	Minimum
Duration of child-care leave	1.482652	0.3863291	1	2
Replacement rate of income				
Support during child-care leave	47.64501	20.08322	20	75
Entry condition to day care for children				
'Waiting list'	0.3595445	0.4798991	0	1
'Very difficult'	0.4	0.4899308	0	1
Benefit of caring for children	0.9509433	1.258494	−0.6931472	2.302585
Actual number of children	1.933735	0.935187	0	5
Planned number of children	2.177498	0.7882079	0	5
Age (wife)	39.13731	6.811309	21	49
Age (wife)^2	1578.117	519.8683	441	2401
Age (husband)	42.09584	8.983953	20	99
Labor income (wife)	3.053023	2.522228	0	7.131699
Other income	5.910566	1.611957	0	8.086718
Net assets	−329.8193	2060.129	−18500	20250
Job status (wife)	0.3842035	0.4864389	0	1

Notes: Sample size is 5151 and the number of respondents is 1099. Hypothetical situations are defined as: duration of child-care leave is one year (actual situation), one and a half years and two years; replacement rates of income support during the child-care leave are 20 (actual situation), 50 and 75 percent; conditions for entry to day care for children are 'easy', 'waiting list' and 'very difficult'; financial benefits of caring for children are ¥5000 (actual situation), ¥50000 and ¥100000. The length of child-care leave and the replacement rate of income support during this leave is defined by the actual number; the entry conditions to day care for children are constructed as dummy variables for 'waiting list' and 'very difficult', such that 'easy' is the base condition; and the financial benefit for caring for children is defined by the logarithm of the number of ¥10000.

are few studies in health economics that use conjoint analysis. The exceptional cases are Ohkusa (1999) and Ii and Ohkusa (2001).[3]

Usually, probit estimation with random effects is adopted as the estimation method for conjoint analysis. Because the dependent variable is dichotomous (either 'yes' or 'no' under a certain hypothetical condition), the use of probit estimation is a natural choice. Moreover, as typical respondents reveal their preference in several hypothetical situations, the econometrician can control for individual effects, which are major determinants of the behavior of individuals but not observable explanatory variables.

There are two types of individual effects, fixed and random. However, the fixed effects model cannot be a candidate because information about individuals, such as age, education level and income, which are constant within the same individual cannot be identified. However, it appears that such information is very important for an individual's behavior, and thus the fixed effects model is inappropriate for conjoint analysis. On the other hand, the random effects model avoids this problem. However, in the general random effects model, the ordinary least-squares estimator suffers from inconsistency when there is a correlation between the explanatory variables and the random effect. Panel studies other than conjoint analysis, for example, those using the Hausman (1978) test, are sometimes rejected. Conversely, in conjoint analysis, the hypothetical situations, which vary even for the same individual, are constructed so as to be uncorrelated with the random effect. Therefore, the inconsistency problem is not present in conjoint analysis.[1]

4. ESTIMATION MODEL

While the most interesting variable in this chapter is the response concerning the number of children in the hypothetical cases, the differences between the response and the actual number or the response and the planned number are employed as dependent variables in order to control the true situation completely. The former is appropriate if the respondent has given birth already. The latter variable can avoid such a problem, but the planned number does not necessarily mean the final number in the sense of *ex ante* and *ex post*. Moreover, in some cases, the planned number of children is smaller than the number already born. Hence, the latter is also contaminated by some measurement error. However, these errors are eliminated by individual effects, as explained below.

The explanatory variables are first concerned with the hypothetical conditions. The length of child-care leave and the replacement rate of income support during such leave are substituted directly into the equation. The entry conditions to day care for children are constructed as dummy variables for 'waiting list' and 'very difficult', while 'easy' is the base condition. The financial benefit of caring for children is introduced as a quadratic function of the logarithm of the value.

Other explanatory variables are the actual number of children, the quadratic form of the wife's age, the husband's age, the job status, the labor income, income other than the wife's labor and net assets. These are included in Tsukahara (1995) and Shigeno and Ohkusa (2000).

Since each respondent provides on average an answer in five cases, we can introduce a random effect as an individual effect. Hence, an ordered probit with random effects is employed:

$$y^*_{i,j} = \beta' \chi_{i,j} + \varepsilon_{i,j}, \quad i = 1, \ldots, N, \ j = 1, \ldots, J(i)$$

$$\varepsilon_{i,j} = v_{i,j} + u_i$$

$$\mathrm{Var}(\varepsilon_{i,j}) = \sigma_v^2 + \sigma_u^2 = 1 + \sigma_u^2$$

$$\mathrm{Corr}(\varepsilon_{i,j}, \varepsilon_{i,k}) = 1 \quad \text{for} \quad j = k$$

$$\mathrm{Corr}(\varepsilon_{i,j}, \varepsilon_{i,k}) = \rho = \frac{\sigma_u^2}{1 + \sigma_u^2} \quad \text{for} \quad j \neq k$$

$$\mathrm{Corr}(\varepsilon_{i,j}, \varepsilon_{l,k}) = 0 \quad \text{for} \quad i \neq l$$

$$y_{i,j} = k \quad \text{if} \quad \mu_{k-1} < y^*_{i,j} \leq \mu_k \quad k = 1, \ldots, K \qquad (9.1)$$

where μ_k is the threshold for the kth order and is implicitly defined as $\mu_0 = -\infty$, and $\mu_K = \infty$. i indicates the ith respondent and $J(i)$ represents the ith respondent's number of cases. The likelihood function $L = \Sigma_{i=1}^{N} \log P(y_{i,1}, \ldots, y_{i,J(i)})$ is constructed by $P(y_{i,1}, \ldots, y_{i,J(i)})$ as:

$$P(y_{i,1}, \ldots, y_{i,J(i)}) = \int_{a_{i,1}}^{b_{i,1}} \cdots \int_{a_{i,J(i)}}^{b_{i,J(i)}} f(\varepsilon_{i,1}, \ldots, \varepsilon_{i,J(i)}) d\varepsilon_{i,J(i)} \cdots d\varepsilon_{i,1}$$

$$= \int_{a_{i,1}}^{b_{i,1}} \cdots \int_{a_{i,J(i)}}^{b_{i,J(i)}} \int_{-\infty}^{\infty} \prod_{j=1}^{J(i)} f(v_{i,j}|u_i) f(u_i) du_i dv_{i,J(i)} \cdots dv_{i,1}$$

$$= \int_{-\infty}^{\infty} \prod_{j=1}^{J(i)} [F(b_{i,j}|u_i) - F(a_{i,j}|u_i)] du_i. \qquad (9.2)$$

These random effects in probit estimation are referred to in Butler and Moffitt (1982) and Greene (2000). In actual calculation, the analytical derivatives:

$$\frac{\partial P_i}{\partial \beta} = \int_{-\infty}^{\infty} f(u_i) \sum_{j=1}^{J(i)} \frac{f_{i,k}^{k-1} - f_{i,j}^{k}}{F_{i,j}^{k} - F_{i,j}^{k-1}} x_{i,j} \prod_{j=1}^{J(i)} [F(b_{i,j}|u_i) - F(a_{i,j}|u_i)] du_i$$

$$\frac{\partial P_i}{\partial \mu_k} = \int_{-\infty}^{\infty} f(u_i) \sum_{j=1}^{J(i)} \frac{f_{i,k}^{k-1}[y_{i,j}=k] - f_{i,j}^{k}[y_{i,j}=k-1]}{F_{i,j}^{k} - F_{i,j}^{k-1}} x_{i,j}$$

$$\prod_{j=1}^{J(i)} [F(b_{i,j}|u_i) - F(a_{i,j}|u_i)] du_i$$

$$\frac{\partial P_i}{\partial \rho} = \int_{-\infty}^{\infty} f(u_i) \sum_{j=1}^{J(i)} \frac{f_{i,j}^{k-1} - f_{i,j}^{k}}{F_{i,j}^{k} - F_{i,j}^{k-1}} \frac{1}{[2\rho(1-\rho)]^{0.5}} \prod_{j=1}^{J(i)} [F(b_{i,j}|u_i) - F(a_{i,j}|u_i)] du_i$$

$$(9.3)$$

are used to speed up the process.

5.   EMPIRICAL RESULTS

The empirical results for the responses for the number of children are presented in Table 9.2, the difference between the responses and the actual number in Table 9.3, and the difference between the responses and the planned number in Table 9.4. Although marginal effects can be calculated for each order in the ordered probit estimation, the marginal effect of the expected number of children, which is aggregated over the orders, is indicated in the tables to save space:

$$\frac{\partial E(y|X)}{\partial X} = \sum_{k=1}^{K} k \frac{\partial \text{Prob}(y=k|X)}{\partial X}. \qquad (9.4)$$

The estimated results about the hypothetical conditions are shared in the three estimations. Namely, there are significant differences in the first term for the benefit of caring for a child. A one-year extension of the length of child-care leave would increase the number of children by 0.12–0.14. The replacement rate of income support during the child-care leave would increase the number of children by 0.04 for each 10 percent point increase. The condition for entry to day care for children reduces the number of children by 0.34–0.39 for 'waiting list' and 0.52–0.58 for 'very difficult' in comparison with 'easy.' The second term for the benefit of caring for children is significantly positive, and thus its impact is conversely related to fertility.

Table 9.2 Empirical results for the response for the number of children

	Estimated coef.	z-value	p-value	Marginal effect
Duration of child-care leave	0.1640569	3.448	0.001	0.13170977
Replacement rate	0.0068148	6.871	0.000	0.00547112
'Waiting list'	−0.5247589	−11.777	0.000	−0.42129209
'Very difficult'	−0.8388626	−18.200	0.000	−0.6734639
Benefit of caring for children	0.0171493	0.486	0.627	0.01376797
Benefit of caring for children^2	0.1129475	4.661	0.000	0.09067762
Actual number of children	0.0562013	1.617	0.106	0.04512008
Age (wife)	−0.0791538	−1.444	0.149	−0.06354703
Age (wife)^2	0.0013996	1.942	0.052	0.00112364
Age (husband)	−0.0040048	−0.824	0.410	−0.00321517
Labor income (wife)	−0.043123	−2.342	0.019	−0.03462043
Other income	−0.0351328	−1.674	0.094	−0.02820566
Net assets	1.18E–06	0.098	0.922	9.473E–07
Job status (wife)	−0.1802012	−1.994	0.046	−0.1446TODO
Threshold1	−5.444364	−5.718	0.000	
Threshold2	−3.450216	−3.651	0.000	
Threshold3	−1.124266	−1.187	0.235	
Threshold4	0.3205894	0.337	0.736	
Threshold5	0.5640061	0.593	0.553	
Threshold6	0.5989264	0.630	0.529	
ρ	0.8469237	204.315	0.000	

Notes: Estimation method is ordered probit with random effect. Sample size is 7460 and the number of respondents is 1094. The loglikelihood is −7098.8331, and the likelihood ratio test for the null hypothesis that all coefficients except the constant term are zero is rejected at the 10 percent significance level. Marginal effects indicate the derivatives of the expected number of children.

240

Table 9.3 *Empirical results for the difference between the response for the number of children and the actual number*

	Estimated coef.	z-value	P-value	Marginal effect
Duration of child-care leave	0.1535932	3.262	0.001	0.11238866
Replacement rate	0.0052179	5.279	0.000	0.00381809
'Waiting list'	−0.4522131	−10.238	0.000	−0.33089761
'Very Difficult'	−0.7079501	−15.578	0.000	−0.51802789
Benefit of caring for children	0.0125039	0.357	0.721	0.00914947
Benefit of caring for children^2	0.1009968	4.212	0.000	0.07390233
Actual number of children	−0.0974341	−3.269	0.001	−0.07129539
Age (wife)	−0.1062831	−2.470	0.014	−0.07777047
Age (wife)^2	0.0014368	2.459	0.014	0.00105135
Age (husband)	0.0229693	2.546	0.011	0.01680731
Labor income (wife)	−0.0165234	−1.093	0.275	−0.01209066
Other income	−0.0526571	−3.032	0.002	−0.03853075
Net assets	2.23E−06	0.192	0.847	1.632E−06
Job status (wife)	−0.1736523	−2.248	0.025	−0.12706649
Threshold1	−9.123864	−11.924	0.000	
Threshold2	−7.405047	9.968	0.000	
Threshold3	−5.342403	−7.226	0.000	
Threshold4	−3.987303	−5.397	0.000	
Threshold5	−1.361818	−1.851	0.064	
Threshold6	0.0321172	0.044	0.965	
Threshold7	0.5315817	0.723	0.470	
Threshold8	0.626333	0.852	0.394	
ρ	0.8609571	239.873	0.000	

Notes: Estimation method is ordered probit with random effect. Sample size is 7460 and the number of respondents is 1094. The loglikelihood is −7427.9156, and the likelihood ratio test for the null hypothesis that all coefficients except the constant term are zero is rejected at the 10 percent significance level. Marginal effects indicate the derivatives of the expected rise in the number of children.

241

Table 9.4 Empirical results for the difference between the response for the number of children and the planned number

	Estimated coef.	z-value	p-value	Marginal effect
Duration of child-care leave	0.1912835	3.884	0.000	0.22372841
Replacement rate	0.0059413	5.798	0.000	0.00694904
'Waiting list'	−0.5458621	−11.766	0.000	−0.63844953
'Very difficult'	−0.858088	−17.811	0.000	−1.0036342
Benefit of caring for children	0.0040339	0.110	0.912	0.00471812
Benefit of caring for children[2]	0.12976	5.160	0.000	0.15176949
Actual number of children	−0.146931	−4.697	0.000	−0.17185298
Age (wife)	0.0566788	1.088	0.277	0.06629248
Age (wife)[2]	−0.0004368	−0.626	0.531	−0.00051089
Age (husband)	−0.0020644	−0.510	0.610	−0.00241456
Labor income (wife)	−0.0364066	−1.791	0.056	−0.04258177
Other income	−0.0365606	−1.794	0.073	−0.04276189
Net assets	−0.0000139	−1.119	0.263	−0.00001626
Job status (wife)	−0.214724	−2.096	0.036	−0.25114481
Threshold1	−6.627019	−7.566	0.000	
Threshold2	−5.269921	−6.063	0.000	
Threshold3	−3.20653	−3.701	0.000	
Threshold4	−1.658625	−1.912	0.056	
Threshold5	1.109687	1.277	0.202	
Threshold6	1.966772	2.268	0.023	
Threshold7	2.093589	2.414	0.016	
Threshold8	2.108089	2.430	0.015	
ρ	0.8555326	183.700	0.000	

Notes: Estimation method is ordered probit with random effect. Sample size is 7460 and the number of respondents is 1094. The loglikelihood is −6774.7895, and the likelihood ratio test for the null hypothesis that all coefficients except the constant term are zero is rejected at the 10 percent significance level. Marginal effects indicate the derivatives of the expected rise in the number of children.

242

In variables other than the hypothetical conditions, only the actual number of children is significant in all tables, but its sign lacks robustness; that is, the analysis of the number of children in Table 9.2 is significantly positive, but the analysis of the difference is significantly negative. This discrepancy seems to be due to the actual or planned number of children being included by substruction in the dependent variable. Hence, its marginal effect in Table 9.2 is 0.39, almost equal to one plus -0.53, which is the counterpart in Table 9.3. In Table 9.4, the corresponding number, -0.26, reflects that substruction in the dependent variables is not the actual number of children, but the planned number. Thus, this change in definition weakened the relationship between Tables 9.2 and 9.3.

While the wives' ages in Table 9.3 are significantly negative, their impact is significantly convex in Table 9.4. Since the estimated peak age is about 50, an increase in age increases the planned number of children during the child-bearing years. At first glance, this result seems to be inconsistent. This phenomenon may result from the fact that the actual number of children is almost always less than the planned number, and this gap reduces with increasing age. (Other estimation methods, linear model and/or Poisson regression with random effects, were examined, and are summarized in Appendix Table 9A.1.[5])

6. POLICY SIMULATION

So as to understand the estimation result intuitively, we calculate the necessary increment of the duration of child-care leave, the income support during such leave and the financial benefits, and its 90 percent significance interval, to increase the fertility rate by 0.1. These figures are summarized in Tables 9.5–7, respectively.

The benefit received for caring for a child is subject to a means test and there are only 2.2 million current recipients, which accounts for 30 percent of the population less than six years of age. However, this income limitation is assumed not to exist for the purpose of the policy implications in this policy simulation. If this limitation is assumed to hold, then the additional expenditure reduces by 70 percent, although the fertility rate rises by only 0.3. Table 9.5 shows that increasing the financial benefit by ¥34–40 thousand raises the rate by 0.1. This means that the financial benefit increase would be ¥39–45 thousand. In 1997, since there were 7.2 million children who were less than six years old, the total spending for the benefit would have been ¥280–324 billion.

On the other hand, to raise the fertility rate by 0.1, the duration of

Table 9.5   Necessary increment of financial benefit for raising the fertility rate (¥000)

	Table 9.2			Table 9.3			Table 9.4		
Rise in fertility rate	Lower bound	Median	Upper bound	Lower bound	Median	Upper bound	Lower bound	Median	Upper bound
0.1	18	34	90	20	40	91	19	34	58
0.2	35	50	101	34	62	135	30	46	76
0.3	40	66	175	50	88	185	40	60	95
0.4	53	84	235	67	115	245	50	74	115
0.5	66	105	295	86	155	305	61	89	145
0.6	80	125	375	115	185	385	73	105	165
0.7	95	145	455	135	225	465	85	125	195
0.8	101	165	555	155	275	565	98	145	225
0.9	135	195	675	185	315	685	115	165	265
1.0	145	215	825	215	375	835	135	185	305

Table 9.6   Necessary increment of child-care leave for raising the fertility rate (years)

	Table 9.2			Table 9.3			Table 9.4		
Rise in fertility rate	Lower bound	Median	Upper bound	Lower bound	Median	Upper bound	Lower bound	Median	Upper bound
0.1	n.a.	0.90	3.25	0.25	1.15	3.30	0.15	0.75	1.75
0.2	0.70	1.65	4.70	0.95	2.10	4.75	0.60	1.35	2.55
0.3	1.25	2.35	6.00	1.65	3.05	7.20	1.10	1.90	3.25
0.4	1.80	3.05	6.00	2.30	3.90	8.40	1.55	2.50	4.00
0.5	2.35	3.70	6.00	2.95	4.75	9.60	2.00	3.00	4.65
0.6	2.85	4.30	10.60	3.55	5.60	10.70	2.45	3.55	5.35
0.7	3.35	4.90	11.90	4.20	7.10	12.00	2.90	4.05	7.20
0.8	3.85	5.45	13.20	4.80	7.80	13.30	3.30	4.60	8.00
0.9	4.35	6.00	14.70	5.40	8.60	14.80	3.70	5.10	8.80
1.0	4.80	7.10	16.70	5.95	9.40	16.80	4.15	5.60	21.90

child-care leave should increase by 0.75–1.15 years, which is double the current amount. The replacement rate of income support during child-

Table 9.7   Necessary increment of replacement rate of income support during child-care leave

	Table 9.2			Table 9.3			Table 9.4		
Rise in fertility rate	Lower bound	Median	Upper bound	Lower bound	Median	Upper bound	Lower bound	Median	Upper bound
0.1	22	41	93	27	52	94	23	42	68
0.2	45	60	130	51	81	131	40	62	91
0.3	56	78	160	73	109	164	57	80	113
0.4	72	95	160	96	135	196	73	99	134
0.5	87	111	160	117	160	224	88	116	154
0.6	103	126	160	137	180	254	104	133	174
0.7	118	141	280	158	202	282	119	150	194
0.8	132	155	310	170	226	312	133	162	214
0.9	146	160	338	188	248	340	147	180	236
1.0	160	174	368	206	270	370	156	196	258

care leave, would need to increase by 41–52 percent (that is, three times the 1997 amount and double the current amount) to raise the fertility rate by 0.1.

In sum, public policy can raise the fertility rate, but an increase of more than 0.1 seems to be less cost effective.

7.   CONCLUDING REMARKS

We conducted an original survey about fertility under hypothetical conditions and then analyzed the difference between the responses to the number of children and the planned/actual number of children using conjoint analysis. The empirical results show that increasing child-care leave by one year would increase the number of children by 0.12–0.14. The income support during child-care leave also has a positive effect on fertility, but a 10 percent increase in the replacement rate would increase the number of children by only 0.04. The condition of admission to day-care service has a significant effect; the 'waiting list' and 'difficult' cases would reduce the number of children by 0.34–0.39 and 0.52–0.58, respectively, in comparison with the 'easy' case. An increase of ¥34–40 thousand in the financial benefits for bearing children would be required to increase the number of children by 0.1.

Future research should extend the conjoint analysis with a wider range of respondents and specific hypothetical conditions to achieve more precise results and reliable policy recommendations.

NOTES

*   This chapter is a report of research directed by Professor Tachibanaki of Kyoto University, as one of ESRI's new millennium projects. I would like to acknowledge helpful advice on the questionnaire from Professor Ohtake of Osaka University and staff of the Kansai Institute of Economic Research. I would also like to acknowledge the fruitful discussions with Professor Tachibanaki and other members of the research group, and assistance provided by Tomoko Nagase. I claim responsibility for all remaining errors.
1. Ogura and Dekle (1992), Harada and Takada (1993) and Ohsawa (1993) analyze cross-sectional prefecture data of the number of children, but only Harada and Takada focus on the welfare policy for children. They found that, for every ¥5000 of the benefit for caring for children, the number of children would increase by 0.01.
2. Simon and Simon (1974) adopt the survey for hypothetical situations to analyze the effect of the benefit of caring for children.
3. See also Fukuda et al. (1999), which was presented at the hospital management meeting.
4. If all respondents were to respond to all the hypothetical situations, the inconsistency problem would be avoided. However, this is not the case in reality; a correlation between the explanatory variables and the random effect may exist.
5. Although there are some differences, the main implications hold for the different methods. Therefore, in this chapter, the ordered probit model with random effects alone is discussed in the main text.

REFERENCES

Bryan, S., M. Buxton, R. Sheldon and A. Grant (1998), 'The use of magnetic resonance imaging for the investigation of knee injuries: a discrete choice conjoint analysis exercise', *Health Economics*, **7**, 595–604.

Butler, J.S. and R. Moffitt (1982), 'A computationally efficient quadrature procedure for the one-factor multinomial probit model', *Econometrica*, **50**, 761–4.

Farrar, S. and M. Ryan (1999), 'Response-ordering effects: a methodological issue in conjoint analysis', *Health Economics*, **8** (1), 75–9.

Fukuda, T., H. Kinoshita, S. Takeda and S. Yamaki (1999), 'Conjoint analysis for choice of medical institution' (in Japanese), paper presented at the Meeting of Hospital Management.

Greene, W.H. (2000), *Econometric Analysis*, Englewood Cliffs, NJ: Prentice-Hall.

Harada, Y. and S. Takada (1993), 'Theory of population and its prediction' (in Japanese), in N. Takayama and Y. Harada (eds), *Saving in the Aging Society*, Tokyo: Nihon Hyouron Sha, pp. 1–14.

Hausman, J. (1978), 'Specification test in econometrics', *Econometrica*, **46**, 1251–71.

Ii, M. and Y. Ohkusa (2001), 'Empirical research into the demand for influenza vaccination' (in Japanese), *Japanese Journal of Public Health*, **48** (1), 16–27.

Kaserman, D.L. and A.H. Barnett (1991), 'An economic analysis of transplant organs: a comment and extension', *Atlantic Economic Journal*, **19**, 57–63.

King, G. (1998), *Unifying Political Methodology: The Likelihood Theory of Statistical Inference*, Cambridge: Cambridge University Press.

Liang, K. and S. Zeger (1986), 'Longitudinal data analysis using a generalized linear model', *Biometrika*, **73**, 13–22.

Ogura, S. and R. Dekle (1992), 'Explaining the declining fertility of Japanese women since 1970 through prefectural cohort data', *JCER Economic Journal*, **22**, 46–76.

Ohkusa, Y. (1999), 'The effect of job status and firm on fertility behavior' (in Japanese), Research Report on Employees in Small and Medium sized Firms, Research Institution for Life and Welfare.

Ohsawa, M. (1993), *Charging in Economics and Female Labor Supply – International Comparison with Japan and the USA* (in Japanese), Tokyo: Nihone Keizai Hyouron Sha.

Ryan, M. (1999), 'Using conjoint analysis to take account of patient preferences and go beyond health outcomes: an application to in-vitro fertilization', *Social Science and Medicine*, **48**, 535–46.

Ryan, M. and J. Hughes (1997), 'Using conjoint analysis to assess women's preference for miscarriage management', *Health Economics*, **6**, 261–74.

Ryan, M., E. McIntoch and P. Shackley (1999), 'Methodological issues in the application of conjoint analysis in health care', *Health Economics*, **7** (4), 373–8.

Shigeno, Y. and Y. Ohkusa (1999), 'The effect of child welfare on fertility choice and labor supply' (in Japanese), *Quarterly Journal of Social Security Research*, **35** (2), 192–207.

Shigeno, Y. and Y. Ohkusa (2000), 'The effect of child welfare on marriage and fertility choice' (in Japanese), Research Report on the Effect of Family Structure and Social Security on Household Behavior.

Simon, R. and J. Simon (1974), 'Money incentives and family size: a hypothetical-question study', *Public Opinion Quarterly*, **38** (4), 585–95.

Tolley, G., D. Kenkel and R. Fabian (1994), *Valuing Health Policy: An Economic Approach*, Chicago: University of Chicago Press.

Tsukahara, Y. (1995), 'The effect of public policies on fertility: an experimental vignette approach' (in Japanese), *JCER Economic Journal*, **28**, 148–61.

Van der Pol, M. and J. Cairns (1997), 'Establishing patients' preferences for blood transfusion support: an application of conjoint analysis', *Journal of Health Services Research and Policy*, **3**, 70–76.

Table 9A.1　Empirical results by other estimation methods

Dependent variable as	Table 9.5	Table 9.6	Table 9.7
Linear estimation with random effect			
Duration of child-care leave	0.1300105***	0.1300105***	0.1303930***
Replacement rate	0.0046768***	0.0046768***	0.0046275***
'Waiting list'	−0.381578***	−0.381578***	−0.380953***
'Very difficult'	−0.566430***	−0.566430***	−0.566191***
Benefit of caring for children	0.0218962	0.0218962	0.0197202
Benefit of caring for children^2	0.0712366***	0.0712366***	0.0726639***
Actual number of children	0.3924549***	−0.607545***	−0.321132***
Age (wife)	−0.056721	−0.056721	0.1407842***
Age (wife)^2	0.0005237	0.0005237	−0.001766***
Age (husband)	−0.004977	−0.004977	0.0003909
Labor income (wife)	0.0125089	0.0125089	−0.009953
Other income	0.0033957	0.0033957	0.0208662
Net assets	4.61e–06	4.61e–06	−3.42e–06
Job status (wife)	0.0702722	0.0702722	−0.018533
Constant term	2.410226***	2.410226***	−2.73960***
Poisson regression with random effect			
Duration of child-care leave	0.0588375*	0.0242775	0.0254732
Replacement rate	0.0025976***	0.0009542***	0.0009344**
'Waiting list'	−0.189812***	−0.073801***	−0.078641***
'Very difficult'	−0.295405***	−0.112385***	−0.118660***
Benefit of caring for children	0.018019	0.0048055	0.0039763
Benefit of caring for children^2	0.0328613**	0.0137085**	0.0151133**
Actual number of children	0.2062240***	−0.119028***	−0.064959***
Age (wife)	−0.021330	−0.004028	0.0295155***
Age (wife)^2	0.0001459	1.83e−06	−0.000381***
Age (husband)	−0.002199	−0.000754	0.0002481
Labor income (wife)	0.0072003	0.0022679	−0.002020
Other income	0.0048424	0.0021724	0.0055266
Net assets	3.56e–06	1.38e–06	−1.19e–07
Job status (wife)	0.0470684	0.0183887	−0.000111
Constant term	0.7139128**	1.931523***	1.030664***

Notes: This table shows the estimation coefficient with its significance level: *** 1% significance, ** 5%, and * 10%. All Hausman test for linear model cannot reject the null hypothesis of random effect model at the 10% significance level.

10. The child-care leave system in Japan: development, problems and further reform

Akira Kawaguchi*

1. INTRODUCTION

Harmonization of work and family has been attracting increasing attention in Japan. There are several reasons, one of which is the continuous decline in fertility. During the baby boom after the second world war, the total fertility rate exceeded 4. Since then, it has been declining and recorded a post-war low of 1.33 in 2001. The sharp decline will cause difficulty in funding social insurance, particularly old-age pensions. It is widely perceived that one of the most important factors that caused the decline in fertility is the difficulty for working women in rearing children. The Ministry of Health, Labor, and Welfare have implemented several policies which harmonize work and family. The enactment of the Child-care Leave Law is one of them.

Another reason for the increased attention paid to work–family harmonization is the increasing demand by working women for work–family harmonization programs. Although the proportion of married women in the female labor force has increased, the majority of women who start a family resign from the workforce when they give birth, returning to the labor market when their children have grown up. Upon their return, however, most of them work part-time, partly because it is difficult to find full-time jobs after an absence from the labor market and partly because the working hours of full-time jobs are too long and too rigid for mothers. The lifetime income of women declines sharply due to this career break. A family-friendly policy is necessary to increase the proportion of women who keep working after childbirth and to reduce the gender wage gap.

Many empirical studies have analyzed family-friendly programs including the child-care leave system. For example, Higuchi (1994), Tomita (1994), Higuchi et al. (1997), Morita and Kaneko (1998) and Shigeno and Ohkusa (1998) found that the introduction of the child-care leave system reduces women's quit rate. Kawaguchi (2001) found that family-friendly programs and equal employment opportunity programs are complementary.

Family-friendly firms tend to implement equal employment opportunity programs. Maeda (2002) states that Japanese trade unions are not eager to introduce family-friendly programs, because core members of trade unions are male workers.

In this chapter, we argue that the interruption of women's careers after childbirth is the biggest cause of the large gender wage gap in Japan. Increasing the number of workers who take child-care leave will reduce the quit rate of women after childbirth and reduce the gender wage gap. In order to increase the number of workers who take such leave, employers should introduce a child-care leave system and undertake positive action programs to increase its users. Legislation is required to impel employers to take such action.

The organization of this chapter is as follows. In Section 2, we discuss how child care interrupts women's careers in Japan. In Section 3, the government's policy to promote child-care leave systems is explained. In Section 4, features of child-care leave systems in firms are discussed. Problems with the current child-care leave systems are analyzed in Section 5. Finally, more effective policies to promote such leave systems are presented in Section 6.

2.   CHILDBIRTH AND INTERRUPTION OF WOMEN'S CAREER

Figure 10.1 shows hourly wage rates, the proportion of women employed, the nature of their employment according to their marital status as well as the age of their youngest child. The source of the data is the 1993–97 Panel Survey of Consumers, the details of which will be explained in the next section. Regular workers are usually full-time workers and non-regular workers are usually part-time workers. The employed people include those who are taking child-care leave.

There are three notable points. First, many female workers resign from the workforce before their child is born. Labor market participation by women declines from 90 to 65 percent on marriage, and to 22 percent after having a child. Second, the rate of labor market participation increases as women return to work when their children get older, but most of the women who return to the workforce work part-time. The proportion of regular workers increases only slightly. This is partly because many firms are reluctant to recruit mothers as regular workers, and partly because many working mothers prefer part-time work since the working hours of full-time jobs are too long and too rigid. Third, working mothers' average hourly wage is lower than that of single workers and married workers

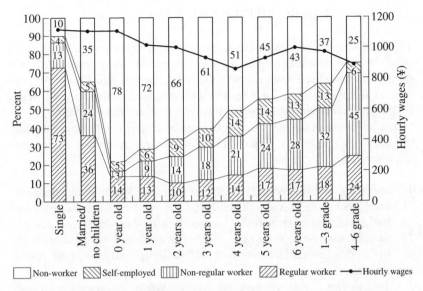

Source: Panel Survey on Consumers, 1993–97.

Figure 10.1   Women's employment and wages by marital status and age of youngest child

without children. This is mainly because the wage rate of part-time workers is lower than that of full-time workers, and the opportunities for pay rises and promotion are limited in part-time jobs.

The first two features are consistent with the 1997 Employment Status Survey (Bureau of Statistics, Office of the Prime Minister 1998). According to the survey, the labor market participation rate of women declines from 85 to 59 percent on marriage. The participation rate for women who have children younger than three years old is 28 percent. Second, the rate of labor market participation increases to 68 percent when the youngest child is aged between 9 and 11 years old, but the proportion of regular workers in this category is only 21 percent.

The labor market participation rate of Japanese women with small children is very low compared to other developed countries. The participation rate of married women with children aged under 6 is only 33.3 percent in Japan, while the corresponding figure is 51.4 percent in Germany, 56.8 percent in France, 60.6 percent in the United States, 61.3 percent in the United Kingdom, and 77.8 percent in Sweden.[1]

3.   THE CHILD-CARE LEAVE LAW

The Child-care Leave Law was enacted in 1992.[2] The law requires employers to offer child-care leave of up to one year. Since then, many firms have introduced child-care leave systems. Initially, no benefit was paid. After 1995, 25 percent of wages were paid as a benefit. This increased to 40 percent of wages in 2001 and is funded by the national employment insurance scheme.

The law requires the government to support employers' policies that harmonize work and family. Based on the law, the government is implementing several subsidy programs:

1. *Subsidy for child-care and family-care support*   When employers assist employees in the payment of child- and family-care fees, two-thirds (one-half in the case of large firms) of the employers' expense is subsidized.
2. *Subsidy for on-site child-care centers*   When employers establish on-site child-care centers, one-half of the setup and operation cost is subsidized.
3. *Subsidy for family-friendly measures*   When employers introduce family-friendly measures, two-thirds of the cost is subsidized. Large firms are not eligible.
4. *Remuneration for returning programs*   When employers establish measures that help those who take child-care leave to return to work, a subsidy of up to ¥210000 is offered. This figure is capped at ¥160000 for large firms.
5. *Subsidy for employing relief workers*   Employers who make regulations and employ relief workers to enable workers to return to the position they held before they took leave, may be eligible to receive a subsidy on the return of the worker to their former position. The subsidy is up to ¥150000 per worker. This figure is capped at ¥100000 for large firms.

In September 2001, the Child-care and Family Care Leave Law was revised as follows:

1. *Treatment of workers who take leave*   Before the revision, dismissing workers who applied for or took leave was prohibited, but other unfair practices were not. According to the 1999 Survey on Female Employment Management (Women's Bureau, Ministry of Labor 2000a), the wage level of employees decreases after taking child-care leave in one-third of workplaces. In these workplaces, there is no guarantee that the worker will receive the wage level they were entitled to previously, after returning from child-care leave. The revised law prohibits employers from cutting wages

and changing work status (for example, switching from full-time to part-time) because a worker has taken leave.

2. *Overtime exemptions for workers with young children* Before the revision, the law restricted employers from requiring workers with children younger than elementary school age to undertake night work. However, it does not restrict overtime. Under the revised law, workers who have children younger than elementary school age are exempt from working overtime in excess of 24 hours a month or 150 hours a year.

3. *Reduced hours for workers with young children* Prior to the revision of the law, employers were required to reduce the working hours of workers who have children under 1 year old and do not take child-care leave. The age was increased to 3 years old by the revision.

4. *Nursing-care leave* Before the revision, the law did not require employers to provide leave for nursing sick children. The revised law requires employers to provide leave for nursing sick children younger than elementary school age.

5. *Consideration of workers' child and family care* When employers relocate workers, they must consider workers' child- and family-care arrangements. There was no such requirement before the revision.

6. *Family support advisors* Employers should endeavor to appoint personnel who will promote work–family harmonization measures. The government offers information and material on work–family issues. There was no such requirement before the revision.

7. *Promotion of harmonization of work and family* Under the revision of the law, the government undertakes to educate workers, employers and citizens on the issue of the harmonization of work and family. There was no such requirement before the revision.

The revised law reflected requests made by working women which will be discussed in the following sections. Working mothers considered the introduction of a nursing-care leave system as most important to their needs and this was adopted in the revised law. The prohibition of unfair treatment for those who take child-care leave is also remarkable. Although not many workers fear wage cuts after child-care leave, taking such leave significantly reduces the opportunity for off-the-job training.

Appointing personnel to promote work–family measures in firms and the government's educational activity ensure that employers and workers understand work–family issues. The most common reason given for not taking child-care leave is that the 'atmosphere of the workplace' discourages women from taking it, and two-thirds of working mothers who did not take leave say that more understanding by their workplace colleagues is necessary to improve child-care leave systems.

The effectiveness of the revisions to the law has limitations. Even if firms revise formal work regulations following the law, there still exist many barriers preventing employees from taking leave. We review these limitations by analyzing several surveys on child-care leave in the next two sections.

4.   CHILD-CARE LEAVE SYSTEMS IN FIRMS

4.1.   Surveys Used for This Research

This chapter draws on the data obtained from four surveys. The first is the 1999 Survey on Female Employment Management (Women's Bureau, Ministry of Labor 2000a), in which workplaces were categorized by size and industry, and a certain proportion of workplaces were selected from each category. In total, 6990 workplaces responded to the survey. The response rate was 70.7 percent.

Another is the 2001 Survey on Women's Work and Family Life (Japan Institute of Labor 2002) implemented by the Japan Institute of Labor (JIL). Some 2160 women who had a child in the period from 2 April 1992 to 1 April 2001 were randomly selected from two wards in the Tokyo Metropolitan Area and two cities in the Toyama Prefecture. The response rate was 67.8 percent. Hereafter, the survey is referred to as the 'JIL Survey 2001'.

The third survey is the 2000 Survey on Employment and Life of Workers Taking Care of Children and Family (Women's Bureau, Ministry of Labor 2000b), hereafter referred to as the 'ML Survey 2000'. Some 3300 firms listed on the Tokyo, Osaka and Nagoya Stock Exchange Markets and 9900 female workers employed in these firms, who have elementary school age or younger children were selected. In total, 846 firms and 1540 female workers responded. Response rates were 25.6 and 15.6 percent, respectively. It should be noted that respondents are biased in terms of firm size and industry. While 41 percent of firms in the sample employ 1000 or more workers, only 3.8 percent of firms employ less than 100 workers, and 50 percent of firms are in the manufacturing industry.

The last survey is the 1993–97 Panel Survey of Consumers, which was conducted by the Household Economic Research Center. Some 1500 women aged 24–34 years old were selected in 1993, and the same women were surveyed every year. In 1997, 500 women aged 24–29 were added to the sample.

4.2.   Features of Child-care Leave Systems

In this subsection, we discuss characteristics of child-care leave systems.

Existence of child-care leave systems

After the enactment of the Child-care Leave Law in 1992, many employers have introduced child-care leave systems. Most workplaces employing 100 or more workers have such a system. However, only about half of workplaces with 5–29 workers have child-care leave systems. It should be noted that even workplaces which do not have the system in operation cannot legally refuse to provide child-care leave if required by the employee.

Child-care leave take-up

The proportion of women who take child-care leave is not large. Only 56 percent of working women who had a child in 1999 took such leave. The figure is higher for large workplaces. On the other hand, the proportion of male workers who took child-care leave is only 0.4 percent.

It should be noted that these figures are for workers who are employed when they give birth. Women who resigned when they gave birth are not included. As Figure 10.1 showed, many women resign from the workforce when they give birth. This implies that the proportion of women who take child-care leave out of the total number of women who bore children is much smaller. According to the figure, 22 percent of women are in employment just after childbirth, which means only slightly more than 10 percent of women who bear children take child-care leave.

Short leave selection

Figure 10.2 shows the length of child-care leave. There are two peaks. One appears at less than 3 months, and the other at 10–12 months. For male workers, the first peak is much higher. Nearly two-thirds of male workers selected leave shorter than 3 months. For female workers, the second peak is higher, but the difference between the first and second peaks is not large. About one-fifth of female workers selected leave shorter than 3 months.

There are several reasons for selecting a short period. First, the marginal utility of such leave declines as the leave becomes longer. Parents often take leave until a child-care center becomes available. Thus, the marginal utility of leave declines after a center becomes available. Second the marginal cost of taking leave does not decline, and may increase, as the leave becomes longer. The cost of taking leave is not only a loss of income, but also the deterioration of skills and knowledge. If the leave is long, workers have to receive training before they return to work. Third, taking a long period of leave may give colleagues and superiors the impression that the workers are not interested in making a career in the firm. This would be a more serious problem for male workers.

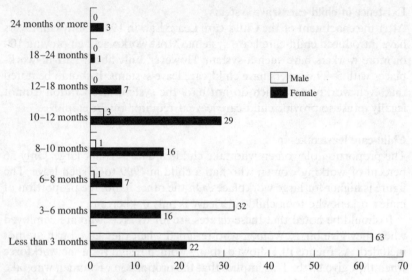

Source: Survey on female employment management, 1999.

Figure 10.2   Length of child-care leave (percent)

4.3.   Econometric Analysis

We analyze which groups are more likely to take child-care leave, using the 1993–97 Panel Survey of Consumers. Table 10.1 shows the probit estimate of the probability of a woman taking leave. (Descriptive statistics are in Table 10A.1.)

Looking first at the data for women (including housewives) who had children from 1994 to 1997, the following characteristics were analyzed: the effect of education, firm of first employment, the worker's age and the year of the survey.[3] Column (1) of the table gives the results.

The first set of dummy variables shows that education has a positive effect on the probability of taking child-care leave. The marginal effect of college education is 8.1 percent, and that of university is 10.9 percent. These are significant at the 5 percent level.

The second set of dummy variables measures the effect of the characteristics of the firms the women were first employed in after graduation. The employers are categorized into private firms and the government sector. The former are further categorized by firm size. The reference group is private firms which employ less than 30 workers. The size of firm the worker first begins employment with has a positive effect with the exception of firms that employ 500 to 999 workers. Female workers who entered firms that employ 1000 or more workers have a 10.4 percent higher probability of taking child-care leave compared to those who are in firms employing less than 30 workers. Workers who entered the government sector have a probability of taking child-care leave 29.6 percent higher than the reference group.

The dummy variables on the wage of the worker and the year of the survey do not have a significant effect on the probability that the worker takes child-care leave. This implies that there is no clear trend over time in the probability of taking leave.

Next, we selected women who were employed in the year just before the birth of their child. The result is in column (2) of Table 10.1. For this group we analyzed the effect of education and the type of employer. The effect of education is again positive, and the magnitude is much larger than column (1). University graduates are 44 percent more likely to take child-care leave compared to high-school graduates.

The government sector has a significant positive effect on child-care leave take-up. Women who are in the government sector have a 62.1 percent higher probability of taking leave compared to workers in private sector firms that employ less than 1000 workers. The large positive effect of employment in the government sector is partly because child-care leave systems exist in almost all workplaces in this sector, and partly because the government itself is promoting the child-care leave system.

In summary, university graduates and workers in the government sector have the highest probability of taking child-care leave. Part-time workers and workers with a low level of education have little chance of taking such leave. In other words, the child-care leave system tends to be used by highly qualified female workers who enjoy a relatively large bargaining power with employers since it is difficult for employers to replace them with other workers. Workers who can easily be replaced by other workers have little opportunity of taking child-care leave.

5. PROBLEMS WITH THE CURRENT SYSTEM

5.1. Overview of Problems

In this subsection, we discuss the problems inherent in the current child-care leave system as found by the Survey on Female Employment Management, the JIL Survey 2001 and the ML Survey 2000.

No child-care leave system exists
Figure 10.3 sets out the reasons for not taking child-care leave, which are quoted directly from the JIL Survey 2001. 'MA' stands for multiple answers.

Table 10.1 Probit estimate of the probability of a female worker taking child-care leave

Explanatory variable	All women who gave birth, 1994–97 (1)			Women employed on a full-time basis in the previous year (2)		
	Coefficient	t-ratio	Marginal effect	Coefficient	t-ratio	Marginal effect
Constant	−1.988**	−2.035	−0.279	−0.943	−4.087	−0.375
Dummy Variable for Education						
High School	–		–	–		–
Technical School	0.533*	1.938	0.075	0.772*	1.882	0.307
College	0.579**	2.357	0.081	0.746*	1.751	0.297
University	0.788***	3.147	0.109	1.108***	2.907	0.440
Dummy Variable for Firm Size (First Job)						
Size 1–29	–		–	–		–
Size 30–99	0.563	1.463	0.079	–		–
Size 100–499	0.600*	1.836	0.084	–		–
Size 500–999	−0.067	−0.127	−0.009	–		–
Size 1000+	0.744***	2.312	0.104	–		–
Government	2.112***	5.841	0.296	–		–
Dummy Variable for Firm Size (Current Job)						
Size 1–999	–		–	–		–
Size 1000+	–		–	0.472	1.192	0.188
Government	–		–	1.563***	3.808	0.621
Age	−0.015	−0.0477	0.002	–		–
Dummy Variable for Year						
1994	–		–	–		–
1995	0.385*	1.663	0.054	–		–

1996	−0.080	−0.316	−0.011	—	—
1997	0.082	0.0297	0.012	—	—
Log-Likelihood Function	−125.7728			−50.6645	
Chi-squared	90.49082			44.48603	
Significance Level	0.0000			0.0000	
Observations	465			103	

Notes: *significant at the 10 per cent level; ** significant at the 5 per cent level; *** significant at the 1 per cent level.

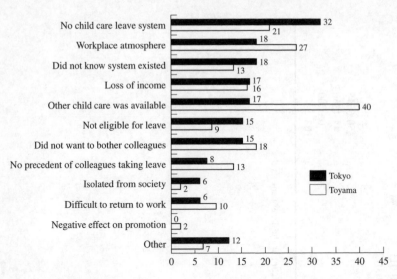

Source: JIL Survey 2001.

Figure 10.3   Reasons for not taking child-care leave (I) (MA, percent)

The figure shows that 32 percent of women in Tokyo and 21 percent of women in Toyama did not take leave because there was 'no child-care leave system'. Moreover, 18 percent of the Tokyo sample and 13 percent of the Toyama sample 'did not know [the] system existed'. Although workers in these workplaces legally have a right to take child-care leave, they would need to exert a greater effort to persuade superiors and colleagues to take it. This would discourage workers from taking leave.[4]

Workplace atmosphere
According to Figure 10.3, 18 percent of women in the Tokyo sample and 27 percent of women in the Toyama sample said that the 'workplace atmosphere' discouraged them from taking leave. This is difficult to interpret. One possible interpretation is that their colleagues and superiors do not understand work–family issues. As stated in Kawaguchi (2001), even though family-friendly programs may have been introduced, corporate culture is not yet family friendly in many firms. This disparity is more significant in large and unionized firms.

Figure 10.4 gives reasons for not taking child-care leave, quoting directly from the ML Survey 2000. The question is similar to that of Figure 10.3. There is, however, an important difference. While respondents in Figure 10.3 are randomly selected from residents in Tokyo and Toyama, those in Figure 10.4 are

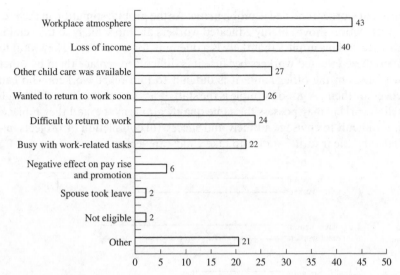

Source: ML Survey 2000.

Figure 10.4 Reasons for not taking child-care leave (II) (MA, percent)

workers in listed companies. Figure 10.4 shows that the 'workplace atmosphere' is the predominant reason for not taking child-care leave. This is because the sample in Figure 10.4 consists of workers in large firms, where child-care leave systems already exist. Once firms introduced a child-care leave system, the 'workplace atmosphere' becomes the largest obstacle to taking leave.

Lack of relief workers
It is often said that workers refrain from taking leave because the duties of their colleagues would increase in their absence. Indeed, another reason women gave for their reluctance to take leave is described in Figure 10.3 as 'did not want to bother colleagues', and in Figure 10.4 as 'busy with work-related tasks'. These can be interpreted as meaning that workers do not wish to be the cause of their colleagues having to do extra duties. This problem may be solved and the perceived atmosphere of the workplace improved if a relief worker was employed so that the colleagues of the worker taking leave did not need to cover that worker's absence.

On the other hand, the employment of relief workers is the biggest problem for employers. Figure 10.5 sets out the problems experienced by employers with regard to child-care leave systems. About half of the employers stated that it is 'difficult to recruit relief workers', and more than 40 percent of employers said that the 'treatment of relief workers' after the original worker returned is problematic. As the probit estimation in the previous section shows, highly educated workers are more likely to take child-care leave. This implies that there is a dilemma for employers. They want to keep these talented workers because it is difficult to replace them by other workers. On the other hand, it is difficult to find relief workers who can cover for them. A good example is the staff of a research institute. Although relief workers may possess the same qualifications as the staff they replace, it is difficult to envisage a timely and successful completion of projects initiated by the institute staff who take child-care leave.

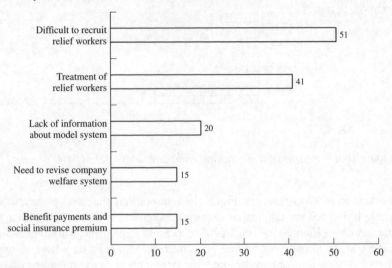

Source: ML Survey 2000.

Figure 10.5   Employer problems in child-care and family-care leave systems (MA, percent)

We doubt, however, that these are critical problems (except for some special cases such as researchers). At this time, the temporary worker market is well developed, and a variety of skills are available in the market. Moreover, workers who take child-care leave tend to be young, that is, late twenties and early thirties, and accordingly, few of them are managers. There are many firms that use relief workers effectively, and it is not difficult to acquire information about those firms. The Ministry of Health, Labor, and Welfare offer a variety of information about family-friendly employment management.

Loss of income
Figure 10.4 showed that loss of income is the second most common reason for not taking leave. This figure may have changed since the benefit increased

from 25 to 40 percent of wages in 2001. However, losing 60 percent of income must still be of significant concern to workers who take leave.

It should be noted that the corresponding figure is much smaller in Figure 10.3, where more respondents are working for smaller firms compared to those in Figure 10.4. This implies that workers in smaller firms tend not to take leave because there is no child-care leave system in their firms. The 'workplace atmosphere' and 'loss of income' become important when firms officially introduce such leave systems.

Inability to return to the same job

Other notable reasons for not taking child-care leave as set out in Figure 10.4 are that workers 'wanted to return to work soon' and it would be 'difficult to return to work' if they took leave. (Again, the figures are much smaller for Figure 10.3.) These may reflect the fact that, in many firms, there is no guarantee that workers can return to the same job they held before they took leave. Figure 10.6 shows the proportion of workers who return to the same section and/or the same job. The figure shows that if the length of leave exceeds 6 months, only half of the workers return to the same job in the same section. There is a clear negative relationship between the length of leave taken and the proportion of workers who were to return to their former job.[5]

Negative effects on pay and promotion

According to Figure 10.3, none of the workers in the Tokyo sample and only 1.9 percent of workers in the Toyama sample who did not take leave stated the 'negative effect on promotion' as a reason for not taking leave. In Figure 10.4, only 6 percent raised 'negative effect on pay rise and promotion' as a reason for not taking leave. This does not, however, imply that taking child-care leave does not affect pay rise and promotion negatively. According to the Survey on Female Employment Management, only 65 percent of firms guarantee workers who take leave the wage they earned previously.

In the next section, we estimate the effect of taking child-care leave on the probability of receiving off-the-job training. The fact that very few women worry about a negative effect on promotion may imply that many of them are not seeking promotion. Working hours for managers are very long, and housekeeping is the wife's role in most families. Hence, promotion would cause difficulty in the harmonization of work and family.

Nursing-care leave systems

Very few firms offer parents leave to nurse their sick children. Therefore, workers have to take paid annual leave in the event that they are required to care for their children. The ML Survey 2000 found that two-thirds of workers who have children under school age took paid annual leave in order to nurse them. This is similar to the proportion of workers who take annual leave for

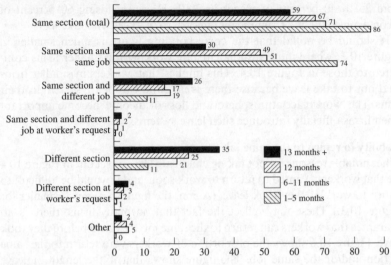

Source: ML Survey 2000.

Figure 10.6   Post-leave work position by length of leave taken (percent)

leisure and recreation. Nursing sick children is a serious problem for working mothers. The same survey found that one-third of working mothers consider the introduction of nursing-care leave systems to be necessary. This is requested by the largest number of working mothers, followed by the longer service duration (23 percent) and the larger child-care leave benefit (23 percent).

Male workers' take-up of child-care leave

So far, we have focused on problems in child-care leave systems for female workers. However, it is much more difficult for male workers to take such leave. Currently, less than 1 percent of male workers whose spouses have had children take leave. This is partly because of the existence of strong gender roles in Japanese society, and partly because male workers are generally paid more than their wives. Households cannot earn enough if husbands take leave. Furthermore, even if a husband wishes to take leave, it may be difficult to persuade superiors and colleagues that this is in fact a good idea.

5.2.   Econometric Analysis

In this subsection, we analyze the effect of child-care leave on wages and opportunity for off-the-job training. As we discussed above, in some firms, wages decline after taking child-care leave. Furthermore, many workers who take leave cannot return to the same job. This may have a negative effect on wages and future promotion.

First, we referred to the 1997 Panel Survey of Consumers, which contains data on women aged 24–38 years old. In total 866 working women were selected. The results are displayed in Table 10.2 with descriptive statistics in Table 10A.2. The dependent variable is the logarithm of hourly wages. Columns (1) and (2) give the results for all employed women, columns (3) and (4) give the results for women employed on a full-time basis, and columns (5) and (6) give results for women employed on a part-time basis.

Columns (2), (4) and (6) use Heckman's two-step estimation procedure to adjust for sample selection bias by including a sequence of adjustment parameters, lambda, that adjust each observation for the sample bias.[6] For column (2), lambda is derived from a probit estimate of participation decision. For columns (4) and (6), lambda is calculated as follows. Women are categorized into three groups, full-time workers, part-time workers and housewives. A model for selecting one of these three groups is estimated by multinomial logit. Using this result, the probabilities of selecting full- and part-time workers are estimated, and these results are used for the calculation of lambda. However, the coefficient of lambda is not significant at the 5 percent level in any of the equations. This implies that there is no sample selection bias, and hence, we shall look at models without lambda.

We used three dummy variables related to child-care leave. The dummy variable 'Child-care Leave System Exists' is applied to employees of firms that have child-care leave systems. The dummy variable 'Colleagues Take Child-care Leave' is applied to workers whose colleagues have taken leave. The final dummy variable, 'Workers Take Child-care Leave' is applied to workers who have taken leave in their current employment position.

'Child-care Leave System Exists' is inserted because family-friendly firms tend to employ more female workers and are more likely to offer equal employment opportunities for women, as stated in Kawaguchi (2001). 'Colleagues Take Child-care Leave' captures firms where workers can actually take leave. As we discussed above, even if a child-care leave system exists, there are many barriers for workers who wish to take leave. 'Workers Take Child-care Leave' captures the pure effect of taking leave.

Column (1) shows that education level and service duration have significantly positive effects on wages. Being employed in a large firm or the government sector also has a positive effect, but the effect is not significant at the 5 percent level. Part-time workers' wages are 6 percent lower than full-time workers. Thus, the result is reasonable.

Among the three dummy variables for child-care leave, only the first one has a significant effect. This means that firms which provide leave offer higher wages. Thus, these firms appear more likely to treat female workers equally

Table 10.2 Estimates of wages (dependent variable is the logarithm of hourly wages)

| | Employed | | | | Full-time | | | | Part-time | | | |
| | (1) | | (2) | | (3) | | (4) | | (5) | | (6) | |
Explanatory variable	Coefficient	t-ratio	Coefficient	t-ratio	Coefficient	t-ratio	Coefficient	t-ratio	Coefficient	t-ratio	Coefficient	t-ratio
Constant	6.751***	70.127	6.750***	70.802	6.431***	41.935	6.437***	42.436	6.983***	51.173	6.723***	33.180
Dummy Variable for Child care												
Child-care Leave System Exists	0.087**	2.327	0.087**	2.345	0.125***	2.612	0.125***	2.651	0.061	1.040	0.070	1.210
Colleagues Take Child-care Leave	−0.023	−0.582	−0.023	−0.586	−0.029	−0.615	−0.029	−0.624	−0.020	−0.265	−0.022	−0.306
Workers Take Child-care Leave	0.047	0.862	0.063	1.015	0.024	0.411	0.009	0.131	−0.013	−0.039	−0.104	−0.316
Dummy Variable for Education												
Junior High School	0.004	0.032	0.007	0.061	−0.847**	−2.399	−0.864**	−2.468	0.077	0.654	0.115	0.983
High School	–		–		–		–		–		–	
Technical School	0.101***	3.002	0.101***	3.009	0.098**	2.216	0.102**	2.283	0.069	1.353	0.048	0.922
College	0.112***	3.506	0.109***	3.394	0.934***	2.206	0.098**	2.261	0.125**	2.599	0.113**	2.402
University	0.271***	7.080	0.266***	6.827	0.166***	3.255	0.176***	3.958	0.462***	7.114	0.433***	6.635
Dummy Variable for Firm Size												
Size 1–29	–		–		–		–		–		–	
Size 30–99	0.001	0.034	0.001	0.022	0.022	0.443	0.022	0.440	−0.034	0.580	−0.030	−0.533
Size 100–499	−0.010	−0.292	−0.011	−0.301	0.018	0.381	0.017	0.366	−0.054	−1.035	−0.053	−1.044

Variable	(1)	(2)	(3)	(4)	(5)	(6)
Size 500–999	0.075 (1.444)	0.074 (1.436)	0.153** (2.330)	0.152** (2.347)	-0.015 (-0.174)	-0.016 (-0.194)
Size 1000+	0.065* (1.845)	0.066* (1.658)	0.102* (1.948)	0.101* (1.957)	-0.015 (-0.228)	-0.027 (-0.44)
Government	0.085* (1.933)	0.084* (1.658)	0.120* (1.890)	0.119* (1.905)	0.050 (0.755)	0.458 (0.712)
Service Duration	0.020*** (4.795)	0.020*** (4.826)	0.020*** (3.895)	0.020*** (3.958)	-0.003 (-0.348)	-0.001 (-0.162)
Experience in Other Firms	0.006 (1.274)	0.006 (1.218)	0.026 (0.304)	0.003 (0.375)	0.007 (1.172)	0.005 (0.913)
Age	-0.003 (-0.074)	-0.002 (-0.606)	0.009 (1.192)	0.008 (0.995)	0.007 (1.172)	-0.030 (-0.533)
Dummy Variable for Part-time	-0.060** (-1.987)	-0.057* (-1.867)	—	—	—	—
Lambda	—	-0.021 (-0.508)	—	0.021 (0.398)	—	0.130* (1.704)
Adjusted R^2	0.22202	0.22134	0.21407	0.21279	0.15248	0.15710
Observations	866	866	533	533	333	333

Notes: * significant at the 10 per cent level; ** significant at the 5 per cent level; *** significant at the 1 per cent level.

relative to male workers. A positive but not significant effect of the third dummy variable implies that taking leave does not have a negative effect on wages.

The estimation of the wage rate of full-time workers (column (3)) gives a result similar to that of all workers. Education and duration of service at the same firm have significantly positive effects, while firm size has only a slightly positive effect. Among the three dummy variables for leave, only that for firms which have a child-care leave system has a significant effect. Taking leave does not have a negative effect.

The equation of part-time workers' wages is quite different from that of full-time workers. In the case of part-time workers, only their education level is significant. Firms' characteristics, for example, size, and the existence of child-care leave systems do not affect wage levels. Again taking leave does not have a negative effect.

Next, we estimate the effect of taking leave on the probability of receiving off-the-job training using a probit model. Cross-section data from 1997 are used for the estimation. The results are given in Table 10.3, and descriptive statistics are displayed in Table 10A.3. The dependent variable is a dummy variable that takes 1 if the individual received off-the-job training in the last 12 months and 0 if this is not the case. Columns (1) and (2) seek to explain the probability of female workers receiving off-the-job training, and columns (3) and (4) explain the probability of full-time workers receiving such training.[7]

Columns (1) and (2) show that education has a significantly positive effect on the probability of receiving off-the-job training. The marginal effect of college education on the probability of receiving training is about 10 percent while the marginal effect of university education is greater than 10 percent. Workers in the government sector have a high probability of receiving off-the-job training. The marginal effect is 23 percent.

The effect of the three dummy variables relating to child-care leave is worth noting. The dummy variable for the existence of a child-care leave system and the dummy variable for colleagues taking leave have positive effects, but the effects are not significant at the 5 percent level. In the survey, however, the question regarding whether colleagues have taken leave or not was asked only of those who said that child-care leave systems exist in their firms. Therefore, if we compare women whose colleagues have taken leave and women whose companies do not have child-care leave systems, the difference is significant. According to column (1), the former have a 15.3 percent (the sum of 8.6 and 6.7) higher probability of receiving off-the-job training than the latter. According to column (2), women whose colleagues have taken leave are 15.7 percent (the sum of 7.9 and 7.8) more likely to receive off-the-job training than women whose companies do not have a child-care leave system in place. This supports the finding that family-friendly firms tend to offer equal employment opportunity for males and females as set out in Kawaguchi (2001).

The effect of taking child-care leave is negative. It is significant at the 5 percent level for column (1) and significant at the 10 percent level for column (2). Those who took leave have a 16 to 18 percent lower probability of receiving off-the-job training.

The estimation results for full-time workers is similar to that of all workers, but the magnitude of the coefficients are larger in most cases. The dummy variable for taking leave again has negative and significant effects. Workers who take leave have a 21 to 25 percent lower chance of receiving off-the-job training.

In summary, we cannot observe a clear negative effect on the wage rate from taking up child-care leave. On the other hand, there is a significantly negative effect from taking leave on the probability of receiving off-the-job training.

6.   FURTHER REFORM

From the discussion in Sections 4 and 5, we can categorize firms into four groups: (i) firms which do not have a child-care leave system; (ii) firms which have a child-care leave system, but it is not easy for the employees to use it; (iii) firms which have a child-care leave system and their employees are using it, but there is no payment from the firm during the leave; and (iv) firms where employees can use a child-care leave system without a significant loss of income.

The Survey on Female Employment Management found that about half of the workplaces employing between 5 and 29 workers and a quarter of workplaces employing between 30 and 99 workers still belong to the first group. For these firms, introducing a child-care leave system is a priority. The Child-care Leave Law should be amended so that the introduction of a child-care leave system becomes an obligation for employers.

However, the introduction of such a leave system is not enough. A majority of the firms which have a system belong to the second group. The 'workplace atmosphere' discourages workers from taking leave. Only 56 percent of female workers and less than one percent of male workers take leave. In order to increase the take-up rate, corporate culture should become more family friendly. The government should legislate to force firms to introduce a program to increase the number of workers who take child-care leave.

Article 20 of the Equal Employment Opportunity Law recommends that employers implement 'positive action'. The article states that if employers take measures towards an equal workplace environment, the government will give them advice and other assistance. Although the law does not

Table 10.3 Probit estimates of the probability of female workers receiving off-the-job training

Explanatory variable	Employed						Full-time					
	(1)			(2)			(3)			(4)		
	Coefficient	t-ratio	Marginal effect	Coefficient	t-ratio	Marginal effect	Coefficient	t-ratio	Marginal effect	Coefficient	t-ratio	Marginal effect
Constant	-0.656	-1.503	-0.230	0.033	0.065	0.012	-0.591	-0.965	-0.235	0.023	0.033	0.009
Dummy Variable for Child-care Leave												
Child-care Leave System Exists	0.245*	1.683	0.086	0.225	1.533	0.079	0.208	1.162	0.083	0.181	0.999	0.072
Colleagues Take Child-care Leave	0.190	1.277	0.067	0.223	1.484	0.078	0.118	0.670	0.047	0.157	0.881	0.063
Workers Take Child-care Leave	-0.504**	-2.188	-0.177	-0.444*	-1.808	-0.155	-0.634**	-2.456	-0.252	-0.517*	-1.841	-0.205
Dummy Variable for Married	0.018	0.132	0.006	0.012	0.089	0.004	-0.066	-0.388	-0.026	-0.104	-0.615	-0.041
Dummy Variable for Children												
No Child	–	–	–	–	–	–	–	–	–	–	–	–
Child	0.106	0.631	0.037	–	–	–	0.223	1.026	0.088	–	–	–
Age 0–2 Years Old	–	–	–	-0.020	-0.103	-0.007	–	–	–	-0.071	-0.289	-0.028
Age 3–6 Years Old	–	–	–	0.060	0.391	0.021	–	–	–	0.217	0.990	0.086
1st–3rd Grade	–	–	–	0.090	0.575	0.032	–	–	–	0.106	0.461	0.042
4th–6th Grade	–	–	–	0.268	1.573	0.094	–	–	–	0.620**	2.509	0.246
Other	–	–	–	0.422**	2.059	0.148	–	–	–	0.196	0.636	0.078

Dummy Variable for Education												
High School	–			–			–			–		
Technical School	0.136	1.018	0.047	0.176	1.312	0.062	0.345**	2.123	0.137	0.368**	2.257	0.146
College	0.271**	2.119	0.095	0.318**	2.454	0.111	0.340**	2.118	0.135	0.367**	2.273	0.146
University	0.312**	1.971	0.109	0.421***	2.587	0.148	0.387**	1.964	0.154	0.474**	2.334	0.188
Dummy Variable for Firm Size (Current Job)												
Size 1–29	–			–			–			–		
Size 30–99	−0.299*	−1.882	−0.105	−0.283*	−1.784	−0.099	−0.320*	−1.688	−0.126	−0.309	−1.625	−0.123
Size 100–499	−0.215	−1.468	−0.075	−0.206	−1.402	−0.072	−0.209	−1.170	−0.083	−0.209	−1.166	−0.083
Size 500–999	0.169	0.878	0.060	0.148	0.764	0.052	0.126	0.528	0.050	0.102	0.423	0.040
Size 1000+	0.129	0.0837	0.045	0.130	0.837	0.046	0.148	0.786	0.059	0.157	0.824	0.062
Government	0.656***	3.633	0.230	0.664***	3.650	0.233	1.022***	4.122	0.406	1.023***	4.095	0.406
Age	0.013	0.681	−0.005	−0.019	−0.841	−0.007	0.015	0.528	0.006	−0.013	−0.384	−0.005
Service Duration	−0.017	−1.105	−0.006	−0.018	0.016	−0.006	0.000	−0.002	0.000	0.001	0.057	0.000
Experience in Other Firms	−0.014	−0.691	−0.005	0.006	0.276	0.002	−0.044	−1.443	−0.018	−0.030	−0.926	−0.012
Dummy Variable for Part-time	−1.027***	−7.963	−0.361	−1.004***	−7.766	−0.351	–		–	–		–
Log-Likelihood Function	−499.9621			−496.4929			−346.7667			−342.9580		
Chi-squared	192.7469			199.6853			86.44721			94.06462		
Significance Level	0.0000			0.0000			0.0000			0.0000		
Observations	934			934			565			565		

Notes: * significant at the 10 per cent level; ** significant at the 5 per cent level; *** significant at the 1 per cent level.

explain details of the measures, a commission set up by the Ministry of Health, Labor, and Welfare recommended changing the traditional gender roles. Increasing male workers' take-up rate of child-care leave is an example of these measures.[8]

We agree with this recommendation. In the case of positive action described in the Equal Employment Opportunity Law, only measures for equal opportunity tend to be focused on. Kawaguchi (2001) states, however, that equal employment opportunity and family-friendly programs are complementary. Thus, firms should introduce these two types of program simultaneously. Family-friendly programs that include child-care leave systems, are essential to achieving an equal opportunity environment that promotes fair treatment of all workers.

In the program, measures to increase male workers' take-up rate of child-care leave should be included. If only female workers take leave and no male workers ever take it, this results in a different type of gender discrimination. The labor cost of women is perceived to be higher than men, and employers may reduce the number of female workers they employ.

Further strengthening of the Equal Employment Opportunity Law is recommended. Under the current law, there is no obligation for employers to take measures to achieve equal treatment between men and women. As a result, very few firms implement positive action. In countries like the United States, Germany, France and Sweden, employers are obliged to implement positive action (or 'affirmative action'). Considering the very large gender wage gap and the very low participation rate of women with small children, stronger legislation is necessary to achieve equality between the genders in Japan. While this may increase the cost to individual firms in the short run, it will partly be offset by improvements in the productivity of female workers. Moreover, society as a whole becomes more effective by utilizing women's talent.

NOTES

*   An earlier version of this chapter was presented to the Fourth International Forum of the Collaboration Projects. I am grateful to Masaya Sakuragawa for helpful comments.
1. The figures for Japan and Sweden are for 2000, while the other countries are for 1999. The figure for Sweden includes single mothers. The data source is OECD (2001).
2. Fujii (1992) explains the process of the establishment of the Child-care Leave Law, 1991. According to Fujii, the establishment of Equal Employment Opportunity Law, 1985 was an important precursor. People changed their perception on women's work. The number of working women increased and the number of women who want to keep working after childbirth also increased. Trade unions set the establishment of the Child-care Leave Law as their next target.
3. Women whose education is limited to junior high school are excluded from the sample since none of them took child-care leave.
4. These figures may be somewhat lower now since this survey covers a long time period from 1992 to 2001. Many firms introduced child-care leave systems in the 1990s.

5. Figure 10.6 is based on individual workers' response. According to the Survey on Female Employment Management, where employers responded, 71 percent of workplaces guarantee that workers can return to the same job. Note also that Figure 10.6 is biased in terms of firm size.
6. See Heckman (1979) and Maddala (1983).
7. For part-time workers, the effect of taking child-care leave could not be estimated since only one part-time worker in the sample has taken leave. Women whose education is limited to junior high school are excluded from the sample, since none of them received off-the-job training.
8. Commission on the Promotion of Women's Activity (2002).

REFERENCES

Bureau of Statistics, Office of the Prime Minister (1998), *Employment Status Survey*, Tokyo: Office of the Prime Minister.

Commission on the Promotion of Women's Activity (2002), *Proposal of Positive Action*, Tokyo: Ministry of Health, Labor, and Welfare.

Fujii, T. (1992), 'Background and outline of the establishment of the child-care leave law' (in Japanese), *Kikan-Rodoho*, **163**, 29–44.

Heckman, J. (1979), 'Sample selection as a specification error', *Econometrica*, **47**, 153–61.

Higuchi, Y. (1994), 'Empirical analysis of child-care leave systems' (in Japanese), in Social Development Research Institute (ed.), *Contemporary Family and Social Security*, Tokyo: University of Tokyo Press, pp. 181–204.

Higuchi, Y., M. Abe and J. Waldfogel (1997), 'Child-care and maternity leave and female employment in Japan, the US and the UK' (in Japanese), *Journal of Population Problems*, **53** (4), 49–66.

Japan Institute of Labor (2002), *Survey on Women's Work and Family Life*, Tokyo: Japan Institute of Labor.

Kawaguchi, A. (2001), 'Work, marriage, childbearing and family-friendly work practices in Japan', paper presented to the Second International Forum of the Collaboration Projects, 18–20 March, Tokyo.

Maddala, G.S. (1983), *Limited-dependent and Qualitative Variables in Econometrics*, Cambridge: Cambridge University Press.

Maeda, M. (2002), 'A family-friendly workplace and labor union efforts' (in Japanese), *Japanese Journal of Labor Studies*, **44** (6), 43–53.

Morita, Y. and N. Kaneko (1998) 'Child-care leave system and service duration of female workers' (in Japanese), *Japanese Journal of Labor Studies*, **40** (10), 50–62.

Organization for Economic Cooperation and Development (OECD) (2001), *Employment Outlook*, Paris: OECD.

Shigeno, Y. and Y. Ohkusa (1998), 'Effects of the child-care leave subsidy on marriage and continuous employment' (in Japanese), *Japanese Journal of Labor Studies*, **40** (10), 49–49.

Tomita, Y. (1994), 'Workplace environment where women can keep working' (in Japanese), *Osaka-furitu Daigaku Keizai Kenkyu*, **40** (1), 43–56.

Women's Bureau, Ministry of Labor (2000a), *Report of the Survey on Female Employment Management, 1999*, Tokyo: Ministry of Labor.

Women's Bureau, Ministry of Labor (2000b), *Report of the Survey on Employment and Life of Workers Taking Care of Children and Family, 2000*, Tokyo: Ministry of Labor.

Table 10A.1   Descriptive statistics for Table 10.1

Variable	All women who gave birth, 1994–97		Women employed on a full-time basis in the previous year	
	Mean	Std deviation	Mean	Std deviation
Dummy Variable for Workers Taking Child-care Leave	0.120	0.326	0.505	0.502
Dummy Variable for Education				
Junior High School	0.000	0.000	0.000	0.000
High School	0.460	0.499	0.427	0.497
Technical School	0.179	0.383	0.126	0.334
College	0.204	0.404	0.185	0.390
University	0.155	0.362	0.262	0.442
Dummy Variable for Firm Size (First Job)				
Size 1–29	0.222	0.416	–	–
Size 30–99	0.131	0.338	–	–
Size 100–499	0.224	0.417	–	–
Size 500–999	0.080	0.271	–	–
Size 1000+	0.245	0.431	–	–
Government	0.088	0.284	–	–
Dummy Variable for Firm Size (Current Job)				
Size 1–999	–	–	0.583	0.496
Size 1000+	–	–	0.136	0.344
Government	–	–	0.282	0.452
Age	30.25	2.920	–	–
Dummy Variable for Year				
1994	0.282	0.450	–	–
1995	0.275	0.447	–	–
1996	0.265	0.442	–	–
1997	0.179	0.383	–	–
Observations	465		103	

Note: 20 women whose education is limited to junior high school are excluded from the sample, since none of them took child-care leave.

Table 10A.2 Descriptive statistics for Table 10.2

Variable	Employed		Full-time		Part-time	
	Mean	Std deviation	Mean	Std deviation	Mean	Std deviation
Logarithm of Hourly Wages	6.941	0.387	7.026	0.387	6.805	0.346
Dummy Variable for Child-care Leave						
Child-care Leave System Exists	0.467	0.499	0.593	0.492	0.264	0.442
Colleagues Take Child-care Leave	0.331	0.471	0.447	0.498	0.147	0.355
Workers Take Child-care Leave	0.067	0.250	0.107	0.309	0.003	0.055
Dummy Variable for Education						
Junior High School	0.010	0.102	0.002	0.043	0.024	0.153
High School	0.411	0.492	0.357	0.479	0.499	0.501
Technical School	0.177	0.382	0.188	0.391	0.159	0.366
College	0.221	0.415	0.227	0.419	0.210	0.408
University	0.177	0.382	0.221	0.416	0.105	0.307
Dummy Variable for Firm Size						
Size 1–29	0.319	0.466	0.236	0.425	0.451	0.498
Size 30–99	0.134	0.341	0.145	0.352	0.117	0.322
Size 100–499	0.191	0.393	0.206	0.405	0.165	0.372
Size 500–999	0.067	0.250	0.077	0.267	0.051	0.220
Size 1000+	0.159	0.366	0.197	0.398	0.099	0.220
Government	0.128	0.335	0.137	0.344	0.114	0.318
Service Duration	4.701	4.253	6.279	4.433	2.175	2.287
Experience in Other Firms	9.313	4.269	9.459	4.401	9.078	4.044
Age	30.16	4.506	29.44	4.344	31.33	4.521
Dummy Variable for Part-time	0.385	0.487	0.000	0.000	1.000	0.000
Observations	866		533		333	

Table 10A.3 Descriptive statistics for Table 10.3

Variable	Employed		Full-time		Part-time	
	Mean	Std deviation	Mean	Std deviation	Mean	Std deviation
Dummy Variable for Off-the-Job Training	0.332	0.471	0.462	0.499	0.144	0.352
Dummy Variable for Child-care Leave						
Child-care Leave System Exists	0.459	0.499	0.589	0.492	0.269	0.444
Colleagues Take Child-care Leave	0.328	0.470	0.448	0.498	0.155	0.362
Workers Take Child-care Leave	0.069	0.253	0.112	0.315	0.000	0.000
Dummy Variable for Married	0.495	0.500	0.368	0.483	0.688	0.464
Dummy Variable for Children						
No Child	0.570	0.495	0.696	0.461	0.386	0.488
Age 0–2 Years Old	0.101	0.301	0.108	0.311	0.079	0.270
Age 3–6 Years Old	0.177	0.382	0.120	0.326	0.261	0.440
1st–3rd Grade	0.186	0.390	0.122	0.328	0.283	0.451
4th–6th Grade	0.151	0.359	0.089	0.284	0.247	0.432
Other	0.091	0.288	0.058	0.235	0.141	0.349
Dummy Variable for Education						
High School	0.415	0.493	0.361	0.481	0.511	0.501
Technical School	0.182	0.386	0.191	0.394	0.174	0.380
College	0.221	0.415	0.230	0.421	0.215	0.411
University	0.166	0.372	0.212	0.409	0.098	0.298
Dummy Variable for Firm Size (Current Job)						
Size 1–29	0.324	0.468	0.237	0.426	0.451	0.498
Size 30–99	0.139	0.346	0.145	0.353	0.125	0.331
Size 100–499	0.185	0.389	0.202	0.402	0.163	0.370
Size 500–999	0.068	0.251	0.076	0.265	0.057	0.232

Size 1000+	0.158	0.365	0.197	0.398	0.098	0.298
Government	0.124	0.330	0.140	0.347	0.103	0.305
Age	30.31	4.523	29.49	4.353	31.55	4.521
Service Duration	4.624	4.245	6.279	4.434	2.144	2.251
Experience in Other Firms	9.316	4.288	9.509	4.376	8.979	4.077
Dummy Variable for Part-time	0.401	0.490	0.000	1.000	0.000	1.000
Observations	934		565		368	

11. Public infrastructures for equalizing capability in an ageing society

Tadashi Yagi

1. INTRODUCTION

In his seminal research, Sen (1985, 1997) proposed the concept of 'capability', which refers to the ability to transform income, service and goods to improve their utility. This concept of capability is of critical importance in a society where there are large differences in capability within the population. As a society ages, the number and share of people who are disabled increases, because the probability of being disabled increases as one ages. Using time-series data, the current number of disabled people, and population forecasts, it has been estimated that there will be over 6 million disabled people in Japan within two decades. Capabilities of the disabled greatly differ depending on how well accessibility (which is not an important issue for those who are not disabled) to services is implemented. In other words, the inequality of capability is dependent upon the state of accessibility in a society, and this inequality of capability is of critical importance in an ageing society.

When we consider the development of social infrastructures in an ageing society, it is important to pay attention to two related issues. One is the building of infrastructures that improve welfare for the elderly, such as home care. Infrastructures such as libraries and museums are very beneficial for the elderly, because the retired have the leisure to utilize these establishments and thus enrich their lives. The other issue is the improvement of accessibility for the disabled, since they are not able to benefit from social infrastructures such as libraries and museums, without easy access. This is an example of inequality in the capability of disabled people to utilize social infrastructures compared to able-bodied people. Without accessibility, expenditures for libraries and museums improve welfare for only healthy (that is, not disabled) people, and therefore expand the welfare gap between the disabled and the healthy.

In this research project, we examine two issues related to infrastructures in an ageing society. One is a theoretical examination of the optimal allocation of public expenditures between building public infrastructures and improving accessibility, using a model in which the benefits from social infrastructures vary according to the degree of accessibility. Since the benefits from improving accessibility differ for disabled and healthy people, the willingness to pay (WTP) for improving accessibility differs for these two groups.

The theoretical examination is somewhat complicated because there are some reasons why healthy people would be willing to pay for improved accessibility. For example, they face the possibility of becoming disabled in the future. Thus, even they have a motivation, 'altruistic motivation', to pay for improved accessibility. In addition, the concept of 'normalization', that all people have the right to move freely and it is an obligation of society to provide complete accessibility for the disabled, further explains people's WTP for improved accessibility. If members of a society accept this idea, regardless of whether they are healthy or disabled, their WTP arises from a sense of obligation as members of society, not from pity for the disabled.

The second issue that is tackled in this research project is that of estimating the degree of willingness among the general population to pay for improved accessibility in terms of the two motivations discussed above. In May 2000 the Japanese government legislated a new law for improving accessibility. However, compared with the Americans with Disability Act (ADA), this Japanese law is not mandatory for existing buildings and the time limit in which accessibility must be improved is not rigid. Therefore, it is important to collect information on the degree of WTP for improving accessibility.

In this study we use the contingent valuation method (CVM) to estimate the degree of WTP for barrier-free investments. In order to design questionnaires for a survey, we estimated the costs for improving accessibility of the public infrastructure in Kyoto City. In our survey, we provided information about the length of time required to complete accessibility improvements and about the various levels of accessibility and asked residents about their WTP for barrier-free investments. The information that we obtained on the residents' choices of length of time and levels of investment will be useful for governments in planning barrier-free investments.

In addition to estimating the degree of WTP for barrier-free investments, we also assessed improvements in the 'capability' of the disabled to use public infrastructures. Capability is a form of power for making infrastructures more utilitarian, and the importance of this concept increases as the proportion of disabled increases in a society, because inequality of capability also increases. Thus, our estimation gives us some information on the role of barrier-free investment in decreasing the inequality of capability in society.

Finally, in an ageing society public investment for improving accessibility is important not only for equalizing capability but also for economic growth. One of the reasons is that improving the environment of the disabled makes it possible for them to become independent, and therefore, participate in the labor market, allowing the government to decrease welfare program expenditures. Moreover, the vitality of the economy in an ageing society depends on how the activities of the elderly are supported. If the elderly spend most of their money on medical expenses, only medical-related industries thrive and the government budget is drained by welfare program expenditures. On the other hand, if consumer activities of the elderly are stimulated through various infrastructures, such as barrier-free public buildings, roads, and stations, the economy will be vitalized and government tax revenue will increase. In this sense, improving accessibility is not only beneficial for the disabled or elderly, but also for the entire population. Concerning the effects of improving accessibility on economic activities, Vickerman et al. (1999) identify some of the major difficulties in defining a simple measure of accessibility, and discuss the role of transportation infrastructure and changes in accessibility on regional economic development. Such empirical studies are necessary for planning public policy for a barrier-free society.

2.   THEORETICAL MODEL OF THE OPTIMAL PUBLIC INVESTMENT POLICY FOR IMPROVING ACCESSIBILITY

2.1.   Model Setting

We consider an economy to consist of two types of individuals and two of social infrastructures, and private goods. The first type of individual (the h-type) is healthy and the second type (the d-type) has a disability. In this model, 'healthy' means 'non-disabled'. We divide each individual's life into two periods. There is a positive probability of being disabled in the second period for individuals who are healthy in the first period, and individuals who are disabled in the first period are assumed to be disabled in the second period.

We also consider two types of infrastructure. The first type provides people with intellectual, educational, and leisure services such as libraries, sport gymnasiums, public halls, museums, and so on. The second type, such as facilities with barrier-free designs, improves the capability of the population to use the first type of infrastructure. We consider the transformation function $\varphi^i(.)$ that generates the utility of the service of the first type of infrastructure for $i(i = d, h)$-type individuals:

$$v^i = \varphi^i (g, m), \; \varphi^h_1 > 0, \; \varphi^d_1 > 0, \; \varphi^h_2 = 0, \; \varphi^d_2 > 0, \tag{11.1}$$

where g is the first type of infrastructure and m is the second type.

This transformation function expresses the capability of the population to use infrastructures. In an ageing society, the concept of capability is crucial because the capability of using infrastructures may differ greatly for people depending on their state of health. The second type of infrastructure decreases the capability differences in using infrastructures. For the healthy individual, an increase in the second type of infrastructure does not increase the utility of the first type. However, for the individual with a disability, an increase in the second type of infrastructure increases the utility of the first type. Thus, the inequality of capability in using infrastructures decreases as the second type of infrastructure increases.

The lifetime utility function of healthy individuals in the first period, U^h, is calculated as follows:

$$\begin{aligned} U^h = u[x^h_1, \varphi^h(g, m)] + (1 - p)\rho u[x^h_2, \varphi^h(g, m)] \\ + p\rho u[x^h_2, \varphi^d(g, m)] + B(m), \end{aligned} \tag{11.2}$$

where x^h_1 and x^h_2 are h-type individuals' consumption of private goods during the first and second periods, respectively, p is the probability of being disabled in the second period, ρ is the time discount rate and B is a sense of obligation to pay for the second type of infrastructure.

The lifetime utility function for individuals with disabilities in the first period, U^d, is calculated as follows:

$$U^d = u[x^d_1, \varphi^d(g, m)] + \rho u[x^d_2, \varphi^d(g, m)], \tag{11.3}$$

where x^d_1 and x^d_2 are equal to the d-type individual's consumption of private goods during the first and second periods, respectively.

The h-type individual's lifetime budget constraint in the first period is shown by:

$$(1 - t^h_g - t^h_m)y^h = x^h_1 + s^h, \tag{11.4}$$

and that for the second period is shown by:

$$(1 + r)s^h = x^h_2, \tag{11.5}$$

where y^h is the income of an h-type individual, s^h is the savings of an h-type individual, t_g^h is the income tax rate for building the first type of infrastructure, t_m^h is the income tax rate for building the second type of infrastructure, and r is the market interest rate.

The d-type individual's lifetime budget constraint in the first period is shown by:

$$(1 - t_g^d - t_m^d)y^d = x_1^d + s^d, \qquad (11.6)$$

and that for the second period is shown by:

$$(1 + r)s^d = x_2^d, \qquad (11.7)$$

where y^d is the income of the d-type individual, s^d is the savings of the d-type individual, t_g^d is the income tax rate for building the first type of infrastructure, and t_m^d is the income tax rate for building the second type of infrastructure.

The amounts of investment to infrastructure are shown as follows:

$$t_m^h y^h = m^h, \ t_m^d y^d = m^d \qquad (11.8)$$

$$t_g^h y^h = g^h, \ t_g^d y^d = g^d. \qquad (11.9)$$

Given the income level exogenously, determining income taxes is identical to determining types of infrastructure or degrees of WTP for infrastructures, as is shown in the above equations. In this chapter, we consider a case where both an h-type and a d-type individual determine their own optimal income tax rates without knowing the other type of individual's optimal income tax rate. Thus, the two individuals' WTP for infrastructures is determined as a Nash equilibrium.

The optimal tax rate for an h-type individual is given by maximizing (11.2) subject to (11.4).[1] In the same manner, the optimal tax rate for a d-type individual is given by maximizing (11.3) subject to (11.5). Examination of the Nash solution is rather complicated because each type of individual has two control variables. For the purposes of making the model operational and clarifying the economic implications of the Nash solution, we assume that the first type of infrastructure is provided exogenously and we disregard charitable motives of healthy people.

2.2. Social Optimality Conditions for Barrier-free Expenditures

As a benchmark case, we examine conditions for social optimum levels of barrier-free expenditures. The social welfare function is defined as:

$$W = \alpha U^h + \beta U^d, \tag{11.10}$$

where α and β are weights for healthy and disabled people, respectively. Social optimum public investment policy is calculated by maximizing the social welfare function (11.10) subject to resource constraints:

$$X_1 = x_1^h + x_1^d + m + g \tag{11.11}$$

and

$$X_2 = x_2^h + x_2^d, \tag{11.12}$$

where X_1 and X_2 are total resources available in periods 1 and 2, respectively. For simplicity, we assume that:

$$\alpha = \beta = 1. \tag{11.13}$$

From the optimality conditions for the social welfare maximization problem, we can derive:

$$\rho p \frac{\partial u^h}{\partial \varphi^d} \frac{\partial \varphi^h}{\partial m} \bigg/ \frac{\partial u^h}{\partial x_1^h} + \left(\frac{\partial u^d}{\partial \varphi^d} \frac{\partial \varphi^d}{\partial m} + \rho \frac{\partial u^d}{\partial \varphi^d} \frac{\partial \varphi^d}{\partial m} \right) \bigg/ \frac{\partial u^h}{\partial x_1^d} = 1. \tag{11.14}$$

The first term of the right-hand side (RHS) of (11.14) is the marginal rate of substitution (MRS) between the barrier and consumption expenditures for healthy people. That is, this term expresses the h-type's marginal benefits of expenditure for barrier-free infrastructures measured by consumption goods. In the same manner, the second term expresses the d-type's marginal benefits of expenditure for barrier-free infrastructures measured by consumption goods. The left-hand side (LHS) expresses the marginal cost of providing barrier-free infrastructures. Thus, equation (11.14) is rewritten as:

$$MRS^h + MRS^d = 1. \tag{11.15}$$

This is the well-known 'Samuelson rule' for public goods.

2.3. The Inefficiency of *Laissez-faire* Equilibrium

In this subsection, we explore the properties of both types of individual's WTP. Since each type is equivalent to a given amount of the other type's WTP, this relationship can be represented as an equilibrium using the Nash solution. First, we examine the inefficiency of *laissez-faire* equilibrium.

From the optimality conditions for the maximization of (11.2) subject to (11.4), we can derive the optimality condition for an h-type individual's WTP for barrier-free infrastructures as follows:

$$p\rho \frac{\partial u^h}{\partial \varphi^h} \frac{\partial \varphi^d}{\partial m^h} \bigg/ \frac{\partial u^h}{\partial x^q_1} = 1. \tag{11.16}$$

The LHS of the above equation is the h-type's marginal substitution between benefits from barrier-free infrastructures and utility form consumption, that is, the marginal benefits of barrier-free infrastructures measured by consumption. The RHS is the marginal cost of providing barrier-free infrastructures. The condition for the h-type's WTP is that $MRT^h = 1$.

In the same manner, we can derive the condition for d-type's WTP as follows:

$$p\rho \frac{\partial u^d}{\partial \varphi^d} \frac{\partial \varphi^d}{\partial m^d} \bigg/ \frac{\partial u^d}{\partial x^q_1} = 1. \tag{11.17}$$

That is, the condition for the d-type's WTP is that $MRT^d = 1$. Thus, the sum of marginal benefits from barrier-free investment for both types of individual is $MRS^h + MRS^d = 2$. Since $MRS^h + MRS^d = 1$ is a condition for social optimum level and MRS is decreasing in m, the *laissez-faire* WTP is smaller than that of the optimal level of m. Recalling that the Nash equilibrium requires the consistent WTP for both types of individuals, expenditure for barrier-free infrastructures at the Nash equilibrium is smaller than that of the social optimum.[2] Therefore, the implications of the WTP expressed by the CVM are cast carefully. The results of this analysis suggest that the optimal level of public expenditure for barrier-free infrastructures must be larger than the WTP expressed by the CVM.

2.4. Equity of Capability and the Optimal Infrastructure Expenditures

In the above discussion, we considered the social optimum by maximizing the social welfare function defined by (11.10). 'Capability equity criteria' requires us not only to maximize the social welfare, but also to equalize the capabilities of the healthy and the disabled to use social infrastructures. The objective function that represents these criteria is:

$$W = \alpha U^h + \beta U^d - \eta[\varphi^h(g, m) - \varphi^d(g, m)]^2, \tag{11.18}$$

where α and β are weights given for healthy and disabled people respectively, and $\eta(>0)$ is the preference parameter for equity of capability.

The social welfare maximization problem is formulated by maximizing (11.18) subject to (11.11) and (11.12). For simplicity, we assume that $\alpha = \beta = 1$. The difference between the social welfare criteria and the capability equity criteria is expressed by the terms:

$$-2\eta[\varphi^h(g, m) - \varphi^d(g, m)]\frac{\partial(\varphi^h - \varphi^d)}{\partial m} \qquad (11.19)$$

and

$$-2\eta[\varphi^h(g, m) - \varphi^d(g, m)]\frac{\partial(\varphi^h - \varphi^d)}{\partial g}. \qquad (11.20)$$

These equations imply that whether the optimal level of public expenditures for infrastructures increases depends on whether the marginal benefits of these infrastructures increase. These two terms express the changes in the marginal benefits. Since it is reasonable to assume that

$$\lim_{m \to \infty} \varphi^d(g, m) = \varphi^h(g, m),$$

then

$$\varphi^h(g, m) - \varphi^d(g, m) > 0.$$

Thus, whether the marginal benefits of infrastructures evaluated by the new criteria increase or not depends on the signs of $\partial(\varphi^h - \varphi^d)/\partial m$ and $\partial(\varphi^h - \varphi^d)/\partial g$. If $\partial\varphi^h/\partial m < \partial\varphi^d/\partial m$ ($\partial\varphi^h/\partial g < \partial\varphi^d/\partial g$), then the marginal benefit of m (g) and the optimal level of $m(g)$ increase, respectively. That is, when the marginal utility of infrastructures increases for the disabled, the introduction of capability equity criteria increases the optimal level of infrastructures.

3. EMPIRICAL ESTIMATION OF WTP FOR IMPROVING ACCESSIBILITY

In this section, we estimate an amount of WTP for barrier-free investment using the CVM. In order to design a questionnaire for the survey, we estimated the cost for improving accessibility of public infrastructure in Kyoto City. In the survey, we asked the WTP for barrier-free investment after providing information about the length of time required for completing the investment and the level of accessibility.

3.1. Sample Design and Survey Structure

Our questionnaire (see Appendix 11A) was sent to a random sample of 2000 households in Kyoto City. The sample was randomly selected from resident registration books in the city ward offices. In order to increase the sample of disabled residents, we sent the questionnaire to homes for the disabled in Kyoto City. Four days after the questionnaire was mailed, a postcard was also mailed.

In contingent valuation methods for evaluating WTP, it is popular to use a dichotomous choice structure (Langford 1994; Takeuchi 1999). Since the purpose of the survey was to collect information on preferences for the length of time that should be spent completing barrier-free investments and for the amount of investment that should be made, instead of a dichotomous choice structure, we made use of a simultaneous choice structure between length of time and amount of investment.

3.2. Survey Results

We received 679 responses by mail, which represented a response rate of around 26 percent. First, we shall present the descriptive statistics.

Sex distribution
Of the sample, 79 percent of the respondents are male and 21 percent are female. The cause for this unbalance in the sex composition is not clear because the samples were randomly selected from the city resident registration books. The higher portion of male respondents may reflect differences in the attitudes of males and females towards responding to this type of survey.

Age distribution
The age distribution of respondents is as follows: the portion of respondents under age 29 is 5.9 percent, age 30–49, 30.0 percent, age 50–64, 44.2 percent, and over age 65, 19.9 percent. Recalling that this questionnaire was distributed randomly, the large portion of middle-aged respondents aged 50–64 reflects the fact that people of this age are more conscious of the issue of barrier-free infrastructures.

Occupational distribution
The occupational distribution of respondents is as follows: 19.2 percent are self-employed, 48.9 percent are salaried employed, 9.9 percent are housewives, 0.5 percent are students, and 22.4 percent are classified as other (which includes retired persons). Since the percentages of housewives and

students are small, most of the respondents are currently paying or have paid income taxes.

Income distribution
Income distribution is shown in Figure 11.1. The shape of the distribution is similar to that of a log-normal distribution, which implies that the income distribution of the respondents is similar to that of the population in general.

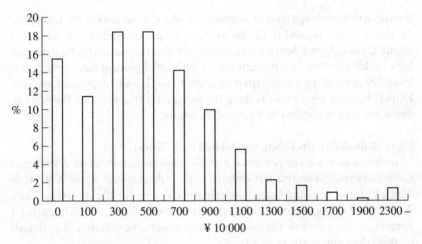

Figure 11.1   Income distribution

Volunteer experience
Respondents were questioned about volunteer experience in order to check for an altruistic motivation bias. Of the respondents, 18 percent have participated in volunteer activities and 82 percent have not. The percentage of respondents who have participated in volunteer activities is not very high, which indicates that there is not an altruistic motivation bias. Among respondents who have participated, 62.2 percent participated in activities related to care for the disabled or elderly, to benefit the community, or to further human rights. Some 20.5 percent participated in international affairs or environmental-related activities and 34.4 percent participated in other types of activity.

Percentage of respondents who have browsed the homepage related to this questionnaire
Information on the estimated costs of improving the accessibility of public buildings and roads in Kyoto City is included in the survey sheet. This

information is necessary for the respondents to make well-grounded judgments in response to the questionnaire items. Furthermore, to improve the reliability of the survey, a website was created in order to provide respondents with information about barrier-free society issues, and the website address was listed in the survey questionnaire. However, survey results show that only 3.6 percent of the respondents browsed the website, suggesting that the method of providing respondents with knowledge through the Internet does not work well.

Barrier-free knowledge level of respondents who did not browse the homepage
To examine the reliability of the answers to the questionnaire, we asked about knowledge of barrier-free issues. Of the respondents, 21.3 percent have no knowledge, 38.6 percent have a little, 30.3 percent have a moderate level, 7.9 percent have more than an average level, and 1.9 percent are very knowledgeable. These results deny the possibility that most of the respondents are very conscious of barrier-free issues.

State of disability (including age-related disabilities)
In order to increase the percentage of disabled respondents we distributed the survey questionnaire not only to randomly selected Kyoto City residents, but also to some homes specifically catering for the disabled. Thus, 20.3 percent (128 people) of the respondents are disabled, which is a greater percentage than that of the disabled in the general population. The details of their disabilities are as follows:

a. Degree of physical disability
    None   59.8%
    Slight   23.8%
    Serious   16.4%
b. Degree of wheel-chair utilization
    Those who do not need it   86.7%
    Those who need it but are able to use it by themselves   2.5 %
    Those who need assistance to use it   10.8 %
c. Degree of visual disability
    None   86.3%
    Slight   12.8%
    Serious   0.9%
d. Degree of auditory disability
    None   76.7%
    Slight   16.7%
    Serious   5.8%
    No auditory ability   0.8%

e. Degree of internal illness
    None   44.6%
    Slight   43.0%
    Serious   12.4%
f. Degree of mental illness
    None   81.8%
    Slight   10.7%
    Serious   7.4%
g. Degree of age-related walking disability
    None   63.8%
    Slight   28.4%
    Serious   7.8%
h. Degree of age-related physical disability
    None   75.2%
    Slight   19.7%
    Serious   5.1%

Frequency of going out
How frequently the disabled go out is an important indicator of their activity levels. By improving accessibility, it is possible to improve activity levels of the disabled. Figure 11.2 shows the current state of activity levels of the disabled.

Public infrastructures frequently used by the disabled
Public infrastructures frequently used by the disabled are summarized as follows:

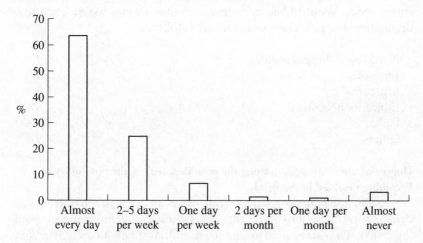

Figure 11.2   Frequency of going out

1. Parks   58 persons (45.3%)
2. Libraries   41 persons (32.0%)
3. Museums   38 persons (29.7%)
4. Community educational centers   23 persons (18.0%)
5. None   53 persons (41.4%)

It is noteworthy that 41.4 percent of the disabled do not make use of any public infrastructures. Examining the reasons for this result would be fruitful for city planning within an ageing society. Lack of accessibility may be one reason for this result.

How frequently are public infrastructures used

More than once per week	21.4%
Once or twice per month	32.1%
Once per 2 to 6 months	19.8%
Less than once per year	26.7%

These results indicate that the frequency with which public infrastructures are used is very small, implying that there is a necessity to reconsider the public infrastructure system in order to improve the activity levels of the disabled.

Public infrastructures not usable because of disabilities
The reasons why the disabled do not use public infrastructures are important for designing public infrastructure systems in an ageing society. This survey asked about public infrastructures that are not usable because of disabilities. The results are summarized as follows:

None (everything is usable)	69.7%
Libraries	3.5%
Museums	11.3%
Educational centers	2.8%
Parks	7.7%
Others	4.9%

Degree of consciousness (among the non-disabled) of the possibility of becoming disabled in the future
We designed the questionnaire for this survey in order to separate respondents' motivations into those that are altruistic and those that are self-interested. The survey item asking the non-disabled about their awareness of the possibility of becoming disabled in the future gives us an indication

of the strength of self-interest motivation (Question 22). The results are as follows:

Not concerned at all	5.0%
A little bit concerned	64.0%
Moderately concerned	18.3%
Greatly concerned	12.7%

These results show that around 70 percent of the non-disabled are not seriously concerned about the future possibility of becoming disabled, and around 30 percent are moderately or greatly concerned.

WTP for investment in improving the accessibility of public buildings
In Question 23, we asked respondents about their WTP for investments in improving accessibility of public buildings. The results are shown in Table 11.1.

Table 11.1   WTP for improved accessibility of public buildings

Years	Total expenditure (¥bn)	Annual tax burden (¥)	Frequency	Ratio	Cumulative frequency	Cumulative ratio
1	3	4900	52	7.9	52	7.9
1	6	9800	66	10.1	118	18.0
2	3	2450	53	8.1	171	26.1
2	6	4900	103	15.7	274	41.8
5	3	980	89	13.6	363	55.3
5	6	1960	162	24.7	525	80.0
10	3	490	63	9.6	588	89.6
10	6	980	68	10.4	656	100.0

Notes: No. of respondents who did not respond = 23. 'Years' refers to the years required to complete investment.

Preferences for the number of years spent to complete improved accessibility investment are summarized as follows:

1 year	18.0%
2 years	23.8%
5 years	38.2%
10 years	20.0%

These results indicate that most residents would prefer that investment be completed within 2 to 5 years. Next, preferences for the extent of investment are summarized as follows:

Level 1 (¥3bn)	39.2%
Level 2 (¥6bn)	60.8%

These results imply that residents prefer full-level investment.

In Figure 11.3, responses to Question 23 are shown in terms of the age distribution of respondents. The graph shows that preference for full-level investment to be carried out within one year (item 2) is highest for the 30–49 age group, and for half of full-level investment to be carried out within 10 years (item 7) is highest for those in the 29 and under age group. The 65 and above age group indicated the largest preference for half of full-level investment to be carried out within one year (item 1), which may reflect that people of this age are most urgently in need of the completion of barrier-free investments.

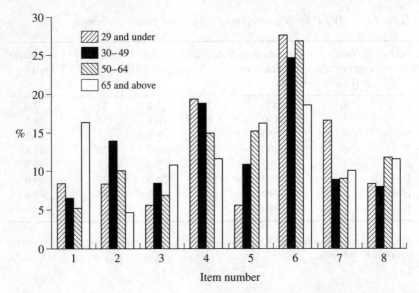

Figure 11.3   Responses to Q23 in terms of age distribution of respondents

The distribution of answers for disabled and non-disabled respondents is shown in Figure 11.4. The figure indicates that those with no disability have a greater WTP for barrier-free investments than do the disabled. At this moment, we cannot ignore the possibility that income factors generate this surprising result. However, interestingly this result could be an indica-

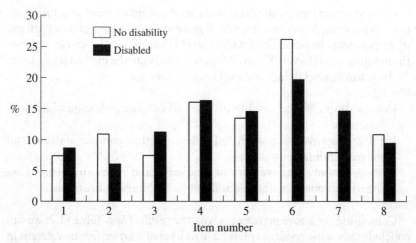

Figure 11.4   Distribution of answers to Q23 for disabled and non-disabled respondents

tion that the general resident population feels a sense of responsibility for building a barrier-free society. In a later section, we discuss this point in detail by using ordered probit and regression analyses.

Evaluation of barrier-free policy
The survey results show that only 3 percent of the respondents think that the current state of accessibility is sufficient. However, 46 percent think that it is sufficient to invest only in frequently used infrastructures, and 50.9 percent think that it is necessary to invest in all infrastructures. Interpretation of these results is not simple, but the fact that more than half of respondents think that the government should invest in all infrastructures is important for policy makers.

WTP for barrier-free investment in roads
Question 26 asks about WTP for barrier-free investment in roads. The distribution of answers is shown in Table 11.2 (see the questionnaire in Appendix 11A1 for the specific items).

Table 11.2   WTP for barrier-free investment in sidewalks (%)

					Item						
1	2	3	4	5	6	7	8	9	10	11	12
8.1	4.7	5.0	5.3	7.9	11.3	9.1	10.2	8.3	10.7	7.3	12.1

Questionnaire items ask about three levels of investment and four time periods for completing investments. Regarding investment level, 30 percent of respondents indicate the smallest level (Level 1), 35.1 percent indicate the medium level (Level 2), and 34.9 percent indicate the highest level (Level 3). Investment level details are explained as follows:

Level 1: Improve accessibility of sidewalks facing public buildings and hospitals.
Level 2: Improve accessibility of sidewalks that connect stations and public buildings or hospitals.
Level 3: Improve accessibility of sidewalks and roads (by networking them) that connect stations and public buildings or hospitals.

Combining the above preferences with the results from Table 11.2, we can conclude that most residents prefer a high level of barrier-free investment in roads and sidewalks that would be carried out over a 3- or 4-year time period.

In the questionnaire we asked the extent to which investment would increase the frequency with which respondents go out. The results are shown in Figure 11.5. For Level 1, it can be seen that the largest portion of respondents would increase the frequency with which they go out by around 20 percent, and the second largest portion would not change the frequency with which they go out. For Level 2, the largest portion would increase their frequency of going out by around 50 percent, and the second largest portion would do the same by around 20 percent. For Level 3, the largest portion would double their frequency of going out, and the second largest portion would increase their frequency of going out by around 50 percent. It is noteworthy that the portion of people who would

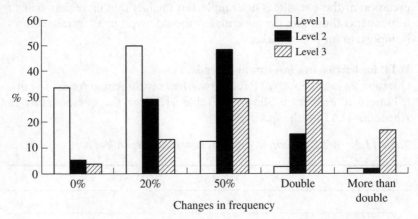

Figure 11.5   Changes in frequency of going out in terms of investment level

double their frequency of going out increases from 1.9 to 17 percent as investment increases from Level 2 to Level 3. That is, the effect of improving accessibility of roads and sidewalks on the frequency of going out drastically increases by networking accessible roads and sidewalks.

Figure 11.6 shows responses to Question 26 in terms of the age distribution of respondents. Figure 11.7 shows investment level selection in terms of

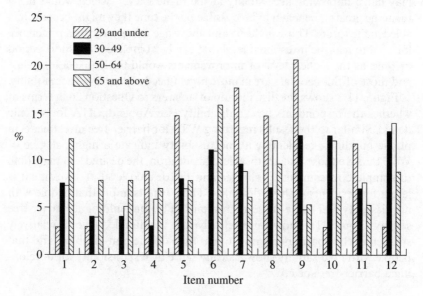

Figure 11.6   Answers to Q26 in terms of age distribution of respondents

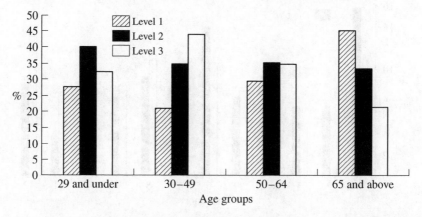

Figure 11.7   Barrier-free road investment level selection in terms of the age distribution of respondents

the age distribution of respondents. From Figure 11.7 it can be seen that the preferences of the 30–49 age group and the 65 and above age group are quite opposite. Those in the 30–49 age group indicate a preference for high-level investment, while the 65 and above age group indicate a preference for low-level investment. These results may be due to differences in judgment about time span required for improving accessibility. Those in the 30–49 age group may judge improving accessibility at the highest level (which would bring them the greatest benefits) to be possible by the time they might become disabled in the future. Those in the 65 and above age group indicate a preference for a more realistic investment level that can be completed in a short period of time, as the highest level of improvements would likely take a long time and those of this age class are in more urgent need of improved accessibility.

Figure 11.8 shows the distribution of answers to Question 26 in terms of whether the respondents have a disability (see Appendix 11A for specific items). Similar to the results regarding WTP for barrier-free investments in public buildings, residents with no disability indicate a higher degree of WTP than do those that are disabled. In addition, the desired length of time to complete investments is shorter and the desired level of investment is larger for residents with no disability. These results imply that people with no disability feel some sense of responsibility for building a barrier-free society. Figure 11.9 shows quite clearly that the disabled favor a relatively smaller level of barrier-free investment than do the non-disabled, and that people with no disability show a strong sense of responsibility for developing a barrier-free society.

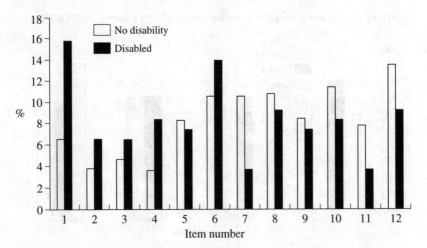

*Figure 11.8   Distribution of answers to Q26 by respondents with and
             without disabilities*

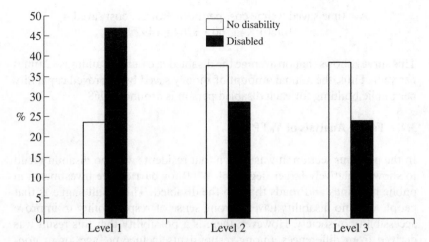

*Figure 11.9   Desired level of barrier-free investment in roads by respondents
with and without disabilities*

3.3.   Improved 'Capability' Resulting from Barrier-free Investment

In the survey, we asked the disabled some questions about what they
expected the time required would be to make improvements in access to
public buildings and about the frequency with which they would use public
buildings. Since we asked for annual income information in the survey
questionnaire, it is possible to calculate the time cost per hour for each
sample. We measured the pecuniary value of improved capability to use
public buildings in terms of the amount of time cost subtracted from
barrier-free investment.

Increases in the frequency with which public buildings would be used
were not observed. The median value of change in the frequency of public
building use per month is 0, and the average value is −0.8. However, time
needed to access public buildings decreases by around ten minutes on
average, and at most by 60 minutes. In addition, the direct cost (transportation cost and so on) decreases by around ¥204 on average, and at most by
¥2480.

The average annual income of the disabled who responded is ¥3 890 000.
Since the average labor hours per week in Japan are 42.5, the average hourly
income of the disabled is around ¥1760. Thus, the pecuniary value of
improved capability per disabled person per use (denoted as A in the following formula) of a public infrastructure is given as follows:

$$A = \text{time saved} \times \text{time cost per hour} + \text{direct cost saved} =$$
$$(10/60) \times ¥1760 + ¥204 = ¥497.$$

This survey shows that on average the disabled use public buildings 12 times per year. Thus, the annual amount of money saved by improved capability per public building for each disabled person is around ¥5968.

3.4. Factor Analysis of WTP

In the previous section, it was shown that residents with no disability tend to show a relatively larger degree of WTP for barrier-free investments in public buildings and roads than do the disabled. This result suggests that people with no disability have a strong sense of responsibility to improve accessibility in society. However, there is a possibility that this result was derived from differences among respondents in income, age, or in non-disabled respondents' worries about the possibility of becoming disabled in the future. In this section, we examine the differences in WTP between the disabled and those without disabilities by controlling for the effects from differences in income, age, and self-interest in the possibility of becoming disabled in the future.

In Question 22, we asked about the possibility of becoming disabled in the future. If there is a strong possibility of becoming disabled in the future, that person may have a large degree of WTP for barrier-free investment due to self-interest. In this analysis, the strength of self-interest is expressed by a dummy variable.

We apply the ordered-probit model in order to explain the selection of investment level in Question 23 (barrier-free investment for public buildings), because the absolute value of level differences has less meaning than does the order of investment level. The model is formulated as follows:

$$y_i^* = \beta' x_i + \varepsilon_i, \ \varepsilon_i \sim N(0,1),$$

$$y_i = 0 \text{ if } y_i^* \leq \mu_0,$$

$$= 1 \text{ if } \mu_0 < y_i^* \leq \mu_1,$$

$$= 2 \text{ if } \mu_1 < y_i^* \leq \mu_2,$$

where y_i is a level selected by respondents. y_i takes a value of 0 if there is no response (23/679), 1 if a response indicates Level 1 (¥3 billion), and 2 if a response indicates Level 2 (¥6 billion). x_i represents explanatory variables, such as annual income (INCOME), a dummy for the disabled (DDISA = 1 for the disabled), a dummy for the strength of self-interest (DSELF = 1 if

Q22 = 3 or 4), *or* age (AGE in quadratic form). ε represents error, and is assumed to be distributed according to N(0,1). μ is a parameter such that:

$$\text{Prob}(y_i = j) = \text{Prob}(\mu_{j-1} < y_i^* \leq \mu_j).$$

The results of this analysis are summarized in Table 11.3. μ_0 is normalized to be 0. These results show that income has a significantly positive effect on the choice of higher-level investment, the dummy for the disabled has a significant negative effect, the dummy for self-interest has a significant positive effect of 12 percent *p*-value, and age significantly affects investment level in quadratic form.

The marginal effects of the explanatory variables on the probability of selecting investment levels are given in Table 11.4 (variables that have almost no effect are omitted). The table shows that being disabled decreases the probability of selecting Level 2, and that self-interest increases the probability of selecting Level 2.

The WTP for barrier-free investment in public buildings is regressed by age (AGE in quadratic form) using the ordinary least squares (OLS) method, and by explanatory variables such as those for annual income (INCOME), a dummy for the disabled (DDISA = 1 for the disabled), and

Table 11.3 Investment level selection of barrier-free investment for public buildings (ordered probit method)

Variable	Coefficient (B)	Standard error (St)	B/St	*p*-value	Mean of x_i
Constant	1.867	0.148	12.53	0.0000	
INCOME	0.655E−07	0.105E−07	6.242	0.0000	5041215
DDISA	−0.285	0.1153	−2.480	0.0132	0.188
DSELF	0.173	0.111	1.553	0.1204	0.276
AGE	0.178E−02	0.737E−03	2.423	0.0154	47.116
AGE2	−0.104E−03	0.325E−04	−3.223	0.0013	2996.86
μ_1	1.74	0.110	15.771	0.0000	

Table 11.4 Marginal effects of explanatory variables on the probability of selecting investment levels

Variable	No answer	Level 1 (¥3 bn)	Level 2 (¥6 bn)
DDISA	0.0166	0.0947	−0.1113
DSELF	−0.0101	−0.0574	0.0675

Table 11.5   WTP for barrier-free investment in public buildings (OLS analysis)

Variable	Coefficient (B)	Standard error (St)	B/St	*p*-value
Constant	2364.71	181.846	13.004	0.0000
INCOME	0.118E–03	0.230E–04	5.132	0.0000
DDISA	−381.987	264.585	−1.444	0.1488
DSELF	406.307	229.316	1.772	0.076

Table 11.6   WTP for barrier-free investment in roads (OLS analysis)

Variable	Coefficient (B)	Standard error (St)	B/St	*p*-value	Mean of *x*
Constant	424.049	30.824	13.757	0.0000	
INCOME	0.185E−04	0.391E−05	4.729	0.0000	5041215.0
DDISA	−68.035	44.849	−1.517	0.1293	0.1885
DSELF	65.666	38.871	1.689	0.0912	0.2768

a dummy for the strength of self-interest (DSELF = 1 if Q22 = 3 or 4). The results (Table 11.5), show that income has a significant positive effect on the degree of WTP for barrier-free investment in public buildings. The dummy for the disabled has a negative effect of 15 percent on WTP.

Finally, we use the OLS method to examine the factors that determine WTP for barrier-free investment in roads. As in the above analysis, we consider age (AGE in quadratic form) and explanatory variables, such as annual income (INCOME), dummies for the disabled (DDISA = 1 for the disabled), and dummies for the strength of self-interest (DSELF = 1 if Q22 = 3 or 4). The results (Table 11.6) show that income and self-interest have a significant positive effect on the degree of WTP for barrier-free investment in roads, and the dummy for the disabled has a negative effect of 13 percent on WTP. In addition, we used the OLS method to estimate the years for completing the investment, but only the dummy for the disabled is significant (*p*-value is 0.048) and has a negative sign. These results suggest that the disabled require a shorter length of time to complete barrier-free investment in roads.

4. CONCLUSION

This survey analysis shows that people with no disability tend to have a strong feeling of responsibility for improving accessibility. This result is robust because it holds true both for barrier-free investment in public buildings and for investment in roads. Furthermore, it holds even after the effects of income, self-interest and age are controlled for. These findings provide policy makers with useful information for using tax revenue to carry out barrier-free investment, and for determining the investment levels and time periods for carrying out investments.

The results of our theoretical analysis suggest that the WTP for barrier-free investment is smaller than the social optimal level when the disabled expect the non-disabled to pay for the cost of improved accessibility and the non-disabled expect the disabled to pay. This finding implies that a government should invest more than the amount indicated by residents. In addition, the finding that the disabled have a smaller degree of WTP than do those who are not disabled may reflect the idea that the cost of barrier-free investment should be borne by people with no disability.

It is noteworthy that the frequency with which the disabled indicated they would go out increases drastically when they indicate support for barrier-free investment in roads to guarantee accessibility between stations and public buildings.

NOTES

1. Although this model accounts for overlapping generations of a population, for simplification, we disregard generational gaps. It is assumed that the degree of social infrastructure that was invested in by the parents' generation is given exogenously. In this case, the setting in which the contribution of one generation determines the total amount of infrastructure is essentially the same as that in which some part of the social infrastructure has been paid for by the parents' generation.
2. Existence of the Nash equilibrium can be confirmed by examining the slopes of response functions for both types of individuals.

REFERENCES

Langford, I.H. (1994), 'Using a generalized liner mixed model to analyze dichotomous choice contingent valuation data', *Land Economics*, **40** (4), November, 507–14.
Sen, A.K. (1985), *Commodities and Capabilities*, Amsterdam: North-Holland.
Sen, A.K. (1997), 'From income inequality to economic inequality', *Southern Economic Journal*, **64** (2), 384–401.

Takeuchi, K. (1999), *Evaluation of Environment and Application to Policy Design –
Reliability of CVM and Travel Cost Method* (in Japanese), Tokyo: Keisoshobo.
Vickerman, R., K. Spiekermann and M. Wegener (1999), 'Accessibility and
economic development in Europe', *Regional Studies*, **33** (1), 1–15.

APPENDIX 11A SURVEY QUESTIONNAIRE ON
                 BARRIER-FREE INVESTMENT IN
                 PUBLIC INFRASTRUCTURE
                 (ORIGINALLY IN JAPANESE)

For detailed information about barrier-free issues, please refer to http://
yagi.doshisha.ac.jp/.

Please answer the following questions concerning yourself (please circle
the applicable number or fill in the blanks).

Q1. Sex
    1. Male   2. Female
Q2. Age ( )
Q3. Area where you are living (   ) city, (   ) ward
Q4. Occupation
    1. Self-employed   2. Salaried employed   3. Housewife
    4. Student   5. Other
Q5. Last year's income (before tax): in dollar calculated at $1 = ¥100
    1. none   7. $100 000–$120 000
    2. up to $20 000.   8. $120 000–$140 000
    3. $20 000–$40 000   9. $140 000–$160 000
    4. $40 000–$60 000   10. $160 000–$180 000
    5. $60 000–$80 000   11. $180 000–$200 000
    6. $80 000–$100 000   12. $200 000 and over
Q6. Do you have any experience participating in NPO (Non-profit organ-
    ization) activities?
    1. No   2. Yes
    If No, please go to Q8. Otherwise please go to Q7.
Q7. What kind of NPO activities did you participate in?
    1. Activities for aiding the disabled or elderly, or improving the com-
       munity or human rights
    2. Activities related to international affairs or environmental
       issues
    3. Other
Q8. Have you browsed the related homepage http://yagi.doshisha.ac.jp/?
    1. No   2. Yes
    If No, please go to Q10. Otherwise please go to Q9.
Q9. To what extent did you browse the homepage?
    1. A little   2. Most of it   3. In detail
Q10. To what extent do you have knowledge about barrier-free issues?
    1. Not at all   2. A little   3. Average
    4. More than average   5. A great deal

Q11. Do you have any disabilities (including disabilities from ageing)?
　　1. No　　2. Yes
　　If no, please go to Q22. Otherwise please go to Q12.

Q12. Please indicate the degree of disability
　　a. Physical disability
　　　　1. None　　2. Slight　　3. Serious
　　b. Wheelchair
　　　　1. None　　2. Can operate by myself　　3. Need help
　　c. Visual disability
　　　　1. None　　2. Slight　　3. Serious
　　d. Auditory disability
　　　　1. None　　2. Slight　　3. Serious　　4. Cannot hear at all
　　e. Internal illness
　　　　1. None　　2. Slight　　3. Serious
　　f. Mental illness
　　　　1. None　　2. Slight　　3. Serious
　　g. Difficulty in walking as a result of ageing
　　　　1. None　　2. Slight　　3. Serious
　　h. Physical disability from ageing
　　　　1. None　　2. Slight　　3. Serious

Q13. Please indicate the frequency with which you go out
　　1. Almost every day　　2. 2–5 days per week　　3. Once per week
　　4. Twice per month　　5. Once per month　　6. Almost never
　　If your frequency of going out is less than once per week, please go
　　to Q14. Otherwise please go to Q16.

Q14. Please indicate your method of going out
　　1. Wheelchair　　2. On foot　　3. Subway
　　4. Railway　　5. Bus　　6. Taxi

Q15. Please indicate the reason why you go out infrequently
　　1. Difficulty using buildings
　　2. Difficulty using roads and sidewalks
　　3. Difficulty using public transportation　　4. Toilets
　　5. High cost of using taxis　　　　6. Lack of information
　　7. No helper　　　　8. Mental problem

Q16. What kind of public buildings do you use frequently?
　　1. None　　　　2. Library　　3. Museum
　　4. Educational center　　5. Park　　6. Other

Q17. How often do you use the public building you indicated in Q16?
　　1. More than once per week　　2. Once or twice per month
　　3. Once per two to six months　　4. Less than once per year

Q18. What kind of public buildings do you have difficulty using?
1. None   2. Library   3. Museum
4. Educational center   5. Park   6. Other
Please answer the following question unless you indicated '1' in Q18.
If you indicated '1,' go to Q22.

Q19. How much time and expense are required to access the public building indicated in Q18?
1. Time needed to access the building (   ) minutes
2. Direct cost of accessing the building (   ) yen

Q20. How much time and expense would be required to access the public building indicated in Q18 if barriers to access were removed?
3. Time needed to access the building (   ) minutes
4. Direct cost for accessing the building (   ) yen

Q21. How frequently would you use the public building you indicated in Q18 if barriers to access were removed?
1. More than once per week   2. Once or twice per month
3. Once every two to six months   4. Less than once per year

Q22. How concerned are you with the possibility of becoming disabled in the future?
1. I am not concerned
2. I am a little concerned
3. I am moderately concerned
4. I am seriously concerned

We would like all respondents to answer the following questions.

Q23. The current state of access barriers in public buildings is summarized in the table. It is estimated that the cost needed to remove these barriers is 6.4 billion yen. The number of households in Kyoto City is 612018. Please select the item numbers indicating how you would favor your tax money to be spent for barrier-free investment.

Item number	Years needed to complete the investment	Total expenditure for the investment (¥bn)	Total tax burden per household (¥)	Annual tax burden per household (¥)
1	1	30	4900	4900
2	1	60	9800	9800
3	2	30	4900	2450
4	2	60	9800	4900
5	5	30	4900	980
6	5	60	9800	1960
7	10	30	4900	490
8	10	60	9800	980

Q24. How do you evaluate the current state of accessibility to public buildings in Kyoto City?
1. Sufficient
2. Not sufficient, but only frequently used buildings should be
improved
3. Not sufficient and all the buildings should be improved

Q25. Please indicate any preference for criteria to determine barrier-free
investment in roads and sidewalks. The following six criteria are often
used: (1) Importance of traffic (2) Size of commercial buildings and
number of shops (3) Existence of public buildings (4) Major tourist
attractions (5) Existence of large hospitals and welfare buildings (6)
Existence of schools

Q26. It is necessary to determine the level of barrier-free investment in
roads and sidewalks and the number of years spent completing the
investment. Investment levels are defined as follows:
Level 1: Improve the accessibility of sidewalks that face public buildings and hospitals
Level 2: Improve the accessibility of sidewalks that link stations and
public buildings or hospitals
Level 3: Improve the accessibility of sidewalks and roads (by networking) that link stations and public buildings or hospitals

Please select the item numbers indicating how you would favor your tax
money to be spent for barrier-free investment. Investment in one area per
ward is assumed.

					Supplement	
Item number	Level	Cost (per area)	Years to complete	Annual tax burden/ household (¥)	Total cost	Total tax burden/ household (¥)
1			1	327		
2	1	¥200m	2	164	¥2.2bn	3595
3			3	109		
4			4	82		
5			1	980		
6	2	¥600m	2	490	¥6.6bn	10784
7			3	327		
8			4	245		
9			1	1797		
10	3	¥1.1bn	2	899	¥12.1bn	19711
11			3	599		
12			4	449		

In relation to each investment level, how much do you expect you would increase the frequency that you would go out?

	0%	20%	50%	Double	More than double
1. Level 1	|—————	|—————	|—————	|—————	|
2. Level 2	|—————	|—————	|—————	|—————	|
3. Level 3	|—————	|—————	|—————	|—————	|

Index